More Owen

More Owen

Searching for Traces of a
Son Gone Too Soon

A Memoir

Mary Klinger

PORTLAND, OREGON

More Owen: Searching for Traces of a Son Gone Too Soon

ISBN (hardcover): 979-8-9943106-2-5
ISBN (paperback): 979-8-9943106-0-1
ISBN (ebook): 979-8-9943106-1-8

Library of Congress Control Number: 2026904299

Published by Panther Creek Publishing, Portland, Oregon

Cover design by Kimberly Parks, ANDIOMA
Book design by Olivia M. Hammerman, Indigo: Editing, Design, and More
Author photograph by John Davenport, For Eyes Photography

To Dustin, all ways and always

To Gabe, Frances, and Owen,
being your mom has been the best part of my life

Contents

Introduction

Owen in Maui November 2014

Surviving close personal loss not only changes a person's life indelibly; it also changes their identity. The English language offers us words to describe someone who has experienced the loss of their parents (an orphan) and the death of their spouse (a widow or widower), but the English language has no word for a parent who has lost a child. So, what does that make me?

My son Owen died during his freshman year at the University of Portland (UP), in 2019. He left his dorm room on a Sunday evening six weeks into the school year and his body was found two weeks later in a nearby river.

Since then, I have been experiencing my life in this unexpected and new way: as a bereaved mother (the best term the English language can come up with). As I come into this new identity, I have been trying to translate my experience to many, many people—basically anyone who will listen.

Why? Perhaps because Owen's disappearance and eventual loss was very public locally, and my family (our nuclear family, which includes my husband and Owen's two siblings, as well as extended family) received such an outpouring of support from the community. I have wanted to share my grief journey publicly, so my work to heal myself and my family may also help to heal everyone else who felt the loss of Owen alongside us. I want to offer comfort to those who have experienced a loss like ours and understanding to those who haven't yet.

Through the following essays, reflections, letters, and poems, I have been attempting to examine and translate all the facets of the experience, such as being a mom who failed at shepherding a child safely into full adulthood—and yet still has to (gets to) continue mothering, because I have two other young adult children to love and support. Losing Owen ramped up my anxiety about the safety and well-being of my other kids; I am afraid I will smother them. I am afraid I will lose them, too.

I try to explain how not knowing why or how we lost Owen—Suicide? An accident? Foul play?—continues to haunt me and frustratingly robs me of an enemy to fight.

Writing about the isolation and loneliness of grief—how even in a roomful of friendly faces, I can feel a gaping distance between what I deal with and the "normal" worries many others carry—helps heal my loneliness. While my heart was breaking apart in the first years after we lost Owen, it was also filling up with more love and compassion for others who are suffering. For good or for bad, this grief creates a direct connection to all the other pain in the world.

I've learned that there can be seemingly infinite and endlessly surprising nuances to life as a bereaved mother: how every day can feel like losing Owen all over again, how strong the pull to end my own life can be, how I struggle with feeling irrationally responsible for his death, how every change of season can be an achingly painful reminder of his loss, and how much I fear I will forget things about him.

I reflect on aspects of Owen's life that have come into sharper focus since his death, sharing bittersweet memories of the joyful ways he filled out the middle of our family.

I write about nature as a balm that helps me bear my unbearable sorrow. The enduring presence of tall trees in a dense forest, the power of water rushing over rocks in a mountainside creek, and the roar of ocean waves sweeping over a sandy beach remind me my grief is just a small part of a more complicated—and beautiful—world. Feeling rain or wind on my skin somehow soothes me, and writing about it helps put my pain in perspective.

I expose my fledgling efforts to connect with Owen's spirit and energy. I interpret my discovery of thousands of heart-shaped rocks and seemingly random coincidences as proof that his love is all around us. Talking about "woo-woo" stuff like spiritual mediumship and psychedelic medicine is uncomfortable, but if sharing my experience can help even one other person find some peace, I will persist.

I confess to feeling guilty when moments of joy slowly slip back into my days because it felt so right to feel wrecked after we lost Owen. I share my determination to love more fiercely, soak each moment in more deeply, and forgive more easily.

These essays, reflections, letters, and poems are sacred medicine for my shattered heart. I wrote each piece separately, each a unique work for that moment's pain. Once I started thinking my writings could come together in a book, the word that kept coming up was "patchwork." These words form a patchwork of grief and memories; it's part scrapbook, part journal, part diary. It's roughly chronological, but it's not a complete picture, and it doesn't flow evenly from the beginning to the end—and that's fitting, because grieving the loss of a child (or anyone) isn't linear either. Grief can, in an instant, rip me from sweet reminiscences of childhood birthday parties and drop me into dark, painful places of fear and anxiety. So I arranged this collection in a way that felt organic to me, echoing these unpredictable tides of grief. It can be read however one wants.

And this isn't the whole story. We still don't know what happened to Owen. We might never know. We aren't done healing and never fully expect to be. This work was stitched together as a place to celebrate Owen, to explore my love for him as well as my pain and grief at our loss of him. I wanted and needed to write these pieces to help heal myself, to find ways to continue living, loving, and mothering.

These essays don't relive the entire, involved search for Owen or our interactions with the Portland police. I can't go there yet. I was inspired by the poet and author Maggie Smith's book, *You Could Make This Place Beautiful,* a memoir of her divorce she calls a "tell-mine," not a tell-all. I don't know it all, so this book can't be a tell-all.

I don't include much about Owen's brother and sister because they are doing their own healing and processing in their own ways, painfully and joyfully remembering their brother (and possibly mourning the different mom and dad they knew before this loss) while they carry on with their own lives. They were in my heart as I wrote every word. I hope that with time they will be able to tell their own stories of Owen.

My husband Dustin is here with me every day, missing and reminiscing about Owen, but he processes in his own way, so this isn't his story either.

Losing a child is like nothing I could have imagined—and something I hope you or your family never have to endure. By offering readers some insights into my experience and my journey to find "More Owen," I hope all of us who have been touched by his story can share greater understanding and compassion in our lives.

Knowing Owen,
Then Knowing Nothing

Owen was our peace-loving middle child who loved Hot Pockets and the art of Vincent van Gogh. Born in 2001, Owen never knew a life without family surrounding him, sharing a room with his older brother Gabe and very quickly becoming a big brother himself when his sister Frances was born seventeen and a half months later. Owen was an active and curious child; energetic, mischievous, and hardworking; musical, thoughtful, and loving.

Owen loved to move his body in all kinds of ways and played many sports: soccer, baseball, football, lacrosse, and water polo. He liked skiing, beach volleyball, family tennis, and golf. He was a devoted teammate who almost always sported a team T-shirt, sweatshirt, or jacket. He was humble about his own athletic abilities, but his dedication and efforts were appreciated by teammates and coaches alike, several of whom shared that appreciation with me over the years.

From the time he was a little boy, Owen liked working. Sweeping, raking leaves, or washing windows around the house turned into mowing lawns and doing bigger yard work projects for his grandmas and our neighbors. In high school, he even wrote a whole essay about why he loved chopping wood. (I share this essay in a later chapter.) He actually whistled while he worked, and he carefully saved the money he earned.

As he grew older, Owen was a supportive friend, buying a classmate's ceramic berry bowl at a high school sale when no one else was buying anything, cheering on the school's baseball pitcher at away games, going to a friend's amateur photography exhibit, and sharing his musical instruments with others who wanted to try one out. Owen was always the one bringing his friends together to hang out and organizing them for fun outings to the beach or our cabin. Owen liked to make people laugh, and people liked Owen.

He was also a deep thinker with a sensitive soul. My journals from his young childhood years are peppered with the surprising things he would ponder. When he was four years old, he asked, "Do you only have to be *old* to be an adult, or do you have to be *smart*, too?" and "Why did people invent money instead of just sharing everything?" A few years later, he wondered, "What do people who don't have kids do with all their money?"

Dustin and I met while attending the University of Notre Dame in Indiana, and we brought our kids up in the Catholic church. When Owen chose to go to college at UP I was so proud of him. UP is considered a sister school of Notre Dame, sharing professors, Holy Cross priests, and a similar Catholic ideology. UP, like Notre Dame, was also an academically challenging choice. The familiar feel of the residential campus eased my mind, and I was excited he would make new friends in his all-male dorm. His sporty side could find an outlet playing club lacrosse and dorm-league soccer. I knew there would be plenty of opportunities for college partying—it's not like I thought Owen was going to become a Catholic priest—but it seemed like a safe place.

I knew from experience with our eldest son that there is a loss of control when a child leaves home: I would go from knowing so much about Owen and his everyday life to knowing far less about many things as he forged his own path. I would no longer be packing his lunch every day or serving him a hearty dinner after football practice. I wouldn't know how often he was going to class or playing video games or what he was drinking or smoking. I wouldn't hear him singing in the shower or playing his guitar. I was sad about having less Owen in my days, but I thought I was ready to face this loss of control. I did not know that it would lead to losing Owen.

I will probably never know why Owen went out that Sunday night before midterms in October 2019. And I will likely forever wonder what exactly happened to him after he left his dorm.

My husband and I went to campus the next morning, after we got a phone call from one of Owen's roommates telling us Owen hadn't come back to their room the previous night. Things quickly got very surreal and very serious. We met with campus security and talked with the dorm supervisor. We consoled Owen's frazzled roommates—boys we had only met once at orientation a few weeks prior—while we surreptitiously grilled them, trying to decide if we could trust them, if they were somehow to blame for Owen's disappearance, if they knew more than they were telling us. They hadn't known Owen very long, but they already knew it was very out of character for Owen to be out of touch.

I remember walking aimlessly, bewildered, along the bluff above the Willamette River next to campus that first morning with Dustin, the long grass brown from the summer's heat yet cool and wet with early fall dew. My feet in thin canvas slip-ons were growing damp and cold, and I felt like I was walking in someone else's shoes, someone else's life. Mysterious and potentially dark and dangerous things like this didn't happen to me or to my sweet, loving family that played by the rules, paid our way, worked hard, went to church, and volunteered. None of us just left home and didn't come back. It was baffling and extremely uncomfortable. I wondered if (and hoped) his disappearance would be resolved in a fairly innocuous manner, or if I would ever feel comfortable again.

That first day we were introduced to alien things like police protocols, search parties, and notions that just one day earlier would never have crossed our minds. I didn't fully know it yet, but that first day was when my journey and new identity began: the identity of a parent who has lost a child—which is so wholly defining but still doesn't have a name.

Owen's body was found two weeks later in the Willamette River. There were no clear-cut injuries to his body, and the autopsy would take months to return what felt like inconclusive results to me: no broken bones or obviously fluid filled lungs; only traces of cannabis in his system, no evidence of heavy drugs. The cause of death was "most likely drowning," and many people—including the police and the campus security people we had been leaning on for support—seemed to believe that Owen committed suicide; that he purposefully ended his life by jumping off the nearby St. Johns Bridge. I still find that very hard to believe or accept. I have spent hundreds of hours poring over Owen's Google searches, his YouTube history, his email accounts, and his own writings and found nothing that leads me to believe he was depressed or suicidal. His friends from high school and his new friends from college echo my belief that Owen loved his family, loved his life, and was making lots of plans for future fun and studies.

I thought I knew Owen so well, but when it mattered most, that familiarity didn't bring me any closer to the answers we needed, and needed quickly. All of a sudden, it seemed as though I knew almost nothing about him and his new life. I didn't know why he went out alone that night. Was he planning on coming back to his dorm? He had bought a week's worth of snacks at the campus convenience store that evening (a box of donuts, a big bag of trail mix, his favorite crackers)—why would he have bought all that food if he wasn't planning on coming back to his dorm? I didn't know why he stopped at the ATM and got out $150 cash or why that cash wasn't in his wallet when his body was found. I didn't know if he had turned off his phone, or if his phone ran out of battery, or if he lost it. I didn't know if he was under the influence of alcohol or drugs. I didn't know if someone had threatened him or accosted him. I didn't know if I could trust his roommates' account of what Owen had said when he was going out the door that night.

I didn't know if I would ever find the answers to these questions and all the never-ending questions since then, or if I could find peace with not knowing. I didn't know how I would get through a single day without my sweet middle boy, let alone how I would survive the rest of my life in a world without his laughter and spark. I didn't know how my other kids would handle this traumatic loss of the heart of our family or how my marriage would stand up to this unimaginable grief Dustin and I were facing. It turns out that I knew next to nothing about Owen and so many other things, just when I needed to know so much more.

A Funeral and "More Owen"

On October 30, 2019, we gathered for Owen's funeral in the Chiles Center on the campus of the University of Portland. Almost two thousand students, friends, and members of the community joined our family for a funeral Mass with thirteen priests, many of them professors at the school, presiding at the makeshift altar inside the basketball arena.

Campus event planners reserved parking spots close to the doors for our family and designated a quiet room where we could wait in private until the procession started. News media were not allowed to broadcast or record the Mass, but before the ceremony began, Dustin and I stood with Frances and Gabe and shared our family's statement with a crowd of local reporters in the hallway.

Dustin started: "A lot of people are asking us for details of Owen's death," he said, "but the honest answer is we don't know how or why we lost our son, and knowing won't bring him back. All we know is that he was fiercely loved by all of us and that we dearly miss him now. Please join us in celebrating how Owen lived—with laughter, passion, a huge smile, and a big kind heart."

I continued, "We remember how delighted he was when he smelled bacon cooking at breakfast or when I made his favorite Philly cheesesteaks for dinner. He loved buying chocolate milk after practice with his brother and eating ice cream whenever possible. We remember all the joyful ways he moved his body: dancing, jumping, goofing around, and playing all the sports he loved, with his long hair flowing behind him. We remember the quiet pride he took in all the yard work and jobs he did for others, the enthusiastic shoveling of snow for the neighbors and his precise lawn mowing. We remember his kindness and empathy for others. We loved the way he gathered friends together and we will keep all of his friends in our hearts. We are grateful for all the smiles and laughter that Owen brought to our family and are amazed by how many people Owen's life has touched. He will always be with us. Thank you for remembering Owen, too."

It wasn't possible in that short press conference back then to say more, and I wished everyone who had supported us during that unfathomable time could've heard the comments Dustin and I shared in the eulogy during the Mass. It's where the idea of More Owen began. I'm happy to finally retell that here.

Once inside the heart of the arena, and after we had somehow endured most of the service, I climbed up to the podium on shaky legs and stood next to Dustin at the microphone. I looked out at the crowd of faces, unable to focus on anyone familiar, feeling alone in the giant space filled with my family and friends. I knew that our words were what everyone had been waiting through the long Catholic Mass to hear. I opened the leather folder holding our notes and made a joke to settle my own nerves and lighten the mood: "They said we could offer a 'short reflection' about Owen, but it's good no one looked in here to see how many pages we wrote. It still won't be enough. It's called 'More Owen.'" I let the love filling the room hold me up and I started to read, alternating sections with Dustin.

Owen Patrick Klinger joined our family in July of 2001. Like many new parents, we taught him to use Baby sign language before he could talk. Owen's favorite sign was "more," and he used it all the time. He wanted more food, more kisses, more dancing, more music, more outside time, more reading. Owen brought us more opportunities to love and laugh. We want More Owen and we want everyone to have More Owen.

Owen was such a happy, charming, and delightfully chubby baby. He was so easy that Dustin and I thought, "We should have another baby!" "MORE!!!" So we had Frances, and Owen became a big brother when he was only one and a half. (Gabe, who was three and a half at that time, became the self-proclaimed "huge brother.") Three kids under age four made our house pretty chaotic at times, but those were sweet, busy days, and by looking back at them we realize how much "MORE" Owen brought to our lives. More Owen.

More visits to the Emergency Room—Most of our family ER trips over the years were either to patch Owen up or patch up someone else after Owen-related incidents. He got medical glue for a cut lip, eyebrow, and finger; hid his broken hand from us for 12 hours; fainted during a scary dehydration incident; and badly sprained his ankle. Owen accidentally rammed a stick into his sister's eye and knocked out his brother's tooth with a shovel. Owen's enthusiastic style of play also caused a toy mail truck to crash and sprain his sister's wrist. More Owen.

More music—Singing, dancing, and drumming made little Owen happy and he continued adding music to our lives with trumpet, trombone, ukulele, and guitar. We loved listening to the music he brought into our house. He enjoyed singing in Japanese class with such enthusiasm that the teacher sometimes abandoned her lesson plan. We cherish the song Owen wrote about Panther Creek and performed as a surprise on Dustin's birthday. He had promised to write a song for me too when I sold him my guitar last month. More Owen.

More physical comedy and laughter—Owen loved to make others laugh and was a smiling, mischievous boy, sometimes disruptive or distracting in situations where he was supposed to be paying attention. He was asked to leave Kendo class, Sunday school, and the junior high youth group because he was expressing a little "more Owen" than was appreciated. We are grateful to teachers who worked with Owen's enthusiasm and gave him extra math worksheets, a speaking part in a group presentation, or a solo line in a Japanese song to engage him. More Owen.

More sports—Owen played many sports: baseball, soccer, swimming, basketball, skiing, golf, tennis, water polo, beach volleyball, football, and lacrosse. Never the biggest, the fastest, or the strongest, Owen loved moving his body and being part of a team. His cleats in soccer were perpetually untied and his body made a frightening thump when he hit the floor in basketball (more often than you would think possible!) All the hits and tackles from lacrosse and football were heart stopping. He was a tenacious outside linebacker and would dive and latch onto the ankles of guys twice his size to make a tackle, getting dragged along like a boat anchor. I loved watching him play all the games and did a lot of knitting while watching to remain calm. We will all remember his hustle and determination. I loved it when, at the end of a season, one coach asked if we had any more Owens. More Owen.

More jobs done—A squeegee was one of his favorite Christmas gifts, and Owen loved sweeping and raking too. I took advantage of his help around the house for sure. Once he started working for other people, the secret of Owen was out and I had to share him. But I was so glad that others appreciated his hard work and loved the joy he took in seeing a job all the way through to completion. Owen liked working hard and loved getting paid well. He saved and squirreled away his money—even offering loans to his less-thrifty siblings. More Owen.

More responsible—Owen was excited about driving and hauling his friends around town. Two summers ago, he organized a golf outing with four friends (including a German exchange student). They stopped at Pizzicato (a local pizza chain), but Owen drove in through the parking lot's exit so his parking angle was off. Owen tried to straighten out. Looking back over his shoulder and pressing on the gas, he did not realize a small tree branch was wedged into the front bumper. He added more acceleration until the whole bumper pulled off, much to the surprise of everyone—including spectators enjoying their pizza at the outside tables. Owen got out, picked up the bumper and wedged it into the back of the already pretty full car on the laps of his friends. When I got home, he gathered up $700 of his own saved cash and neatly piled it on the kitchen counter.

(We just happened to know the price of a new bumper because his brother had replaced it four months earlier after clipping a tree.) Owen owned it and was more responsible than any sixteen-year-old I knew. Last summer, on his own, walking up to a job fair booth, he got a job doing manual labor with Peter Corvallis Productions and savored the rewards of long overtime. More Owen.

More bacon—I found a notebook of Owen's with a list of dates, weights, and sports practices or workouts. Owen wanted to gain more weight, to be stronger, and bigger for his sports. He desperately wanted to grow taller than his brother Gabe and he was almost there, but had to settle for the middle and just taller than his dad. I always tried to feed him well, but when looking through old photos, we found a picture of Owen drinking bacon grease! His last entry in the notebook was in July of this year when he weighed 156 pounds (even though he told everyone he was 165). More Owen.

More love and friends—We wouldn't have our dog if it wasn't for Owen. He missed his brother Gabe during Gabe's eighth grade trip to Japan, and we finally gave in to the idea of a dog: more love, more fun, more snuggles. During high school, Owen filled our basement and our hearts with his friends. We loved having groups of boys here watching movies, playing video games, listening to music, eating pizza, and drinking all of our La Croix. Instead of taking dates to the senior prom, Owen's friends came to our house for a fancy home-cooked dinner and crème brûlée. The same crew also made memories around the campfire at our cabin. More Owen.

Through all of his adventures, ups and downs, and real successes, Owen was unassuming, modest, and genuinely reticent about his place in the world and if he deserved it. I never heard him brag, except about how much bacon he could eat at his grandma's house. It often took several rounds of encouragement to get him to try out for a team, go for a position, or take harder classes. Maybe it was the shadow of his older brother, or that he really had to work harder because things often did not come as easy for Owen, but he was genuinely a humble and unsure kid in many ways. So whoever is on duty at Heaven's Gates, please listen for the timid knock—that may be Owen. We promise it will be a better place for everyone with More Owen.

Anger Stage?

November 2019

Since losing Owen, I have learned a lot about grief. One of the surprising things I learned is that the famous five stages of grief—denial, anger, bargaining, depression, and acceptance—made popular in the writings of Elisabeth Kübler-Ross were originally based on her research done with terminally ill people facing their *own* impending deaths, not on people who were experiencing the loss of a loved one. I got angry when I read that, and then I sheepishly had to admit that she might have been onto something. And that maybe there was some crossover after all, especially for those of us who lose someone unexpectedly—and if that someone is a child, a one-time part of ourselves.

So: anger stage? You bet. The university security person we were trusting to investigate Owen's disappearance was a recent hire, a woman who had retired from the Portland Police Bureau and moved into the job at UP to finish her career. She seemed to have her mind made up from the beginning that Owen took his own life and didn't really do much of anything to help our search for his body or answers. The university administration reluctantly told us that one of Owen's roommates was facing charges of sexual assault (the boy also told us this himself); this seemed like it would have been something important Owen would have been pondering, something important for us to know about. After we asked several times for a report of their investigative activities, the university gave us a list of data points showing when Owen and his two roommates were using their key cards to scan in and out of the dorm and other campus buildings over that weekend. We accepted all the help they offered, but it didn't feel like enough in many ways.

I recently revisited a clearly frustrated email I wrote to two friends who had been helping us search for answers about Owen's disappearance a month after his body was found. Maybe I was angry simply with losing Owen, but many actions (and non-actions) by others no doubt contributed to my rage. How awful it was to feel such sadness and anger. I still feel it surge when I think about the roadblocks, delays, red herrings, confusing reports, and holes we were presented with during the investigation. And how many things felt (and still feel) unresolved.

Monday, November 11, 2019
Subject: Ramblings about Owen

Dear Kimberly and Colleen,

Just read a comment on Facebook that made me steam up! "The family has been tight lipped." WOW! What are we supposed to say when we don't know what happened?

We have been trying to focus on sharing memories of Owen and how he lived his life (#moreowen) while we are grieving this profound loss. That being said...

"**No** evidence of foul play has **not** been discovered." This is our favorite quote from Portland Police Bureau's update #1 about Owen Klinger. (And the only one I saw about foul play.) This was in the second press release from the police about Owen. I can't see the date of it in the Police news archives as it is just buried under their last "update" about his disappearance which was on October 18 and in their amazing system they don't show the dates of any of the previous releases. Dustin and I were looking at police press releases this morning to see if they had said anything about closing the case. They did post on 10/22 about the body in the river being found and identified as Owen, but haven't made any public statements since then. This also brought back many of the other things they got wrong and went public with that were frustrating—like how they said it was confusing to issue a correction when one of their early press releases said Owen was seen last at Lombard and Portsmouth when Detective Fonken should have said "Willamette and Portsmouth!" I know what they mean: corrections are sooooo confusing! Way more confusing than the truth! Am I right?

We have been told that we have to wait twelve to fourteen weeks for the Medical Examiner to finish and release their report to us. That means that until then we will not know how Owen died. When the police confirmed Owen's identity they told us that there was water in his lungs, but they did not officially tell us the cause of death. The police recently told us that they are closing Owen's case (perhaps to focus on the large number of people still missing in Portland), but we still have a lot of unanswered questions. We feel like we are stuck in limbo. Learning the answers to our questions won't bring Owen back, but it might help us understand how and why he is no longer here.

Why did Owen buy donuts on Sunday night at dinner time? Was this a usual purchase or unusual for him? Did he eat them all or take them with him when he left the dorm at 7:30? Were his roommates in the dorm for the rest of the night? Was anyone else from the lacrosse team absent from practice that night? Was Owen going to meet anyone? Why didn't Owen's roommates check with Sam (Owen's close friend, a girl he liked) when Owen didn't come back to study in the room later that night?

Who was sending group texts to his phone on Sunday between 4 and 5:30 p.m. (or any other times through the month)? We cannot see any of the numbers that were in group messages with him. We also cannot see any of the content of any individual text messages people had sent him. Would anyone who was texting with Owen in September or early October share those texts with us?

Would anyone who saved any snapchats with Owen want to share their content with us?

What happened to the money Owen took out of the ATM? It wasn't found with his body (though his wallet with the ATM card in it was). Did he buy drugs from someone or something at a store? Did he give the money to someone? Did he put the money in his backpack? (This seems unlikely as the bank card had been replaced in his wallet.) Did he burn it like the guy in "Into the Wild"? Did he have a lighter with him?

Where is his phone? Did he have it in airplane mode when he left campus? Not sure how that would show up on the T-Mobile tower report—oh that's right the police didn't request the full amount of time needed to show the time until Owen's phone had stopped sending and receiving messages and data because they messed up the time zone in their original request. They apologized but said they couldn't make another request.

Where is his backpack? I would love to find this to see what was really in there.

What about the videos the police have of someone that could be Owen walking *away* from the St. Johns Bridge on the night of October 6th? Where were those taken? What time? Is it Owen? Can we really figure out which direction he was walking? Are we really getting them from the police now that the case is closed?

Was he suicidal? Doesn't seem like it to most of us who knew Owen closely and/or had interacted with him recently. He seemed happy, was making plans for fall break, to write more songs (bought my guitar on 9/27). It does sound like he was trying to stop smoking and vaping and that he might have been feeling guilty about that difficulty. It's possible that the situation with his roommate was upsetting him, but he didn't tell any of us that this was weighing on his mind. If he was going to go to the river, why did he cross Willamette Blvd to be on the side away from the bridge? (from the TriMet video on 10/6).

What happened at the dance on Friday night? What about his friendship/love interest Sam? Does Justin (one of Owen's roommates) know more about what was going on with Owen than he has shared? Why has the other roommate's family not communicated with us AT ALL since Owen's body has been found? Will we ever hear more from the University about the sexual assault case and Owen's potential involvement in it?

That's all for now. I know you don't have these answers, but thanks for letting me vent. I'm going to pet my dog for a few minutes and lower my blood pressure.

Let's talk soon,
Mary

Owen Loved Chopping Wood

December 2019

Owen always enjoyed tasks that other people thought were odious chores—sweeping the driveway, shoveling snow, squeegeeing windows, and chopping wood. When he mowed the lawn, he never stopped until he had finished edging, swept up all the trimmings, and stowed the equipment carefully back in the garage. He was such a thorough and thoughtful guy! As he was growing up, I worried I was taking advantage of his attitude by giving him the jobs I knew Gabe and Frances would complain about. He would comply with a smile. He genuinely liked helping out in these physical ways.

When we lost Owen, I was filled with questions about who he had been and whether I had really known anything about him at all. Was he unhappy or was he struggling? What had I missed? Didn't he love his life? It sure seemed like he was doing well. So many people—including the police—came at us with their own theories and questions that it was easy to succumb to the rising waters of doubt and uncertainty about who Owen was and why he was gone. It was confusing and sad. We had physically lost our beautiful son, and then our own memories of who he was and what values he possessed were being treated with skepticism. Maybe I was being naive, but I thought I really knew Owen. This is one of the reasons I started my quest for More Owen. I wanted to discover everything I could about Owen and the person he was.

A few months after we lost him, Owen's Japanese teacher worked with his high school's leaders to grant us access to his high school Google drive account. Finding more of Owen in his own words in assignments he had written and turned in over the years for all his different classes was an amazing gift. I love reading what he wrote for his freshman English class (even all his typos, which I have left uncorrected for your pleasure)! Every word I read reveals that I really did know him very well. I wish he could have found some wood to chop at college if he had been feeling stressed out.

Owen Klinger

4 December 2015

Per.1 WW McFaul

I love Chopping Wood

The first time I chopped wood, I was about ten and I was at my Grandma's house. As I recall, it was a fairly small piece of tree and it took me about 6 tries to split it. But on that sixth time, I learned what the most amazing feeling in the world felt like, cleaving a log in two.

That was back in 5th grade. Now, I chop wood that is quite sizable. Every once in awhile, I go out to that same Grandma's faded red house and cleave timber. I don't just do it for the money, although that is quite a big bonus. I do it so she can stay warm during the winter among other things, as her heat comes from burning trees.

Cleaving wood takes my mind off everything, almost like i'm sleeping. This helps me deal with anger, stress, sadness, even boredom. I recall one weekend in particular, when I had been very stressed out about school and sports. I just went out to my Grandma's and did what I loved. I was so happy then, with no worries.

I feel that hewing lumber is more than just something you do to get money, or just something to do. It means something more. You are being productive and contributing to society. You are getting stronger. But more important than that, you are being persistent, you are not giving up. You could stop at any moment and tell yourself that you will do it later, but no. I believe that that is what cutting timber really is, persistence.

I love the simplicity: just chop it in half. This simple act can take your mind off anything. You don't think you just keep on slashing as the world melts around you leaving only you, the axe and the timber. It is not numbness that you feel, it is a feeling of bliss.

The smell of fresh cut trees relaxes you. The feeling of the axe in your hand as it takes hold of you. These are the things I love about splitting lumber. The axe keeps you moving in the same motion for what seems like forever. Only stopping occasionally to get another piece of timber. It has already taught me the benefits of stress-relieving activities.

I love more than just the hacking of the logs, but the persistence that it requires. I hope that it can help me become a better, more persistent person.

Spotify Playlists Resurrected

January 2020

Owen was only eighteen years and two and a half months old when he died. The summer after his senior year of high school (when he turned eighteen) was a busy one filled with work at his first official job, camping trips with friends, family dinners on the front porch, and preparing to move to college. One of the items he tackled on that checklist was getting a debit card.

Owen already had a savings account after participating in his elementary school's "Bank Day" years earlier. When Owen needed to open a checking account, it made sense to go to the same bank so we went together to Umpqua Bank on NE Fremont Street. Owen was stoked to get his debit card and quickly set up his online bank access. He arranged for the paychecks from his job setting up rental tables and chairs for events to be directly deposited into the account and he was off and running. Because I was a signer on Owen's original "bank day" account, the bank kept me connected to Owen's new account and I was able to look at his purchase history after he died.

One of the first purchases he made with his debit card in June of 2019 was a premium Spotify subscription: three months for $0.99. This premium subscription allowed him to listen ad-free and download his own playlists, keeping songs in the order he wanted to hear them. I liked learning that he had treated himself to this literally "premium" music service: it showed me he believed music was important.

When Owen went missing in early October of 2019 and we had no idea what had happened to him, we looked at his Spotify account to see what he had been listening to. My older son, Gabe, whose computer skills helped us do a lot of digging around in Owen's apps and accounts, said Owen was unusual in that he had a few really long playlists (one called "Good Music" is almost seventeen hours long!) and not lots of theme-specific ones.

We took a brief look to see what he had been listening to that last weekend on campus. My heart jumped when I saw a recent playlist called "sad boi"! Was Owen sad or depressed? It's possible, though we didn't have much else to support this theory. "Surrender" by Cheap Trick was on this list, along with melancholy tracks from The Replacements. "Let Her Go" by Passenger, Pink Floyd's "Wish You Were Here," and Green Day's "Wake Me Up When September Ends" explored themes of yearning and loss, but not "my life is over" vibes. Gabe and his sister Frances assured me that everyone, even the happiest and most well-adjusted of their friends, keeps a playlist of sad songs to cry to. They didn't think that Owen's playlist was evidence of suicide.

I saw the playlists as proof of Owen's love of music and his unique sense of what was worth listening to. The Beach Boys, John Denver, and The Beatles mixed with Ween, Weezer, and Wilco. Country tunes from

Home Free, an acapella vocal group, contrasted with AC/DC, Queen, Neil Young, and the Pixies. Owen's tastes were not limited to one musical genre. His dynamic personality shone through, even in the inclusion of the silly barbershop quartet ditty "Enormous Penis" by Da Vinci's Notebook and 23 versions of Johnny Cash singing "Ring of Fire."

I saw that these playlists were there while we were searching for Owen. Once Owen's body was found in the river, I didn't listen to much music for a while. I just couldn't. A few months later, thinking it would be a good time to listen to his "sad boi" playlist since I was already crying all the time, I tried to login to Owen's account but my access was denied. Spotify said there was no account associated with Owen's email address! I panicked as I felt another bit of Owen slipping away. We had lost so much when we lost him, and I was desperately grasping at any fragments of Owen still around, to preserve anything and everything about him. Perhaps it's irrational, but once I knew that Owen's life was over, that he wouldn't be having any more experiences, or making more memories with our family, everything I had of his took on more importance. Losing access to these playlists was another blow, and I didn't want to accept any more loss.

When I couldn't access his Spotify account, I took a deep breath and dove back into the dangerous ocean of Owen's email. Exploring his inbox is always difficult for me: I need to search for more proof of Owen, that he lived an engaged and satisfying life, but I never know what message will spawn a rogue wave of sadness that could sink the unstable life raft I'm drifting on. I found the email showing he paid for the premium Spotify subscription with his new debit card and I entered "Spotify" in the search box to see if there had been any messages regarding account access.

Sure enough there was an unread message dated 10/28/2019. It was in Indonesian! Yes, that's right the message was written in the language of the country of Indonesia so it had gone into a spam folder and I didn't see it. When Google Translate (what an amazing tool!) transformed the Indonesian text into English, it read, "We would like to inform you that the email address on your Spotify account has been changed recently." The message went on to say, "If you really want to change it, no need to worry. You can continue using Spotify as usual. If this *isn't* your email, email us at account-details-changed@spotify.com to let us know. We will investigate what happened."

I felt violated by this takeover of something precious. I was angry at these Indonesian hackers (or was this language just a red herring?) and wondered what was even the point of their hack. I was not very optimistic about regaining access to these treasured glimpses of Owen's musical soul, but I had to fight back.

I emailed Spotify customer service in January of 2020. Luckily, the people at Spotify were my allies in this battle and shared my belief that the music Owen had chosen to save and listen to revealed things about him and his life that words could not express. The customer service agent's message quoted Hans Christian Andersen, "Where words fail, music speaks," and they seemed to understand how important the recovery of Owen's playlists was to me.

After providing Spotify with details of Owen's phone (which we were sadly unable to recover) and the computer browsers where he would have been logged into his account, along with the receipt from his $0.99 payment from his Umpqua debit card, they restored Owen's account for me. I was able to listen to the 23 different versions of "Ring of Fire" again. Scrolling through these lists to hear his favorite tracks like Lynyrd Skynyrd's "Sweet Home Alabama," Toto's "Africa," and John Prine's "Paradise" is like spending time with Owen again. I know I can listen to his "sad boi" playlist anytime I need music to cry to.

I'd like to share Owen's playlists here too. I don't think he would have minded. I think that he, like me, would want others to enjoy the music lists he so thoughtfully curated to reflect his varied interests and moods.

Here are links to some of Owen's playlists:

https://open.spotify.com/playlist/1cHjiq2NucBKcy9fkkhdld?si
=36930cfaa5e943eb

https://open.spotify.com/playlist/5x9Jxc7OCsw4ivvpahVjai?si
=915b07b968b945d8

https://open.spotify.com/playlist/1FhoEMLtnAxO2oFRpehsWT?si
=5255970fa7e4490f

https://open.spotify.com/
playlist/7alILFFDoMeIboHOeJto2M?si=e7b4921621ec4ba6

Discovering Quotes Left Behind

March 2020

One of the ways I processed some of my emotions and discoveries throughout my grief journey was by writing longer emails to the group of supporters who had volunteered to help search for Owen through a findowenk@gmail.com email list our friends created in October 2019.

At first the "Find Owen" group emails were updates on Owen's search. Later, after his body was found and then when we weren't able to get together with friends due to pandemic restrictions, sharing my feelings with this email group—and hearing back from many people—was a helpful part of my healing. I am including some of these messages throughout this book. And while the name of my Facebook page has changed to "More Owen," I haven't yet migrated these email addresses to a new place or name, so this group name still remains as "Find Owen." Maybe I will change it someday, although maybe it will remain as it was originally created, and that's OK. And, yes, I still write to this special group of people. More often than not, I simply address them as "Dear Friends."

to: findowenk@gmail.com
date: March 20, 2020
Subject: Quotes from Owen's Desk

Owen and my dad, Grandpa John, posing with the newly built loft bed/desk 2006

Dear Friends,

Yesterday was the five-month anniversary of Owen's passing and I thought it would be a good time to reach out to this group of helpful people who continue to send love and support us in many ways.

What crazy times we are living through! I hope that this message finds you well, staying home as much as you can with people you like to be with. Waves of uncertainty create a constant flow of anxious thoughts in my head, but when I stop and take a breath I am grateful to be spending so much time at home with my family. I love having our older son, Gabe, home from college and our daughter, Frances, now on spring break, nestled in her bedroom where she logged into her digital classroom all last week. I hope that even in this unprecedented and stressful situation, you can find gratitude for the people in your life.

Of course being all together makes it obvious who we are missing. I think of Owen constantly and look for signs of him every time I turn around. Until a few weeks ago, we hadn't really touched anything on Owen's side of the bedroom that the boys shared. To prepare for Gabe's homecoming, I had done a lot of cleaning on Gabe's side of the room and Dustin replaced Gabe's childhood loft bed/dresser/desk combo (one of two my dad built for the boys in 2006) with a new bed, but Owen's loft bed still stood, dominating the room. It seemed like we could take some steps to make the room seem less Owen-focused. I packed Owen's stuff into bags, bins, and boxes to sort through at another date and Gabe got out tools and carefully started taking Owen's bed apart.

As a little boy, Owen loved tools and helped assemble this loft—how could we undo the physical manifestation of his sweetly earnest efforts? We knew there was a spot under the mattress where Owen added his name in 2006 below my dad's dedication and signature: "Dear Owen, May all your dreams come true. Love, Grandpa John." It was very moving to see that, and I almost put a stop to the deconstruction. We pushed on, and I am so glad we did. What we didn't know was that over the years, Owen had been writing all over the beams that framed the built-in desk.

Did he scribble swear words or fart jokes? No. "Mom is driving me crazy"? or "Dad is being mean"? No. Gabe discovered that Owen, in his terrible hand-writing, had painstakingly carved a variety of inspirational quotes on every inward-facing surface. Gabe brought all these pieces down to the living room and lined them up for us to see. I couldn't believe my eyes.

These are the quotes Owen wrote:

```
"When the rich wage war it's the poor who die."
```

```
"Try not to become a man of success, but become a man of
value."
                                        —Albert Einstein
```

```
"Mankind must put an end to war before war puts an end to
mankind."
                                        —John F. Kennedy
```

```
"If you think you can do a thing or you think you can't do
a thing, you're right."
                                        —Henry Ford
```

```
"The only place success comes before work is in the
dictionary."
                                      —Vince Lombarty (sic)
```

"Far better is it to dare mighty things, to win glorious triumphs, even though checkered by failure than to rank with those poor spirits who neither enjoy nor suffer much because they live in a gray twilight that knows neither victory nor defeat."

—Theodore Roosevelt

"Nearly all men can stand adversity, but if you want to test a man's character, give him power."

—Abraham Lincoln

"A smart man makes a mistake and learns from it, and never makes that mistake again, but a wise man finds a smart man and learns how to avoid mistakes altogether."

—Roy H. Williams

"It is not in the stars to hold our destiny but in ourselves."

—William Shakespeare

I try to imagine middle-school Owen sitting in his desk writing these quotes when procrastinating and I feel even more deeply the loss of his sensitive and thoughtful soul. Being a parent is so mysterious and humbling: we are granted 24/7 access to our kids' lives and think we know everything about them and then some new aspect of a child is revealed and it can absolutely blow us away.

We asked Micah Kassel (the parent of a classmate of Owen's) to create an art piece to preserve and display the parts of the bed/desk Owen had written on. I moved the pieces of wood outside for Micah to pick up and grabbed the headboard in case he could use that piece in the creation too. When I picked up the headboard, I found more quotes along the bottom part that had hung down into the desk area. I was excited to discover more evidence of Owen's inner life and squinted at the scratchings to decipher what else he had written:

```
"Success is not final, failure is not final(sic). It is the
courage to continue that counts."
                                        —Winston Churchill
```

```
"I say what I want to say and do what I want to do. There's
no in between. People will either love you or hate you."
                                                   —Eminem
```

```
"While I thought I was learning how to live, I have been
learning how to die."

                                      —Leonardo da Vinci
```

This flattened me. What young boy would take such time to carve and trace all of these letters, contemplating the meaning of life? Owen's head wasn't just full of thoughts of bacon and sports. I was astounded, and then I had to laugh that Eminem's lyrics were included with such deeply philosophical and revered names. Inspiration can come from anyone, and I know I need to keep letting messages from Owen reveal themselves.

I realize I may never have answers to the questions I still have about how and why we lost our son. It is very hard to carry on without Owen and without knowing why he is gone. I will work on summoning "the courage to continue" that Churchill (and Owen) say is what counts. I do this with an increasing appreciation for Owen and all he brought to our lives and the lives of so many people. I am grateful that Gabe came home to stay with us and took apart Owen's bed. Discovering all this about Owen is opening my eyes to the unique ways *all* of my kids have improved my life. It is humbling to watch Gabe and Frances grieving the loss of their brother knowing that I can do little to lighten their load. I can walk alongside them, letting them lean on me as I shift the weight of my own heavy grief. And I can help make something beautiful from these pieces of Owen's bed.

Please take care of yourselves. Keep taking care of each other too.

With love and longing for More Owen,
Mary

* * * *

Update Posted on Facebook
May 13, 2020

"#moreowen arrived on Mother's Day with the delivery of the finished artwork from Micah Kassell. I love how this turned out and am so amazed by how Micah artfully imagined combining these special pieces of Owen's bed with some of Owen's other words. Thank you, Micah. Thank you, Owen, I am so glad I am your mom. Gratitude to Dustin, Gabe, and Frances for helping me feel special and appreciated on Mother's Day."

Part sculpture, part painting, it's really big and I'm not sure what to call it, but it's full of More Owen. Micah reverently traced Owen's words, darkening them with ink so they are easier to read. The pieces of loft that framed the desk area now surround a beautiful canvas the size of the twin bed Owen slept on for thirteen years. It proclaims "More Owen," with colors and symbols that evoke memories of him. Words and notes from Owen's song adorn the headboard above the last quotes we discovered.

Mere Owen by Micah Kassel

Skydogs and Panther Creek

March 2020

Owen at Panther Creek September 2017

Dustin and his brother Seth, along with a few of their Klinger cousins, are co-owners of some timber property in Southwest Washington, the place we call Panther Creek. Their small forest is adjacent to national forest lands that have been in conservation since 1908 when Theodore Roosevelt established the Columbia National Forest (now called the Gifford Pinchot National Forest). An old hunting cabin built by Dustin's great-grandpa in the 1930s sits under the protection of tall Douglas fir trees just above the high water mark along the banks of Panther Creek, a cold, spring-fed stream that cuts through the property and feeds into the Wind River. (Current laws do not allow construction of a dwelling so close to a waterway, but I guess this one is grandfathered—or great-grandfathered!—in.)

Dustin's mom, Barbara, and dad, Bruce, made this rustic cabin their home when Dustin was a baby and they were "living off the land" in the early 1970s. There was no electricity or indoor plumbing, but they had plenty of running water in the creek out front and 80 acres of firewood all around for the woodstove that heated the cabin. It was a pretty idyllic place to be a little kid, but full of challenges for the parents.

Dustin was eight years old when his mom discovered she was pregnant with Seth and realized she did not want to continue to raise her family in the deep shade of the Panther Creek woods. Dustin's parents separated and later divorced. Barbara moved with the boys closer to town, while Bruce lived in the cabin until shortly before he passed away in 2007.

The old cabin was pretty run down by the time Dustin and I started our own family and moved back to Portland. (Panther Creek is about an hour's drive from the city.) We occasionally visited Bruce (Grampy Bruce to our kids) in the cabin, but we mostly stayed outside as I was always nervous the kids would hurt themselves in the dark climbing on the ladder up to the sleeping loft or falling on an old rusty nail (there were buckets of these all around). After Grampy Bruce passed away, we rarely went in the cabin at all and would instead set up a big tent in an area next to the cabin on our annual Labor Day camping trips. The kids loved cooking over a campfire and even washing dishes in the creek. Fishing, throwing rocks, whittling sticks (inevitably cutting their fingers with pocket knives!), and hiking around our own private forest and creek spoiled us all. (We only camped as a family somewhere else one other time!)

The thing about timber property is that there comes a time when the trees need to be harvested and then trees must be replanted. For the Klinger property at Panther Creek, this time came in 2013. The trees within 250 feet of the creek remained untouched by the logging. Dustin and Seth decided to use some of their profits to renovate the old cabin that was moldering—uninhabited and uninhabitable—under a leaky roof. The refreshed structure kept the initial footprint of the cabin and utilized some of the original beams. It became the setting of many more family memories and was Owen's favorite place in the world.

When Owen went missing, a few of his friends thought he might have gone to Panther Creek. Dustin led a search party out there. I hoped Owen would be found camping out among his favorite trees, but he wasn't. Spending time out there now, knowing he is never coming back to this place or to us, is both heart-wrenching and healing. It's a beautiful place and Owen's deep love of it connects all of us to him and the land.

From my journal: March 21, 2020

I'm at Panther Creek on a spring Saturday with Dustin. Usually we don't come out here much at this time of year. It's too cold and usually too wet; we used to be too busy with commitments in town, but we come out here more lately, and it's where we both feel connected to Owen.

Green is all around us. The bright green tips of new growth on the fir trees reach out optimistically into the open spaces, somehow turning the dark gray winter rains and the heavy northwest volcanic soil into something beautiful and tender. These fragile fingers of life contrast starkly with the hard, craggy limbs and sharp, spiky needles of the tall firs that guard the creek. The trees stretch up to the sky from the canyon's steep banks, reaching heights where the wind blows through the lichen and long mosses clinging to their highest branches, moving like Owen's long hair flowing behind him when he ran.

Panther Creek is clear and cold, even in the summer, but right now it's so cold it makes your hand ache as soon as you reach into the water to test the temperature. It runs fast in spring with snowmelt from Mt. St. Helens, hiding the swirling currents deep below the surface. The rushing water creates a wall of sound, but somehow it's oddly quieter, too. Maybe it's because we are quieter now, not a boisterous family of five frolicking at the side of the creek, calling to each other to be heard over the sound of the water. As the season moves on, the water level will drop and sink down into the channels where it burbles over rocks and through narrow chutes of the blue-green creek bed of Panther Creek. For now the round holes in the rocky bank, usually shallow pools, are full to the brim, appearing like small underwater rooms, a setting for a watery fairy tale. What would it be like to be trapped in a room like that with the creek water rushing over your head? What would the sky look like through the water? What did Owen feel when he was in the river?

I see a fat robin approach a tree that hangs out over the creek. He lands quietly and stays there a long time. Silent and still and then gone. Was that Owen? One of his skydogs?

Owen wrote this song his senior year of high school when he was in an audio engineering class and had formed a band called Head Voice with a few of his friends. I'm sure it was inspired by the birds we always saw at Panther Creek. I continue to think of Owen whenever I see a bird. I love that he called them "skydogs."

Skydogs by Owen Klinger

Birds flying free
Soaring across the sky
High above the trees
Flapping tirelessly

No direction but their own
A new view of the world
Climbing through the atmosphere
Looking out at the world

Fly north in spring
Back south for the winter
Journey never ends
I wanna be a skydog

I wish I was one of them
A family of my own
Gliding in herds of ten
Doing whatever I can

```
A red hawk, a crow or an eagle
I cannot find my beagle
Sparrow, falcon or dove
Everybody says they're in love

Fly north in spring
Back south for the winter
Journey never ends
I wanna be a skydog

Feathers flowin' in the wind
Streaking through the clouds
Crossing the endless oceans
Diving back down to earth

The future is unknown
All we have is the present
And I know in a hundred years of
Furling through the sky

Flying north in spring
Back south for the winter
Journey never ends
I wanna be a skydog

Gliding through forests for days on end
No more worries filling up my mind
The rhythm of my wings and the howling wind
I wanna be a skydog.
```

Owen also wrote his song "Panther Creek" as an assignment for that same audio engineering class. His friends told us that he procrastinated on this song until the deadline was almost upon them. They were impressed and a little jealous at how quickly and easily it came out once he finally started composing. It captures the simple joy of times Owen spent at our cabin by Panther Creek, his favorite place on Earth. When the year-end audio engineering showcase was scheduled on Dustin's birthday, Owen thought he could perform "Panther Creek" as a birthday surprise for Dustin. Unfortunately, the show was also scheduled for the same date and time as his lacrosse state playoff game at a field across town.

Owen performing at the Audio Engineering showcase May 2019

Owen figured out a way he could play in the game (they won against a tough opponent!) and still make it to the auditorium in time to perform if I drove him between the field and the high school and he changed in the car. It was an ambitious plan, but Owen and I made it in plenty of time for him to go on stage and perform with his friends. What he didn't take into account was that Dustin had volunteered to bring our gas-powered generator to the lacrosse field to run the scoreboard and PA system. Dustin didn't want to drive across town with all that gasoline sloshing around in the car—plus Frances and her friend, who had gone to the lacrosse game, were complaining that they didn't want to waste more of their time "watching Owen do stuff." (These were appropriate feelings for a little sister to have about her brother but painful to write about now that he is gone.) So Dustin headed home and missed the performance that was supposed to be his birthday gift from his middle kid. It is one of the saddest things for all of us, but I shared the video I had taken on my phone with Dustin when we got home—he loved it.

When Owen first performed it at the school, the words "Panther Creek" weren't even in the song, though I heard a natural place the words could go. On the way home, I made the suggestion (annoying mom much?) and he liked it, so now that's the last line of the song.

<u>Panther Creek</u> by Owen Klinger

Turn off 14, headed for Carson
Passing the High Bridge to Bear Creek Road
Jump in the creek and it's freezing cold
Hopping across the rocks
It's hot outside so you warm up quick

Spending hours not catching fish
Sharpening sticks—don't cut your hand now
Building a dam out of some rocks
Playing cribbage with my best friends

Sitting around a fire at night
These memories I love

Nowhere in the world that I'd rather be…
Panther Creek

Owen sharpening sticks with Gabe at Panther Creek June 2019

We have a scratchy recording the band made out at Panther Creek of these songs and a few others on an old Toshiba tape recorder that was Grampy Bruce's. You can even hear the sound of the creek in the background.

https://forrestgregor.bandcamp.com/album/panther-creek

Where I'm From—by Owen Klinger

April 2020

U P's literary magazine published a poem Owen had written during his short time as a student there. This was an assignment in one of his classes and the professor sent it to us while Owen was missing. I took it as validation that Owen loved his life and am grateful that we have these words from him. I wrote the following introduction:

Owen is an unlikely person to have his writing published in a literary magazine. He is probably rolling his eyes at me for submitting his poem. He got an F in Language Arts in seventh grade because he simply never started—let alone finished—either of the two required writing assignments. Later in high school, he survived by writing one long paper about income inequality and tweaking it to fit several different classes. I can safely say that Owen hated writing. But without him here now, all we have are our memories of him and his own words. Even though they might be short and simple, or Owen wrote them to do the bare minimum for an assignment, his writings have meaning for us and reveal more about him than we ever knew. It is clear that no matter how much some of us may hate writing, parts of our identities linger in the words we put together.

Where I'm From by Owen Klinger

I am from rain jackets, from wool Pendleton sweaters and the never ending rain.

I am from the steep grassy lawn in front of my house, soft, covered in leaves and still wet from yesterday's downpour.

I am from towering Fir trees, the moss growing on river rocks in the spring.

I am from football Sundays and overly sarcastic humor, from Dustin and Mary and John.

I am from the opportunistic deal finders and the give-it your-all's.

From extra credit is mandatory and explore all your options.

I am from Our father who art in heaven most Sundays until I got busy with high school.

I am from Portland and Slovenian Clevelanders, almond roca and pickled dilly beans.

From my Grandpa's tours in Korea to the four years my parents lived in Japan to the 12 years of Japanese language my siblings and I studied.

I am from the countless scrapbooks, family trees and papers that sit in our bookshelves at home. My family's lives, history, traditions and most importantly the times spent together are captured in those pictures and lines of text sitting on the shelves.

A Tribute to His Dad

When Owen went missing, we were lucky to have many smart friends who volunteered a wide range of skills. They led brainstorming sessions in our dining room, contacted local media stations, coordinated volunteers to search various sections of the city, and checked with businesses in the area who might have video footage of Owen on the night he went missing. They designed and printed flyers, hung them up all over the city, and screened my calls and social media messages. Our family received so much assistance during those weeks of searching for Owen I will never be able to express enough gratitude. But something our friends couldn't help us with was the agonizing search in our hearts to see if something had gone wrong in Owen's life with us, combing through our memories for hints of how we might have changed this tragic outcome if we had done something different in the past.

As a mom I felt like my primary and very important job was (is!) to take care of my kids. The pain of losing Owen blew up my life like a huge, blinding explosion. It's hard to imagine that we could even feel anything else in the aftermath, but I felt a shameful sting that I had possibly failed my son. It was hard for me to not question our parenting. Had we done enough as his parents to raise him to make good choices? In our "zone defense" (two on three) parenting style, had we missed something that would have made a difference for Owen?

Even though we thought things had gone well for Owen at home, we were leaving no stone unturned and searching for any clue about what might have happened. I scrutinized our family scrapbooks and some of the journals I kept when the kids were growing up to see if there was anything that could point to the reason he was now lost to us. Was I too hard on him the time he was teasing Frances and I took away his Gameboy? Did Dustin make Owen feel bad when he got mad about the stupid F on his seventh grade report card? Was being the second son frustrating for Owen?

Owen brought Dustin canned coffee as a souvenir from his 8th grade trip to Japan 2015

I was glad to be a stay-at-home mom through Owen's childhood, chaperoning school field trips, fundraising for the public school foundations, and running the PTA. I took the kids to school and their after-school activities, made them healthy lunches and dinners, and made sure they did their homework (most of the time). I felt like I had a front-row seat to all the drama and excitement of growing up in this family of three kids that were each two years apart in school. And I felt like it was going well. Dustin worked long hours at his law firm but was also a pretty involved dad, making it to most of the kids' sports activities, volunteering on school committees, and teaching them useful skills like building a fire or pruning a tree. Were we good parents? We were certainly trying hard to be.

I know I worried over the years that I was taking advantage of Owen's love of work. It was so much easier asking Owen to wash the windows—a job he loved!—than it was to ask Gabe or Frances, who might complain about having to do it and then not be as thorough (or as joyful while working). Did he resent the role he was cast to play in the heart of our family? Did he feel a heavy burden of parental expectation for excellence? In his "Where I'm From" poem he mentioned he is "from extra credit is mandatory"—maybe this means we pushed too hard. Now he is gone, and we are left behind. Without knowing what happened, it's hard not to blame ourselves for whatever might have gone wrong in Owen's life for him to either have left us on purpose or to be making decisions that put him in harm's way.

I think because Owen is not here to answer in person that we were indeed a positive influence on his life, we have to trust the writings he left behind. This tribute speech he worked on and presented in his speech class at UP is one of the few assignments we found after he was gone. Being able to read Owen's words of gratitude when we struggle with so many unanswered questions has helped us a little. We know he knew of our love for him, and in this speech we can feel his love for his dad (and me—in a little shoutout in his conclusion).

These are his notes, so it's not all written out in prose and again any grammatical errors here are his.

Owen Klinger: A tribute to my Dad

Christmas is usually a time of family, friends and giving gifts. Another common tradition is stockings. As I am sure most of you know, you usually get little gifts or candy. Well 10 years ago "Santa" left me and my siblings gobstoppers in our stockings. Now I had never had a gobstopper before in my life and I didn't know that you were just supposed to suck on them. So I popped one in my mouth and immediately started choking. Within a split second of me making a noise my dad jumped up and did the Heimlich maneuver on me very effectively. My dad has had such an impact on my life and aside from saving my life, he has shown me what hard work can get you, how to respect other cultures and how to look out for others.

Body:

A. Showed me what hard work means
   A. He worked long hours when I was little, and I didn't get to see him much. As I got older, I started seeing him more but even when we were on a trip somewhere or on vacation somewhere, he would get a phone call and he would be buried in work again.
   B. After my second year of middle school, he changed firms and finally started having more free time to take us to school, go to my brother and I's football games or see my sister's ballet recitals. The change in my dad was so visible after he moved jobs, he was happier, more energetic and moved a little slower through life instead of always pushing forward to the next thing. My dad showed me how important it is to keep a balance in life in everything you do. Don't work too much but always work hard.
   C. Now the real way I learned how to work wasn't just from watching my dad, it was from working alongside him. Despite his busy schedule, he almost always found time on the weekends to clean up the yard or fix up the house. We spent countless hours together doing yard work on those rainy weekends in the fall or spring. While yard work might not seem like the most profitable skill, it

taught me how to work towards a bigger goal. The hours spent raking and mowing may have seemed fruitless by themselves, but when you are done you get to see with your own eyes the work that you accomplished.

B. Taught me about Japan and cultural differences
  A. After college, my dad spent four years in Japan, and convinced my mom to come over as well while they worked to pay off his student loans. This is where my dad realized his deep appreciation of Japanese language and culture.
  B. After moving back to the US and buying a house in Portland, my parents found the Japanese immersion program which taught both English and Japanese from K-12 and enrolled my brother, sister and I in it.
  C. At first, I hated learning another language, it seemed like it was forced on me and I had no say. But after visiting Japan in 5th grade with my school trip, I understood why my parents had put us in that school. Seeing firsthand the differences in everyday life almost five thousand miles away still has a lasting effect on my perspective of the world. I have my dad and his crazy Idea to move to Japan to pay off his student loans to thank for my outlook on the world.

C. Advised me to look out for others
  A. Whenever my dad ended up dropping me off in middle school he would tell me as I was getting out of the car to say hi to someone who looked lonely. Given I was an anxious middle schooler at the time I didn't take his advice to heart and only said hi to a few people. But looking back, those words make me think about how you don't know what anyone you see in your life is going through. I try to follow his example now and say hi or just give a quick smile and even though it's not much, it still brightens their day.

B. My dad was always kind to strangers and struck up a conversation if we were waiting in line for something. And he always stopped to help people on the side of the road if people had car trouble and gave them a jump or helped them change a tire.

Conclusion: Just to be clear I am not choosing a favorite parent and I could write the same speech about all that my mom has done for me and to be honest it would probably be longer than this one. My parents have both had a huge impact on me, but my dad inspired me to work hard in everything, respect differences and always be kind to people. Thank you for listening to what inspired me, I look forward to finding out about what inspired all of you.

A Pandemic Birthday

July 2020

Below is an email I sent to the Find Owen group on what would have been Owen's 19th birthday.

to: findowenk@gmail.com
date: July 23, 2020
Subject: Owen's Birthday is today

Dear Friends,

It's a summer Thursday in the midst of a pandemic. Beautiful flowers, leaves, and herbs appeared outside our front door overnight, lovingly arranged in a sweet tribute to the nineteenth anniversary of Owen's birth, the first of such celebrations since we lost him. He was born at 1:48 a.m. on July 23, 2001 in a relatively peaceful and non-painful way. (Remember I have two other kids so I know what I am talking about with this one!) This day is much harder.

We have seen this day looming on our calendars and wondered how it would go. Because of pandemic restrictions on social gatherings, our plans to share Owen's birthday with friends and family had to be postponed, leaving a bigger void on our already empty calendar, but I wasn't sure what I would feel like doing. Would I want to be alone? Be near friends? Honestly, the day is here now and I still don't know. More than anything I want this day to feel "normal" and unremarkable and easily survivable. At the same time, I want this day to be more special than ever before and I want everyone to remember Owen and be thinking about us. The pandemic messed up all the birthday parties this year–Dustin and I each turned fifty earlier this summer with very little fanfare–so it's no surprise that Owen's birthday is weird too.

My grief often sends me mixed signals. If I look at it from a certain perspective, maybe today can be both things: special *and* unremarkable. Life without Owen is our new normal now and I am trying to make the choice to celebrate and find comfort in anything I can. So I got up early, fed our dog, ran the dishwasher and put in a load of laundry, finding peace in these comforting domestic rituals. I left the house early to play tennis (with a community I'd been involved in for years; this counts as therapy, people!), came home and drank more coffee, had some avocado on my toast, and tried to not let the coronavirus death count in the news pull me under. It's just like so many other days we have had, and yet everything today has more meaning.

There is simultaneously nothing and a lot going on. This July 23 is another day in Oregon when people are trying to stay safe and healthy in the face of the ongoing pandemic but still trying to get some stuff done and perhaps enjoy a bit of a "normal summer" experience. This July 23 people are trying to make decisions about school in the coming fall or how to show up safely for important ongoing Black Lives Matter protests. This July 23 people are struggling with their health or hunger or joblessness or frustration and worry about the current political situation. Owen isn't here for any of this, but I am trying to think that his absence can help me be more present for everyone and everything else around me. (I'm still not all the way there yet, but I am still working on it!) I am grateful for the tennis and the coffee and the avocado on my toast. I am grateful for the health of my husband and the two other children sleeping in upstairs. (Yes, I did all those little household things and went and played tennis and am now writing this message while they are all sleeping. It's not fair! Sleep is still so hard for me.) I feel blessed to have a caring circle of friends who are sending us photos of Owen and messages of support, and who made the beautiful flower mandala outside my door overnight, a breathtakingly loving monument to a special boy who is gone.

Owen's birthday was always one of the best days of the summer in many ways. This day brings perfect weather to Oregon almost every year, and Owen's birthdays were full of swimming, water balloons, frozen treats, and delicious grilled dinners. When he got older, the celebrations featured goofiness, laughter, and music making with friends around campfires. We might not be able to celebrate as we used to with these heavy hearts, but we can all hug the people we are with today and share a smile for the boy who loved his birthday and who loved his life.

Please keep reaching out to us. We need your support more than ever.

With love and thanks,
Mary and family
#moreowen

Make a Contribution to the Group

September 2020

to: findowenk@gmail.com
date: September 14, 2020
Subject: Owen's Contribution to the Group

Dear Friends,
Hope this finds you somewhere safe and not too smoky.

Somehow we are making it through this year of grief and unimaginable loss, but it has not been easy. I know now more than ever that no one knows what to say in situations like ours, but that's OK and by at least trying to say something you are remembering Owen, seeing us, and acknowledging our pain and this helps. Maybe this is why I spend so much time immersed in memories of our days with Owen: it helps me remember all the things we learned and experienced as a family of five—more of everything because Owen and his beautiful energy was in the middle of it all. It helps me appreciate the rare but sweet moments we can still create together as a family of four, even in the midst of a pandemic and catastrophic wildfires. I have heard from many people that this helps them, too.

Most recently, I have been poring over the memories of the end of last summer, when we took Owen up to the University of Portland and moved him into

Christie Hall. Last week I saw this photo from Orientation weekend for the first time, and it took me right back to all the proud, happy, sad, and nervous feelings I had when we were sending Owen off to college.

Owen's dorm room August 2019

What a gift to discover another special moment captured. During events that weekend, Dustin and I met Owen's two roommates and their families. We unpacked and arranged furniture while chatting about siblings, sports, music, and potential majors. A student media team came through the dorms to document this rite of passage, taking this photo and asking me if I had any last words of advice for Owen. My family sometimes calls me "Helpful-Suggestion-Woman" as if it's my superpower, so I leapt at the chance to impart some helpful suggestions and advice to Owen and his cohorts.

Since he was attending a college in our own town, I really wanted Owen to immerse himself in the college residential experience and give new friendships the time they needed to grow. I didn't want him coming home all the time (oh, how I wish I could take that back!) or just hanging out with all his Portland friends. Off the top of my head I said, "I just want them to be present in the moment. Be here, be with this community, and make…make a contribution to the group." The boys in the room were not really listening, but little did we know they would have another chance to hear my advice.

Later that weekend, a video of "Freshman Move-In 2019" was shown on the huge screen to the entire group of incoming freshmen and their parents in the Chiles Center. (Yes, the same place where we would gather just a few months later for Owen's funeral.) Imagine my surprise when it was my voice that opened the video!

I punched Dustin's arm, saying, "That's me! That's my advice for Owen!" I looked up in the bleachers where the students were sitting to see if I could catch Owen's eye, but I couldn't find him in the sea of freshman faces. Later, Owen said he and his new friends knew it was me right away. I am not sure if he was proud or embarrassed, but at least I knew he heard me. At the time, I was elated that my words were chosen to be the opening comments in that video, that what I said had resonated with the film editors, and it validated my feeling that UP was a great fit for Owen. (Later, the fact that my voice out of all the parents recorded that day was the one used at the beginning of that video seemed like an eerie and haunting coincidence.)

When Owen went missing, and his body was eventually found, it was these words that came back to me when I was trying to come up with something to say to the reporters after the impromptu Memorial Mass UP put together for Owen on October 22, 2019.

As I told the reporters then, and recall again today, Owen's "contribution to the group" was revealing how connected we are and how much we need each other. The experience of searching for Owen and mourning his loss when his body was discovered united the UP community and our Portland community in that unique way that mutually experienced trauma can.

Connections were revealed and strengthened as we received different types of help from the network of friends, business contacts, and strangers who came forward to aid in our search for Owen. New links were forged as individuals teamed up in spontaneous ways to lead searches, help with social media, or canvass the neighborhoods around the school. I know that several new collaborations came out of this stressful time—diamonds created by the pressure of the situation? Friends shared stories of their own traumatic losses that I had been naively unaware of, deepening our bonds and mutual understanding. I am trying to be grateful for all of these new connections even as I am struggling to accept the loss of a huge part of my heart.

Now I am trying to be present in the moment—"one day at a time" seems like a pretty brilliant approach, whoever thought of that!—but I am worried about the weeks and months to come with overwhelmingly sad memories waiting in the wings as we approach the anniversary of Owen's disappearance. I will try to take my own advice and "be here," remembering what finding Owen did for us all.

During this time of grief, this pandemic, this climate crisis and wildfire disaster, this election cycle: what's your contribution to the group?

Thank you for continuing to remember Owen and to appreciate the people and blessings in your own lives. Please keep reaching out to us.

With love,
Mary
#moreowen

Owen in a Word

October 2020

On October 7, 2020, we held an online celebration to remember Owen, one year after we learned he had gone missing. The social gathering restrictions put in place due to the Covid-19 pandemic kept us from getting together in person with many others that loved Owen. We still felt it was important to mark that day and are grateful that so many friends and family joined us on Zoom to share stories, laughs, and tears.

While people were signing on, Sarina Saturn, a psychology professor at UP who had become a sympathetic friend of mine and was serving as the emcee and moderator for us, asked everyone to put in the chat one word that described Owen. For some folks, one word wasn't enough to describe Owen so they wrote in twice. More Owen!

This is how Owen is remembered:

From Mary: Gentle
From Stuart: Selfless
From Scott: Kind-hearted
From Carrie: Smiling
From Scott (again): Responsible
From Kevin: Joyful
From Sheli: Free spirit
From Kevin (again): Fun

From Bobby: Impressive
From Dustin: Giving
From Bill: Gentle
From Shauna: Playful
From William: Committed
From Bobby (again): Loved
From Michele: Loving
From Karen: Courageous
From Shannon: Joyful
From Barb: Soulful
From Everett: Caring
From Jen: Smiley
From Mark: Fearless
From Michelle: Joyful
From Julie: Hardworking
From Steve: Genuine

Losing My Body

December 2020

A few weeks after Owen left for college, I started to notice a lump in my lower belly. It seemed to only be there when I was waking up in the morning and lying on my back. Like a dummy, I thought, "Wow, my bladder must really be full to be sticking out like that. I better go to the bathroom!" What I didn't think was that I needed to go to the doctor.

I *did* need to go to the doctor, but then Owen went missing and my world fell apart. I forgot about my bladder and my lump, and I wasn't really sleeping so I wasn't waking up to see it. It feels strange to say we are lucky that Owen's body was found only a few weeks after he went missing. Lucky? That's not the right word because, of course, finding a lifeless body was not what we were hoping for, but it did solve one part of the mystery and gave us a little peace. (I have met parents who have never found their children, even ten years after they went missing, and honestly I don't know how they keep going.) The rest of 2019 passed in a blur as I was dazed and numb and I didn't know yet how hard it would be to keep going without knowing what happened to Owen, or how my family would continue our lives without him.

One of my friends who does energy work and physical therapy would say things like "you aren't in your body" as she shared her healing touch with me. I didn't really get it, but looking back I think now I understand what she meant. I was so caught up in the storm of emotions, charting the tides of my fresh grief, worrying about my other two kids and my husband's shattered heart that I was unable for months to feel anything corporal. My eating and sleeping were terribly disrupted. Nothing tasted good, but I knew I had to eat. Playing tennis—something I had been doing five or six days a week since my kids were in full-time school—was difficult to get back into. I didn't feel the passion and the drive to chase a yellow ball.

I was not able to pay any attention to what was happening *inside* my body either.

And then the pandemic swept into our lives, bringing isolating social restrictions and terrifying scenes of overflowing hospitals and funeral homes. I was paralyzed with fear and anxious that we could accidentally kill someone we loved if we weren't vigilant about limiting our exposure to others and the virus. We stayed home and stayed safe. Other than obsessively checking to see if I had a fever or had lost my sense of smell, I was still not in my body.

Then something at one of the socially distant meet ups with my book club in the summer of 2020 brought me back around. I met my friends on a warm evening at a local park, and each of us brought our own snacks and drinks. We sat in a big circle on individual blankets with a lot of space between us, and what we hoped was a safe distance from other people gathering in the park. I don't think we talked about a book that time because none of us were really able to concentrate on reading anything other than the terrifying daily news reports, but we caught up on each other's lives and tried to enjoy each other's company like we used to, finding comfort in our mutual anxieties. After a while, someone had to go to the bathroom. And the public bathrooms were closed (and if they had been open we were probably too afraid of the coronavirus to go in). This led to a funny discussion about who was going to discreetly pee in the park and who was going to hold it until they got home. I said I thought I could hold it and then remembered the bump I had seen in my lower belly when my bladder was full. I mentioned that to my friends and learned from my physical therapist friend who specializes in women's pelvic bowl issues that there is really no way that was my bladder sticking out and I might need to get that checked out.

I finally made an appointment to see my doctor. I arrived at the clinic wearing a mask that hid my nervous smile and had my temperature taken by a nurse at the door to make sure I wasn't secretly harboring the dreaded coronavirus. I followed freshly-taped arrows down the hallway to the check-in counter where the masked assistant behind a plexiglass window keyed in my name and date of birth. Most of my doctor visits in the past had been just routine checkups, so these special pandemic procedures seemed to heighten my anxiety and concern. I wept in the exam room, which alarmed my doctor—was I in a lot of pain?—no, I had to explain, I was just weepy all the time because my son had died. And now I was scared I was going to die, too. The doctor's touch was gentle as she examined me, and her voice was calm as she confirmed that something was growing in my uterus. I would need to go to another doctor for further tests.

In a different office, on a different day, after following similar arrows to a waiting room with chairs placed carefully six feet apart, I met the doctor who would eventually remove my uterus and the fibroid tumors growing there. She assured me they were likely benign, but that pathology would look at the tumors to make sure there was no cancer. I wept in that office, too. After suffering tremendous loss, I was losing even more: a physical part of my body that for many years I thought had defined me. And I was losing forever the opportunity to have another child, a longshot given I had recently turned 50, but it was a thought I had when we lost Owen: let's have another baby! Now it seemed like my uterus had done its job and was ready to be retired.

I had never had surgery before the day in November 2020 when Dustin dropped me off at the day-surgery center. I was scared, but my older brother works as a nurse anesthetist and my mom is a retired nurse who worked in the surgical recovery room for 20 years, so I had knowledgeable family members who had helped answer my questions about the procedure and how I might feel. What I was not prepared for was the tremendous outpouring of emotions the cocktail of medications released in me as I came out from sedation. Whoa! I think I scared the nurses with my wailing—they thought I was suffering physical pain from the operation. When I was able to talk, I blubbered on and on about how I was a grieving mom who was missing her son, only a year from the loss, how I wanted to not wake up so I could be with him. (Super scary for them to hear, I'm sure, but that's how I was feeling!) I told them that every time I went to sleep—and the anesthesia for the procedure was deep, deep sleep like I hadn't experienced since we lost Owen—and woke up, it was like losing Owen all over again. And now I had lost the womb that had miraculously grown my three children so perfectly. My uterus made me a mom. My uterus made Owen. I went on and on. It was a lot. The pain assessment tool with those smiling and anguished faces was useless. I was inconsolable. They moved me into my own space rather quickly so I wouldn't disturb the other patients coming out of surgery and left me alone with my grief—oh, and some applesauce.

Compared to the pain ripping my heart apart, the physical aftermath of the procedure was nothing. I felt weird pressure on my insides and an annoying tugging when I shifted my position in the bed. They said my bladder was having a hard time "getting organized" again after the removal of a tumor that was close to where the bladder was (maybe I wasn't so stupid to think the bladder was involved after all!) so I stayed overnight.

The pathology report revealed that these were in fact benign tumors and there were no cancer cells detected in any of the tissue they tested. I was going to be OK, but without a womb and without one of my children. Realizing that the pain of losing Owen was greater than other physical pain I would experience in my body throughout the rest of my life actually made me feel better about everything. I wonder if this is why so many bereaved moms get tattoos! Nothing can hurt as much as losing your child! I had survived a whole year being smothered by the unbearable pain of child loss. I was still here. I could carry on. Even without my womb I could still be a mom to Gabe and Frances, and I believe I will always be Owen's mom, too. I came away from that surgical experience with a fearlessness I hadn't felt before. The most terrible thing I could imagine had already happened: I lost one of my precious children. Living in a super careful way wasn't going to protect me from that pain—or the pain I will eventually experience as other loved ones die in the future. My body is here to help me experience physical aspects of this human life. I might as well do what I can physically as long as I am able to. Losing Owen so early in his life revealed that these days—with a womb or not—are not to be taken for granted. Maybe it's time for me to get a tattoo for Owen.

Missing Kids and a Box of Crackers

February 2021

More Owen by Justin Tong

to: findowenk@gmail.com
date: February 10, 2021
Subject: More Owen-missing kids and a box of crackers

Dear Friends,

I have been thinking about what to write to all of you for many months. I know that we need to connect with each other, especially when our interactions are so limited, and writing these emails has been a good way for me to feel like I am staying in touch even when my grief makes me feel I am all alone. It's hard to say how we are doing in terms of grieving and healing. Some days I can look at Owen's pictures and smile or laugh, recalling fun family moments he made possible. Other times, something simple like a box of crackers sets off waves of anger, sadness, and questions. Last night it was the box of Chicken in a Biskit crackers I saw in our kitchen. Owen loved these crackers and they were among the items he purchased at Mack's Market on the night he went missing. Seeing those crackers just reminded me how it never made sense that he would buy all those snacks (supplies for the week of midterms?) and then not return to his dorm to enjoy them. I just wish we knew what happened.

Grief interferes with so many of my plans—that is if I can even get *through* the plan making stage. I am fortunate to not have a very full calendar of commitments at this time so I start a typical day with some modest goals: a shower, maybe laundry, writing in my journal, a vague plan for dinner, and some tennis if I am lucky. So what actually happens? A short walk with the dog, a half-hearted online barre workout, hours lost as I search through old family photos for that one of Owen I was trying to find, and scrounging in the fridge for leftovers for dinner. I try to be gentle with myself (and with Dustin and Frances, too) but I feel like a whole year has passed me by while I have been able to do very little. I get so mad and feel like it's just not fair! But then I feel bad about how I feel knowing that many people have basic needs that aren't being met and here I sit with time for reflection in a quiet, peaceful house. My mom stayed in our house for six weeks over Christmas while she was healing a broken leg so our small circle of activities shrank even more during that time. She is getting stronger and living back at her own house now, so I have felt better about playing tennis indoors again (wearing a mask, of course) and have started back to work as a college tennis umpire. With these baby steps back to "normal," I was thrown for a loop when all my "progress" recently was undone by a simple box of crackers.

I don't always know what will bring on a fresh wave of grief, but some things I can anticipate will be triggering, like missing kids! Last week we received word that my friend Elizabeth's son (a K-8 classmate of Frances's) and his girlfriend were missing in Southern Oregon. They had gone on a short road trip to visit some natural hot springs and were no longer communicating or sharing their location with their parents.

They are safe at home now, but for the two days they were stuck in the snow on an infrequently traveled forest road out of cell phone range, I felt anxious and helpless. (Someone told me that this is how everyone felt when Owen was missing: anxious and helpless.) I also felt useless when Elizabeth reached out to me for help. I was only able to offer just a few suggestions about how to interact with media and law enforcement. I wanted to hide under a blanket; I didn't want to be a local expert in searching for missing children. When the missing kids were found, I was extremely happy for Elizabeth *and* I cried for hours, with big, ugly sobs of despair and anger. Why couldn't our search for Owen have brought a similarly joyful conclusion? Why Owen? Why us?

Then last night, I saw the box of crackers in my kitchen and fell apart all over again. I was instantly back in October of 2019 when Dustin spied a similar distinctive box in Owen's dorm room while looking through his computer for clues. We knew he loved these crackers, and his roommates confirmed they were Owen's. The university provided us with a list of Owen's UP meal card purchases and we saw he had bought them that last night at the campus convenience store. A wave of helplessness washed over me again—I wish I understood what happened to him that night. Why didn't he get to come back to the dorm and eat his favorite crackers? His donuts? His trail mix? All I could think about was Owen's interrupted life and I left the box of crackers unopened on the counter. I used to love those crackers, too, but I couldn't eat them.

I spend a lot of time worrying about how to best support Gabe, Frances, and Owen's friends: young adults whose lives were interrupted and dreams diverted by his disappearance and death. I can only guess at the forces they must grapple with to find enough courage to carry on living each day when their kind and cheerful brother and friend is no longer attacking life with the gusto they relied on him to bring to every adventure—AND at a time when their daily activities have been depressingly restricted by the pandemic. I hope that the friends can lean on each other and find solace in knowing that others are feeling the loss of Owen deeply—and that it's OK to laugh, make music, play games, and find joy again.

Even though his time on campus was short, I am grateful that Owen made some deep friendships at UP. One of Owen's roommates, Justin Tong, recently made a very touching poetic tribute video. I loved being able to experience the way Owen came across to new friends when he went to college through Justin's reflections. The video captures our yearning for More Owen and leaves me with some hope that these connections we have formed can blossom into something beautiful—all because we all loved Owen.

With love and longing for More Owen,
Mary

Here's an excerpt from Justin's video, which he shared in November 2020.

"I tried to act tough...like there was nowhere, no experience, no feeling that I hadn't been at.

And you were just so humble. You probably didn't want my bragging to fall flat so you just said, 'Hey I could probably learn a lot from you.'

Looking back now it was you I learned a lot from...

You taught me humility and how to acknowledge my deficiencies with nobility.

You taught me grit and persistence; how to be dedicated to everything you do and to do it with conviction...

I know that our paths will cross again and until then...the seeds you have planted in all of us will blossom and flourish magnificently. We will thrive together."

—Justin Tong

Do Not Work as a Referee

May 2021

to: findowenk@gmail.com
date: May 5, 2021
subject: be gentle with yourself–do not work as a referee

Dear Friends,

I hope this email finds you well. We have somehow made it through eighteen months without Owen's physical presence in our lives. Every day since we lost Owen has been long, hard, and much quieter than we used to experience in our family. In some ways it seems like Owen was just with us and at other times he feels far away. There are some signs of hope: Frances has returned to in-person school four days a week to finish out her senior year of high school, and we have all received covid vaccines (Frances will be the last to get a second shot next week). Exciting and good, but I can see it won't be a quick or easy return to all that we used to do, and I am beginning to see more new ways losing Owen has forever changed us.

In late February, I received a text from Father John Donato, Vice President for student affairs at UP. He sent me a photo of the small leaf buds emerging on the tree planted on campus to honor Owen. Watching this tree grow and change with the seasons has been part of my grieving process, and I was so grateful for this photo. I also appreciated Father's message to me, "Continue to be good and gentle with yourself." It was a bit of a wake up call. I was not being either of those things in the winter, and the message came at a time when I was having a difficult time with my work as a college tennis official.

Owen's tree at UP–Father John Donato

"What is it about our family and the rules?" Frances asked in the spring of 2018 when both Owen and I were getting ready to go off to our jobs as referees one weekend. (He was refereeing youth lacrosse and I had recently trained to be a tennis official for youth and adult tennis competitions.) I was excited about this career path and the potential for future travel and fun experiences. I mostly worked at junior tournaments and helped at high school districts. I knew all the rules and enjoyed teaching young players about good sportsmanship.

I eventually added the certification I needed to work college tennis matches and did a lot of shadowing at Division 1 and worked a few Division 3 events in 2019. In the strange daze of fresh grief, I began working Division 1 college matches early in 2020 before the pandemic led to the shut down of the tennis season. I barely remember those matches, and, honestly, I can't recall details from that time. I was numb and going through the motions, doing what was expected of me, what I thought people wanted to see me doing. I got through it and wasn't too disappointed when the rest of the season was canceled.

One long and lonely pandemic year later, college tennis was starting up again. I deliberated about the safety but decided to say yes to being back on the schedule to work at matches for UP, Portland State University, and even a few matches for the University of Oregon. It felt like something I **should** get back to doing, since I had trained and prepared for it—and because it was something I had originally really wanted to do. I was nervous about Covid but appreciated the protocols in place for officials and players. I made sure I had the right uniform, masks I could speak clearly through, and fresh batteries in my stopwatch. I re-watched training webinars and re-read the rule book to hopefully avoid some of the most common rookie mistakes.

What I encountered, however, went beyond new-job jitters. I lost sleep in the days before a match, suffering nervous tummy issues and other symptoms of anxiety. Being at matches where coaches were yelling at their players was very unsettling: These were young men like Owen, playing a sport they loved with their school name on their chests. I didn't like that yelling. Nor did I like it when the coaches argued with or yelled at *me*! Yikes! I should have seen this coming, but somehow I hadn't remembered that this was indeed part of refereeing at this level. I was doing everything I could think of to calm myself: aromatherapy, breathing meditations, physical exercise, and vigorous review[s] of the rules so I would be prepared for anything. Still, the anxiety continued and worsened. I found myself one morning in the Chiles Center lobby nervously pacing around awaiting the results of my pre-match Covid test. It struck me that this was the very place where we had gathered for Owen's funeral Mass. It was a difficult day.

Around this time, I received the message from Father Donato reminding me to "continue to be good and gentle with yourself." It got me thinking and I started talking about how I was feeling with my family and friends. I ultimately made the difficult decision to step back from working as a tennis official for now; supportive co-workers took my remaining scheduled matches, and I was able to take a deep breath. This job that I thought would be such a good fit didn't fit who I am now, and that's OK.

We have all gone through a year (or eighteen months) of experiencing many different levels of grief and loss, so I want to remind you all to "continue to be good and gentle with yourself."

It's difficult to know how this year of fear and isolation has affected each of us, but I know it has. As much as it feels like giving up or being lazy, taking it easy on yourself might be the best way to show yourself love. I imagined Owen giving me his signature two-thumbs-up when I made the decision to step away from refereeing. Know that he would also give you a two-thumbs-up for being gentle with yourselves.

With love,
Mary
#moreowen

Owen's Camera

July 2021

Many of my thoughts about losing Owen don't have cute smiling photos to match.

How can I show the absence of his joyful energy? What image would fully reveal the empty hole in our family?

While I enjoy revisiting pictures of all the things he did and what made him Owen, I think about the missing snapshots from his life: the college experience he didn't finish, jobs he didn't have, music he didn't write or play, lawns he could have meticulously mowed and edged, love he might have known, and enriching or infuriating interactions with his siblings that won't take place.

I don't just miss the silly boy we laughed with and the strong young man we watched at football and lacrosse; I ache for the man he would have become and the whole life he would have experienced. It's more Owen I seek every day, everywhere. I find some of it when I look at the photos he took with his digital Nikon camera. I see more Owen in the subjects (many of which were nature) he chose to explore, and in the images of the people he photographed, including himself.

Owen was twelve when he received the Nikon as a Christmas gift in 2013. I took lots of snapshots with our basic digital camera in those years, but Owen had seen the wonderful photos my mom's boyfriend at the time, Ron Cooper (a onetime photojournalist), took of our family celebrations with a *real* camera, and Owen wanted a real camera too. Ron taught Owen the basics and spent lots of time helping him frame shots and then upload and edit the digital images on his iPad. The next year when our first dog (Bella the beagle) joined our family, she was one of Owen's most frequent subjects. Trips to Crater Lake and Hawaii gave him the chance to play with exposures, shutter speeds, and aperture. The camera had many automatic programs, but Owen prided himself on learning how to manually adjust the settings and used the timer feature to set up family portraits like my favorite from our family trip to Maui in 2014.

Dustin's brother, Seth, hired Owen to photograph some of the events at his wedding in 2015, and Owen took the assignment seriously. He captured some sweet spontaneous moments (like the groomsmen taking shots of bourbon before the ceremony) and gained a reputation throughout the family as a talented photographer. I think he was proud he could make an important contribution to the occasion.

As Owen's life got busier with high school, his photo shooting changed to quick snaps of his friends or his food with his cell phone camera for Snapchat. He used his Nikon less and less. He dusted it off to take Gabe's senior portrait, capture professional images for my LinkedIn profile, and do a photo shoot with his friends when they were seniors. I like that his Nikon was one of the things he took along to his dorm room. Photography was something he planned on continuing to explore. I know he spent some time at UP in the fall of 2019, taking photos of a spot he hung out at by the Willamette River, though I haven't been able to look at those photos yet.

I love to find photos of Owen behind the camera, scrunching his face up in concentration or smiling about how a photo turned out as he checked the digital screen. Photos of the photographer in action give us an alternate point of view of the photo being taken.

Thinking of all the occasions and places Owen *didn't* get the chance to photograph multiplies the grief that sweeps through my days like sudden cold rainstorms. The already acute pain intensifies, insofar as that is possible. Darkness gets darker. I think of the medicine cabinet mirror in my mom's bathroom and how you can angle it so that the image in the mirrored wall seems to repeat infinitely. When Owen's life ended, and our family was shattered, these potential views disappeared. How many unique, Owen-experienced photos did he miss out on by leaving us so early? We are left with a broken mirror and a small collection of photos.

I wish I could ask Owen, "What were you looking at through your lens? What did our family look like? Did you see the love? And how proud of you we were?

"Did you see how your friends smiled at you? I know you took some of the best pictures of me and Gabe.

"Did you see the beauty of the sunsets and the places we traveled? Where else did you want to explore?

"What did you see on that last weekend at school? Do I want to see what you were looking at?"

I wish Owen had been able to take Frances's senior photos this year. I wish I had been able to do it myself with Owen's camera, but It's still too soon. Maybe someday I will be able to pick up his camera and hold it up to my eye to glimpse things the way he might have seen them or to capture images unique to my own experience. I think he would like that.

Emotional Baggage

July 2021

When summer days get really hot and sunny in Portland, we escape to the Pacific coast. Temperatures can be 20 or 30 degrees cooler next to the sea due to some kind of weird weather phenomenon where the high pressure system over the Willamette Valley can lead to foggy and cool—or even cold—days at the beach. It's almost always at least sweatshirt-weather at the Oregon coast. Beaches there are for walking on or doing something active where you are moving around, like playing frisbee or volleyball, or digging in the sand and building sand castles. They aren't the kind of beaches where you lie in the sun or snooze on beach chairs. I can count on one hand the number of times I have been hot on an Oregon beach. I love having this cool retreat just an hour and a half's drive west—especially since our hundred-year-old house in Portland does not have air conditioning—and we are lucky to have a free place we can always stay.

My mom, who my kids call Nona, bought her beach house in 2000, just a few months after Dustin and I as new parents of Gabe had moved back to Portland (from Japan and Seattle). A mini family reunion the previous summer at a Central Oregon resort inspired Nona to look for a place where we could continue to make intergenerational family memories.

Built in the late 1960s in a forested community a short walk from the beach, Nona's beach house has a funky retro vibe complete with a sunken wood-paneled great room with high ceilings and cushy wall-to-wall light blue carpet. Within sight of the kitchen, just down a few wide, carpeted steps, this space was the perfect playroom for our young kids when rainy weather at the beach kept us indoors. It was big enough to contain indoor wrestling, golf putting practice, gymnastics shows, and many hours of family board games. When the kids were in high school, it was big enough for them to bring a few friends. The house was unique, quirky, and just right for our family's changing needs.

I often took the kids out to the beach house by myself in the summer when they were younger and Dustin had to stay in his hyper air-conditioned office in the city working long hours as a young law associate. One particular trip stands out in my memories. As we crossed the Oregon Coast Range of mountains, the final major barrier on our drive, and descended towards the sea, the external temperature also started to drop. Mile by glorious mile the temperature on my minivan's dashboard thermometer sank downward, back to a much more comfortable range for a mom with three young kids. I hoped the more temperate surroundings would ease the kids' crankiness, help stop their squabbling, and give me more patience to handle their high energy level.

When we got to the beach house, I let the kids run around in the cool great room while I got a few things out of the car for the night. I unzipped the duffel bag containing the kids' pajamas and clothes and was surprised that they still felt warm to the touch from when I had packed them on the steamy second floor of our old Craftsman bungalow back in Portland. It was the weirdest feeling that the clothes were still hot, even though the beach house was so chilly inside I was going to be making hot cocoa and lighting a fire in the fireplace that night.

I thought of this recently when I was at the beach house with hopes of taking a break from grief, of escaping the heat of painful memories that surface in spring when neighbors hire other kids (or professional yard workers) to mow the lawns that Owen used to care for. Every jarring gasoline-powered engine is a reminder that he's not here anymore, carefully maneuvering his manual edger along the tree lawns on our street or flicking the power cord of his electric mower in a practiced lasso-like throw over his head when he made a turn. I wanted to be somewhere without lawn mowers, so I went to the beach.

But once I was there, I realized that the grief had followed me. And that the grief will follow me wherever I go. Just like the warmth of the hot city permeating the pajamas in the suitcase I packed for the kids those many years ago, memories of Owen and things we are missing will forever be emotional baggage I carry.

Almost Doing Laundry with Dog Food

August 2021

Frances playing "Heart and Soul" with Owen playing "Jingle Bells"

to: findowenk@gmail.com
date: August 28, 2021
subject: End of summer–almost washing clothes for college with dog food

Dear Friends,

After our crazy heat waves, these cool cloudy days we have had lately feel good, but at the same time the cooler weather is unsettling, because it means fall is coming. And it was fall when we lost Owen. Somehow my body seems to know this. These crisp mornings as we near the end of summer bring back the feeling of wet grass on my bare ankles when I was searching along the bluff for Owen the first morning he was gone. I am feeling like I could use a little more summer before we plunge into those feelings of fall.

It was a quiet summer with lots of time at home, some time at the creek and out at the beach. I had a few overnight trips for tennis, Frances had a few get-togethers with friends, and Dustin played many rounds of golf. Gabe stayed in Corvallis working at the university and taking a few classes. We watched the Tokyo Olympics on TV and I knit one and a half afghans–one for Frances in the dark green and white colors of Sarah Lawrence College and half of the orange and blue one I'm trying to finish for my nephew Maxwell before winter hits at Syracuse University. (With each stitch of these blankets, I thought of the purple one I knit for Owen before his move to UP in 2019.) All summer long, a heap of college supplies slowly grew in our living room waiting for Frances to pack them off to New York. I felt restless watching the approach of her sendoff, harboring an uncomfortable ache that we cannot hold onto her or this moment forever.

Our flight to New York leaves in two days. We need the pile of stuff on the couch to be packed. The perfect college duffel bag waited up in the attic. It's ancient–dating back to my college freshman year in 1988–and it's indestructible. It folds down flat and small when empty. But it wasn't empty. It was still full of clothes from Owen's dorm room that Dustin and Gabe packed when they were moving all of Owen's stuff back home.

The other day I opened the attic and dragged it out into Gabe and Owen's room. I took a deep breath and slowly let it out as I pulled the chunky zipper open to reveal some of Owen's favorite clothes. It felt important to touch and honor each of these items he had packed for college. I cried over his Pendleton shirt, his black sweatshirt, his aqua polo shirt (worn for almost every dressy occasion) and the madras shorts it matched. New Christie Hall shirts and UP swag mingled with stained Grant HS and Peter Corvallis Productions T-shirts from his last job (his first job); the well-worn Trailblazer pajama pants peeked out from under the new Prana jeans and khakis we had bought together at the Columbia store the summer before he went to college. (Did he even get to wear these new pants at all?) Though he just played one season of water polo, it was well represented with his long-sleeve team T-shirt, a sweatshirt from his first tournament, and the monogrammed towel presented to seniors at the end of the season. Lacrosse T-shirts, hats, and shorts filled out the bag. I cried when I started and found more tears awaited when I got to the bottom of the bag. There was no more Owen to unpack. I know it's just stuff, but it is *Owen's* stuff and that makes it precious to me.

Now the duffel bag is ready to be filled with a new set of college clothes and travel with Frances to New York. How do we do this? Sending a youngest child to college is bittersweet for many parents but how are we supposed to send another precious child away to college to live in a dorm room with strangers after we lost Owen just a few weeks into his freshman year? We already lost so much through the last eighteen months of grief and restricted living. I don't want to be ruled by fear and I don't want Frances to miss out on anything because we are afraid we will lose her like we lost Owen. (There, I said it!)

I want to help Frances pack and it's not just me being kind—it's a little selfish. I want to have a chance to touch the shirts, jeans, and sweatshirts that are special to her: her favorite thrift store pants, a skirt from France, ridiculously fuzzy fleece sweats, cut-off jean shorts, and the sweatshirt from Carson with the goat on the front. I want to soak her all in before she moves on, knowing that this moment is fleeting. It's just stuff, but it's her stuff—the way she is choosing to present herself to the world. She is precious to me.

There are moments when I think, "This is how it is supposed to be—it will be OK." And then I do something like put dog food instead of laundry detergent in the soap dispenser while washing Frances's clothes for college! I caught my mistake and was able to get all the dog food out and replace it with our family's favorite lavender and eucalyptus-scented detergent. I hope when Frances unpacks her own emotional baggage in New York, she will smell all my love.

With love,
Mary #moreowen

List of Fun

September 2021

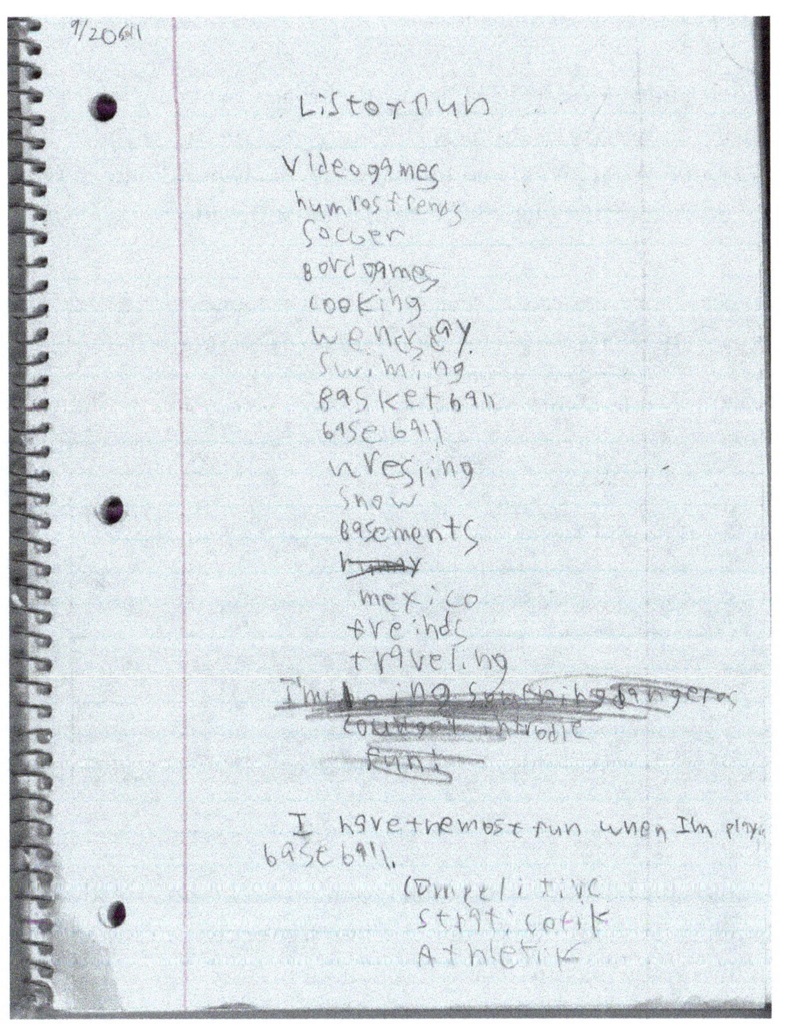

In my ongoing searches for More Owen, I shift boxes around in the attic, dig through Owen's desk drawers, and flip through books and notebooks on his bookshelves to see if anything I haven't seen before comes to light. I had more time at home alone after Frances left for college, and that's when I found this list Owen wrote in an otherwise unused spiral notebook left in his closet. I wish I could remember why Owen wrote this. It's dated September 20, 2011 so I think it could have been part of a homework assignment, but I don't remember reading it before. I love what ten-year-old Owen wrote—and also think it's funny what he crossed out. Here's my translation of his little kid spelling and some reflections on some of his favorite things:

Video games—We had a PC set up in the kids' playroom with some basic games they could play. Does anyone remember the online pet game Webkinz? Owen had a virtual dachshund named Otto for that game. It's where his love of gaming began.

Humorous friends—I love that Owen prized humor. He loved to laugh and make others laugh. He had some pretty funny friends in fifth grade (pictured), and throughout his life.

Soccer—Around this time, Owen was playing soccer on rainy fall days and muddy spring weekends. In the winter, he played outside in the cold and inside in a chilly indoor futsal warehouse. (Futsal is a type of soccer that's played indoors on a much smaller artificial turf court.) Summer soccer camps and fun family kick-arounds filled any gaps in his soccer schedule. His cleats were always coming untied. We were *always* asking him if he had enough water because he fainted after becoming dehydrated one spring weekend that featured several soccer and baseball games. This is around the time Owen requested I bake soccer ball-shaped birthday cakes. He could never seem to get enough of that game.

Board games—Family game nights are legendary in our household. In case it's not been made clear yet, I'll just say that we are competitive, game-loving people. I still have the Sorry game board Owen taped up after ripping it in half following a particularly frustrating round. He really was sorry, as the game belonged to Gabe, who got pretty mad! (I also have a bad reputation for quitting a family game of Pit, but that's a card game, not a board game, so I don't have to tell that story here.) Life, Settlers of Catan, backgammon, and Monopoly were played in heavy rotation. Owen even read a book about how to win at Monopoly, and then took great pleasure in wiping us all out. We had a special *Star Wars*-themed Monopoly set featuring extra rules and bonuses for different tokens that spent years on a "time-out shelf" because it caused too many tears. Owen's favorite board game was one we don't play anymore, since we're without him: Axis & Allies, a very complicated World War II strategy game that requires great patience to set up and even more patience to play. Rounds could go on for days, but Owen really loved this game, as his big smile at our Panther Creek cabin shows, and I'm glad we have the memory of playing it with him.

Cooking—Owen didn't do that much cooking when he was ten, but we did a few things together in the kitchen that made lasting memories. The two of us stirred up a special tomato soup from scratch, and he liked sifting the flour for my Grandma France's potica (a traditional Slovenian pastry often made for holidays). When he was older, he learned to make gnocchi and baklava from my mom, and cheesecake from my dad. Dustin's mom (who the kids called "Granny B") taught him something really amazing: to form bacon (remember, his favorite food!) into taco shells and bowls to hold yummy fillings. Cooking isn't always fun, but I think Owen made it fun. After his high school graduation, Owen traveled to New Orleans with my mom for a special trip she had purchased at a fundraising auction. Owen was the youngest participant in the Cajun cooking class they took there. He brought back the recipes and some special spices, but we never got to try them together. Maybe my mom and I need to cook those recipes for Owen.

Wednesday—This is less obvious, but I think the fun factor stemmed from the late start we had for school on some Wednesdays when he was that age. Owen enjoyed the more relaxed morning routines on those days, and there was time for big family breakfasts with, of course, bacon.

Swimming—I'm glad Owen thought swimming was fun because I feel like I forced my kids to take year after year of swimming lessons whether they wanted to or not. (Here five-year-old "Otter" Owen frolics at Grant Pool in July of 2006.) Again, I think it was Owen who made this fun and knew how to truly enjoy the non-lesson swimming opportunities he was given. The kids all loved swimming in the above-ground pools Granny B put up for them at her house in the summer, and also the swimming pond and slide she built for them. I remember family fun in many hotel pools and hot tubs when traveling, and Owen loved swimming in the ocean in Hawaii and Mexico, too.

Basketball—Owen brought his passion for basketball to several different teams during his hoops "career." He was relentless when going for a loose ball or trying to get a steal. His middle school team once played at the Moda Center before a Portland

Trail Blazers game (he's #0 in the photo below), a tremendous thrill for the kids to shoot at the baskets of their sports heroes. When I stand at my kitchen sink today, I often long to see Owen shooting baskets in our driveway with Gabe, playing the rough one-on-one type of basketball they would enjoy most nights after dinner until someone got hit in the balls (yes, this happened more than you'd think!).

Baseball—This one was interesting because I wasn't sure if Owen thought baseball was fun. We often just signed him up for the same activities that Gabe did without much forethought, as Owen seemed to want to do what Gabe did anyway. Compared to the other sports Owen played, baseball was slow, and there was a lot of sitting and standing around. It might have not been the best fit for his wiggly, young boy energy, but it seemed like he made good friends in the dugout and always enjoyed the pizza parties at the end of the season.

He had big plans for his baseball "career" too. In my "More Owen" search, I found another notebook in which he had recorded all kinds of sports plays, drills, and team records for a few months. Nine-year-old Owen wrote, "I want to play catcher in minors. I am going to have 2 outs at home. I am going to catch 3 pop flys. I am going to buy Big League Chew at Dollar Tree." The notebook also has a note he wrote but never gave to his coach asking if he could be the catcher and saying he was going to be a "power hitter."

Wrestling—This was never something Owen did in an organized way, but it was a big part of everyday fun in our house. As I mentioned earlier, Gabe and Owen shared a bedroom, and so, as many parents of boys may attest, there was a lot of wrestling. Before he could talk, Owen had even made up his own baby sign language identifier for wrestling to communicate with us what he wanted: More wrestling! He would grasp his hands together and bend his wrists back and forth while breathing heavily. This was definitely a dad-and-kids activity; I wasn't involved in the wrestling, except probably to stand on the sidelines saying, "Be careful!"

Snow—Snow is rare in Portland, especially snow that sticks. Owen loved playing in the snow whenever it happened, though, so I'm not surprised it made this list, even months out of season. When he was little and we got snow, he would stay outside with Gabe and Frances as long as possible, only coming in to warm up a little, drink some hot cocoa, put on dry mittens, and head out again for more fun. When he got older, building sledding jumps and shoveling snow were his passions on snow days.

Basements—It's true, our basement was pretty fun. We had a "big boy toy area" where Gabe and Owen could play with Legos and toys while keeping small pieces away from baby Frances. We put up indoor play tents for cozy games. We had a stage area with a big curtain for scene changes, a chalk wall for the backdrop, and many dress-up costumes to change into. It's also where we had our only TV set. As the kids grew up, the basement became the place for video games and jam sessions with friends.

Money—Owen wrote this and then crossed it out. I suppose he had a complicated relationship with it, as many of us do. He was pretty savvy about money early on and liked to save rather than spend. When he did spend money (like buying Big League chew for baseball season!) it was often on something everyone could enjoy or on gifts for others. On one family trip to Ashland, Oregon, for example, Dustin gave the kids each a few dollars to buy snacks at the local Grocery Outlet. Owen was very excited to find a case of chocolate pudding cups, thinking he could eat a lot of them himself and still have some to share or trade with Gabe and Frances. Unfortunately, he did not see the word "sugar-free" on the packaging; the pudding was disgusting, even for a kid who loved all kinds of treats. Maybe that's why he crossed out money…he knew he couldn't always buy fun.

Mexico—I'm sure Owen would have found a way to visit Mexico again, but his only time there was when he was six years old. Our family stayed at a resort outside of Cancún with my brothers and their families to celebrate Nona's retirement. It was a long way for our small kids to travel, but once we got there, Owen loved body surfing in the warm ocean water and drinking virgin piña coladas.

Friends—This is on the list twice, with his note of Humorous Friends above. Owen clearly valued friends deeply, and I think he was aware even at this tender fifth grade age that some friendships were going to change, as everyone was growing up. Yet, many of Owen's friends in high school were the same kids he had been friends with since kindergarten.

Owen and Nick at kindergarten graduation in 2007

and on an eighth grade field trip to Mt. St. Helens in 2015

Traveling—Owen was always up for taking a trip, whether it was just to a grandma's house to spend the night or across the country to visit New York City. Road trips around the Pacific Northwest or to California were always more fun with Owen in the car, and he brought his unique sense of humor on family trips to Kentucky, Hawaii, and Texas. When Owen wrote this list, he and his classmates were preparing to travel to Japan on their fifth-grade exchange visit. He went to Japan again in eighth grade and flew to New York by himself in 2018 to meet my dad for a skeet shooting and culinary adventure (this photo is from when I dropped him off at the airport for that journey).

His post-graduation tour of New Orleans with Nona in 2019 was his last time out of the Pacific Northwest. Where else might Owen have traveled as an adult? He was thinking about studying abroad in Australia during college. I'm sure he would have had many adventures out in the world, with his *joie de vivre*, pleasure in making friends, and fondness for goals and planning. I'd like to think of him out and about, spreading good energy and More Owen.

"I'm doing something dangerous (could get in trouble) fun!"—This is also crossed out, but I believe Owen really did think that kind of stuff was fun. Owen talked too much in class, getting in a little trouble with his teachers, but I don't think anyone thought of Owen as a "bad" kid. He was a jokester who got caught creating fake Facebook profiles for his friends when they were only ten, trying to get away with something they weren't allowed to do at their age. Parents don't always know what their teenagers are up to, but I imagine (and hope) that Owen's adventures with his friends through high school and beyond fell into this category of fun. After he was gone, I saw videos saved on his Snapchat account of him daringly crossing Panther Creek hanging from a cable above the frigid water and performing other silly stunts at playgrounds after hours. Not understanding exactly what led to his death kind of sneaks into my thoughts about what Owen thought was "fun." Maybe he left campus that night to do "something dangerous" and got into more trouble than he bargained for and it wasn't any fun. I guess I am glad he had crossed this out in 2011.

I have the most fun when I'm playing baseball.

Competitive

Strategic

Athletic

Well, there it is in Owen's own writing: he really did like baseball. And not only that, but at least at this age he had the "most fun" doing it! It's surprising to me, then, that he didn't play any more baseball after the spring of 2011. In middle school, though, while he continued playing soccer, he added football and lacrosse (which ran through the spring, formerly baseball season). These quickly became his new favorite sports. I believe Owen had fun playing any sport or doing just about anything with anyone—and I myself had so much fun being his mom.

Owen's Baby Blanket

January 2022

I found Owen's baby blanket sometime after his body was recovered from the river. After he left his dorm room that October night in 2019, wearing his new Carhartt hoodie. After two weeks of agonizing, terror-filled days and nights of hoping, searching the Portland neighborhoods near his campus and along the Willamette River.

It was after I knew he hadn't hitchhiked out to our cabin at Panther Creek in Washington or hopped a train to Alaska. After we figured out the police weren't going to be any help at all. When I was imagining the worst (suicide or murder) and struggling to comprehend Owen wasn't ever coming back to our family's cozy bungalow on Holladay Street.

I looked for the blanket when I needed to find evidence that Owen had loved and been loved. That I had done all that I could have done as a mother, that this tragedy was not my fault. I couldn't remember when I had seen it last, but I knew I hadn't seen it in a while. When had he tucked it away? When did he grow up?

When I saw Owen's blanket neatly folded in the back of his dresser drawer, I fell to my knees, overcome with my grief and humbled by this tattered and threadbare testament to Owen's transforming life and love. I knew Owen's blanket had been ripped and torn over the years, and I remembered him asking me to repair his blanket, but after losing Owen, the ragged beauty of this patched-up quilt shocked me and struck me as physical proof of the way Owen's love had rubbed off into all of our days.

Patchwork Quilt

In a basic patchwork quilt, selected fabrics are cut into squares, laid out in the desired pattern, and stitched together to form the quilt top. Next, a layer of batting is sandwiched between the quilt top and a solid fabric bottom. The three parts are quilted together usually by hand stitching. Finally, binding seals the edges of the quilt, providing a finished look.

In the beginning, the blanket was a simple patchwork quilt made with love by a friend for the birth of my second son. Not too heavy or too light and just the right size to cover a lap at story time or wear as a cape, the blanket became known as "Fuzzy." Fuzzy was Owen's favorite.

As the peace-loving middle child, Owen was the fluffy batting adding so much dimension and warmth to our family quilt. Boy-boy-girl, each two years apart in school, we stitched our quilt squares of kids neatly together and naively expected life would go according to our plans. I didn't know how much loving—and then losing—Owen would change us over the years.

Owen threw himself passionately into whatever adventures filled our busy days, and his blanket friend Fuzzy was there through it all. Little Owen loved digging, dancing, running, and any kind of physical playing. He scraped his knees and elbows racing down the sidewalk on his scooter with Fuzzy trailing behind him. He bloodied his face— twice!—climbing the bookshelf in the playroom while Fuzzy tried to cushion his fall. Fuzzy healed Owen's ouchies alongside me, as I doled out hugs and kisses, Band-Aids, and cookies as needed. The blanket sustained many scratches and cuts in these activities too and Owen asked me to add patches of fabric and stitch up the rips.

Fuzzy also added a layer of quilted comfort to Owen's rare quiet moments, warming the chilly hardwood floor under his desk as he did homework and shielding him from prying eyes when he was sad or embarrassed. Owen was generous with his love. He sometimes tucked Fuzzy around our beagle for a snuggle or shared the healing powers of his blanket with his sister (especially after he had accidentally hurt her). Fuzzy lined his hammock when we camped out by Panther Creek, providing extra grip for the slippery sleeping bag, but enduring several more rips from the friction of Owen's vigorous bumper-car-style hammock swinging. Owen continued to bring Fuzzy on family trips into his adolescence and never let the blanket too far out of his sight when he was at home after exhausting days at middle school and exciting sports practices or games.

Owen didn't want Fuzzy to be "broken." He wanted repairs made and new bits added. He wanted Fuzzy to be reinforced with extra stitches. Did Owen know he was burning through Fuzzy's love at an accelerated pace? It comforts me to remember that he wanted Fuzzy's ability to provide warmth and cheer to continue. The quilt's fuzziness—the special loving softness—dissolved into the love of Owen's days and all our family memories, but Fuzzy's look and composition changed as more patches and stitches were added. I didn't realize that I was also changing.

<u>Crazy Quilt</u>

Not based on specific geometric patterns, crazy quilts are one-of-a-kind artistic textile creations made from irregularly shaped pieces of fabric joined in a random manner. They can be simple or very intricate and often feature embellishments like beads or buttons sewn onto the blanket and decorative embroidery. They rarely contain the layer of batting that usually defines a quilt.

The original green and yellow flannel fabric squares now hang together by tattered threads. Only a few seam allowances between the old pieces remain like a skeleton, hinting at the original patchwork grid. It looks like weathered window frames with the panes badly cracked or missing altogether. Bits of quilt batting float where the fabric is just gone, like wispy, cotton candy clouds stretching across the summer sky. This blanket looks wretched and wrecked. I was gutted when we lost Owen. People who unthinkingly asking, "How are you?" heard my constant refrain: "It feels right to feel wrecked." Losing Owen wrecked me, fracturing all the glass in my windows and tearing my heart apart like Owen's blanket.

But now there are patches. Blue peace-sign fabric leftover from a bathrobe I sewed for Owen anchors one corner. (Owen used to sign the O of his name as a peace sign and touching this spot–in the blanket's upper right corner–makes me smile.) Large patches of Chicago Cubs fleece left over from homemade Christmas gifts shore up the sides and support Fuzzy's failing infrastructure. Fabric with graphics of different states spans some of the most gaping holes, reminding me of the distant places our family traveled to like New Mexico, where Owen filled his swim shirt with air in the hot tub and then jetted around like a noisily deflating balloon.

Owen's Blanket photographed by Beth Nakamura for *The Oregonian* 5/6/2020

I run my fingers along Fuzzy's wonky zigzag reinforcement stitching and remember how Owen's various trips to the ER, that surprise F in seventh-grade English, and the way he crashed his body into other players on the field of all the sports he played scared me and stretched my heart. Did Owen rub his fingers along these sutures when he was healing from his own pains? He tenaciously tackled much larger players in football, breaking a few bones in his hand while playing up on Varsity. He hit the floor so many times in basketball scrambling for loose balls that I came to recognize the unique "kathunk" of his wiry body colliding with the gym floor. As a defensive midfielder in lacrosse, he threw his body in front of many attackmen, earning time in the penalty box with pride. It took great courage for Owen to go out for water polo his senior year. Even though he lacked advanced swimming skills, he poured his heart into the team, learning how to get his long hair to stay in the swim cap, and making a significant contribution on defense and as backup goalie. He built muscles where he had never had them before and showed them off in the tiny team Speedo he wore. Do those of us whose lives are shorter somehow shine brighter?

Did Owen know his life would be so short? Was he loving fast and hard to get it all out before he had to leave us? When he was in middle school, I drove Owen to our local nickel arcade for his first date. I tried not to spy on him, but I saw him gallantly helping Maya play a shooting game and luckily caught a glimpse of their awkward kiss by the car before I drove him home. I wish I had seen more special moments like that one. I saw him grow in confidence as he built his lawn-mowing business and landed his first real job. He wrote songs, and I got to see him sing and play one on his guitar in front of an audience. I didn't know it would be the last time. He did so much in his eighteen years, but I feel the void of all he will never get to do. He was looking forward to voting for the first time and filing a tax return, making plans for fall break and future study abroad.

Would Fuzzy have saved Owen's life at college? Since we will likely never know what exactly happened to Owen, why can't we imagine that a blanket's love could have prevented it? I wish Owen had packed Fuzzy in our vintage Lands' End duffel bag and tucked the quilt's protective, loving self under his pillow to console him, to comfort him, to even score some points when a date came back to his dorm. Would that have been enough? Would anything have made a difference and prolonged Owen's life? If only Fuzzy could have been a parachute. If only Fuzzy could have been a life raft.

I try to feel him when I visit the creek he loved. I find more tears there, but I hear the rushing water as if it's Owen's voice saying, "Fuzzy's yours now, Mom. You need Fuzzy more than I do." I see the tall fir trees above me swinging in the wind like his flowing long hair. I breathe in the warm smell of wild blackberries and cedar blowing up the canyon and dip my feet in the numbingly cold, clear water. I wonder about the water in the Willamette: was Owen cold in the river?

For a while, I left Fuzzy in Owen's room, carefully folded on the used La-Z-Boy recliner he bought with his own money. Encountering the well-loved blanket was too painful, stopping my breath tightly in my throat and stirring up too many memories of the special boy I loved so much. I could barely compel myself to move through the days after Owen's death and didn't think I could handle the extra emotional weight of this amazing, love-worn blanket. I also believed Fuzzy was too fragile, too special for daily use, so I treated it with reverence and awe. Keeping it on Owen's altar, showing it exclusively to Owen's grandma, whose friend was the original seamstress.

As I brought Fuzzy downstairs to write this piece, I imagined Owen's younger voice saying, "Fuzzy's lonely. Keep Fuzzy close to you and I will stay close to you, too." The grief of losing a child has stranded me alone on a deserted island. There's no comforting shelter to protect me from storms, no food to satisfy my hunger or water to quench my thirst. Day after day of hot, blinding sun blisters my skin; cold rain at night chills my soul and robs me of sleep. But I have Owen's blanket.

I sit at my desk with Fuzzy on my lap, totally awed by the power of the love of a little boy, the power of the love of a mom. The blanket surprises me with its soothing heft, especially since it has been so worn down. Is that the extra weight of Owen's love? Fuzzy calms me and steadfastly stays on my lap as I type, never shifting or sliding off. Was this what Owen loved about this blanket? Its reliable comfort without any backtalk? No nagging parental reminders or unvoiced expectations to meet, just an unwavering friendly presence. Protection. Reassurance. Fingering the faded shreds of the original flannel squares, I think about how much more of everything

Owen brought to our lives. More love, more joy, more laughter, and also more sadness, more despair, more tears.

The tattered scraps of memory we are left with when we lose someone we love can become something beautiful if we are brave enough.

Fuzzy is my blanket now, and it can be my life raft, my parachute, my shelter, and my comfort as I hold my breath launching Owen's siblings into their future lives at college and beyond. Maybe I will add more embellishments as our one-of-a-kind family story continues. I vow to keep letting Fuzzy's loving fuzziness rub off into all my days, even if it leads to a few more rips or patches.

Last Words

March 2022

Last night, Dustin went to take the dog on a quick walk after coming home from work. We exchanged greetings, a quick hug and a kiss. He said he'd had a productive day. Frances and I did too, in our own way, though we did not find the missing key to Nona's beach house, a task we'd been focused on and only the most recent drama emerging in this chaotic time. We'd worked on sorting and tidying a few areas of our own bedrooms—hers way messier than mine—spritzing on old perfumes and laughing together about past to-do lists we found that said we should clean our rooms, "get organized, and stay organized!"

So despite my plans for the week having been upended by the missing beach house key, I appreciated having an easy day. It arrived on the heels of an emotional Monday—Gabe's birthday—when I was weepy, missing my biggest boy who had just driven back to school in Corvallis on Sunday, and of course missing Owen and all of the ways our family used to spend spring breaks and Gabe's birthdays together.

I was running a little late getting plans for dinner together since Frances and I had gotten lost in the upstairs cleanup projects, and when Dustin came home from work, I'd suggested he walk the dog to give me a little time to forage in the fridge and see what I could come up with. We talked about the new dog treats he had bought for Bella (duck jerky!) to replace the ones that had grown too stale and crunchy even for the usually undiscerning palate of our beagle. He said he would bring some of the new jerky on their stroll to see if he could encourage Bella to do what the walk was intended to facilitate: Poop.

"More poop," Dustin said. "More poop!" was my enthusiastic echo. And they were gone. I chuckled to myself thinking Dustin was making fun of my frequent refrain of "More Owen" and—as grief and trauma have been known to sneak up on me and decimate sweet moments—I was suddenly struck with the thought, What if those are the last words Dustin and I get to speak to each other? "More poop!" What? I panicked a little. That would be terrible. I admonished myself that I should have sent him and Bella off on their walk with love and gratitude. A blessing. But, maybe it *was* a kind of a prayer: More poop.

I was trying then to recall my last physical encounter with Owen and how I wish I knew what exactly we had said to each other. I saw him outside Christie Hall at the end of September 2019, in that circular driveway where we had dropped his stuff off on move-in day the previous month. I was bringing him my Yamaha guitar. He was actually *buying* it from me, he insisted, for $100 and the promise he'd write a song for me in the future. (I still have the $100 bill he proudly gave me.) It was a few weeks before midterms and I know I said those mothering mantras: I hoped he was keeping up with his classes, finding people to study with, sleeping and eating well. I am pretty sure I asked him if he was going to the UP soccer games where the guys from his dorm painted purple letters on their bare chests and chanted with wild abandon. I remember asking him if he was thinking about applying to study abroad sophomore year, as the deadline for applications loomed on the calendar after midterms. What else did I say? What did Owen say?

Along with my guitar, I had a few other things that I brought as a little care package for him that day from the Muji store downtown in a swanky bag from the Apple store. I brought him a 2019-2020 planner—which we later saw he had filled out with all of the semester's assignments, quizzes, and test dates. He was excited about the small microfiber cleaning cloth and lint roller, as he was conscientious about keeping his computer clean and one roommate had dust allergies. Did he make his high pitched "oooh, cookies!" voice? I can't remember. I know we hugged, but I am sure it was brief. I know I didn't say, "More poop," but whatever I did say, it wasn't what I would have wanted my last words to be for my son. I was probably a little preachy with my helpful-suggestion mom-speak.

As I got in my car to leave, I worried that I had come down too hard on him with my "Don't miss the deadline for study abroad" reminders. I stopped to snap a picture of a Ford Pinto parked behind his dorm and sent it to Owen, reporting, "Just saw this. Someone has a cool old Ford pinto parked behind Christie."

He wrote back: "Yeah it must be a student because it's here all the time, pretty cool as long as it doesn't blow up." That is the last one-on-one text conversation we had, but those aren't the last words we exchanged.

The week before midterms, first-year students at UP received letters their parents had written to them at orientation. They were meant to be helpful messages of support arriving when students might be feeling anxious and stressed about exams.

Owen's midterm letter from Dustin:

Hey Bobo—It is an amazing privilege to be your Dad, and watching your journey into the world. You are our treasure and we love you more than you can ever know. When you get this letter it may be fall and the hard work of college hitting you—but it is all good. You know how to work through the hard times and keep pushing to grow and succeed. Breathe deep, make a plan and put in the time to study. I believe in you no matter what—Dorky Dad

Owen's midterm letter from me:

Hi O, Hope you have settled into your "life on the bluff." Dad and I are so proud of you making the choice to study at UP and to challenge yourself to grow in so many ways. Please remember how many people love and support you—we are always here if you need us. Also remember what a difference working with Scott made on your calculus. Don't be afraid to ask for help. Make plans for fall break. I always like having a trip on the calendar to look forward to...beach house? Panther Creek (cold!), New York? Kentucky? Or just hang out here. You got this! Love always, Mom

I know Owen got his letters from me and Dustin before he went missing. There was a three-way text thread with us about this and we found the opened letters among his books and papers. He knew how much we loved him, that we were proud of him, and that there were people around who could help him at any time if he needed it.

Wednesday, Oct 2 · 3:57 p.m.

Owen Klinger

> I got the letters you wrote at orientation today! Can't wait for fall break!

Dustin R. Klinger

> You are a great kid. We love you. Gotta couple of weeks of work to do still before Fall Break. Feeling ok?

Owen Klinger

> Yep, feeling good, getting ready for midterms next week

Me

> Yay! We love you.

Saturday, Oct 5 · 9:38 p.m.

Dustin R. Klinger

> Found this under [the] basement couch. Recognize?

[PHOTO OF BASEBALL HAT]

Owen Klinger

That is Gabe Harris's he left it last time he was here

Me

We will keep it in the basement for his next visit here. Hope you are well.

Saturday, Oct 5, 9:40 p.m.

Owen Klinger

Sounds good, I am doing well!

And those were the last words we exchanged. The next evening, Sunday, October 6, Owen left his dorm room and we never saw him again.

Recovering Perfectionist

Lifelong and Ongoing

I'm not sure how it started, but looking back, I really worked hard on trying to be perfect all throughout my life. When I was a kid, I remember my dad, a pathologist, saying that I had been "mature since age three." It seemed like high praise that I wanted to hear again and again. The young me must have decided that being perfect was one way to do that.

How does a child practice perfection? Well, growing up as the middle child in my family, I probably could have been a little nicer to my two brothers, but I tried hard to keep the peace and I remember being pretty good at splitting a five-piece pack of gum into three equal shares.

In elementary school I was a diligent student, doing extra credit whenever I could, striving always to be the teacher's favorite. I was even kind to the unpopular boy who had a really difficult home life and probably some unaddressed learning challenges. I was nice to him, that is, until he started following me around on the playground and everyone started teasing me that he liked me, so not exactly perfect there, but I did try harder than many others.

I only got in trouble a few times in school over the years. Once it wasn't even really in school, it was *before* school and I was by myself! I lived just down the street from McKinley Elementary in Salem, Oregon, and walked to school every day. One day it was raining hard and there were deep puddles in front of the school. I loved walking in the rain (I still do!) so

I was having a joyous time getting soaking wet splashing through these puddles. As luck (not!) would have it, my dad drove by on his way to work and saw me. Apparently he did not think this was mature or perfect behavior. He called my mom once he got to work and she called the school, where those in charge learned of my imperfection, too.

The other time I remember getting in trouble at school was in middle school Home Economics. Halfway through our six weeks of cooking sessions (which I was really enjoying), the teacher announced we were going to switch to a unit on macrame. Somehow, this really enraged me, and I found it was something I just *had* to speak out about. I don't remember what I said but I ended up in the principal's office. When the school called my mom, she replied, "I think you have the wrong Mary. I'm Mary POZAR's mom." They had to break her heart and tell her that it was indeed her darling daughter, the once-perfect Mary Pozar, who was in trouble for rudely protesting a hippie hemp craft in Home Ec. (I think my mom could see my point, but she was mortified: perfect children do not talk back in class—especially about something so benign!)

I went to church with my mom. Not every week, but more than my brothers did, enhancing my perfect status most Sundays while getting rewarded after Mass with a doughnut. I went through Confirmation, getting a new dress and a middle name in the process—which my brothers never got (neither the dress nor the middle name!).

I practiced piano every day, keeping my nails short because my music teacher, Mrs. Schnelker, said I had to if I wanted to be a serious (and in my mind, perfect) pianist. In high school, I quit volleyball after two short years even though I liked it, because setting the ball was not great for my pianist fingers. In 1986, I went to a summer-long music camp at Interlochen in Michigan to practice a Mozart concerto for a local competition. I wore the ridiculous camp uniform of corduroy knickers and knee socks through muggy summer days and mosquito-filled evenings by the lake. I spent most of that summer in a lonely piano practice room while the other campers were engaged in their group dance classes or collaborative orchestra rehearsals. I missed my boyfriend (who my parents secretly didn't think was perfect for me), but I perfected my part of that Mozart concerto for two pianos and was able to win the competition the next year with my partner.

I flirted with imperfection again through a few teenage experiments. I only skipped school one time, in high school. Our boys' basketball team went to the state finals during my senior year, and we all wanted to go watch the game up in Portland. (They didn't win, but it was still worth it!) I only smoked cigarettes—cloves—one time with my friends Heather and Holly in downtown Salem. (So risky! Any of our parents could have seen us!) I drank alcohol with friends a few times, but didn't go to (or rather, wasn't invited to) the big drinking parties down by "the river"—yes, the same Willamette River where Owen's body was found—which also ran through my hometown. I kissed a few boys, but not so many that I could be considered slutty. That would SO not be perfect! When I had a serious boyfriend, I was a perfectly loyal girlfriend.

I got good grades in high school, did well on the standardized tests, and won some awards for music. I applied to only one college—the University of Notre Dame—and I got in with an early decision from admissions. Perfect, right? I think my dad wanted me (or one of my brothers) to go to Tulane, where he had gone to medical school, but Notre Dame was a pretty big deal for someone from Oregon with Midwestern Catholic roots, so it was quite close to perfect.

At Notre Dame, I continued striving toward perfection. I met my future husband, Dustin, walking on the quad the first day of Freshman Orientation. We didn't date immediately, but still, what a perfect meeting that was! I bonded with my roommates and the girls in the triple room next door and only gained ten pounds instead of the dreaded Freshman 15. I went to weekly Mass in our dorm's chapel and eventually began leading the music group for those liturgies.

I tried to remain a perfect daughter, calling my freshly separated parents separately on Sunday nights, when long distance rates dropped, and listening to them cry over the phone, holding back my own tears while trying to be supportive and understanding about their difficult situation.

I broke up with my boyfriend from back home when I wanted to start dating that perfectly interesting boy (Dustin!) I had met on the first day of college—because that was the right thing to do—even if I later bounced between a few boyfriends for a while. Lucky for me, Dustin stayed interested for three years despite my lack of perfection in juggling my youthful suitors.

I studied hard at Notre Dame, too. I went to all my classes and joined the serious classical choir, Chorale. I sang and danced in the musical *Godspell* in my sophomore year and somehow managed to get even better grades during that semester when every minute was filled with classes, homework, rehearsals, or dates! I also got a job working in the computer lab on campus—word processing on Apple computers was a new thing in 1989, but I knew how to put paper in the printer and use the "Ctrl + Z" command to help frantic peers recover work they had accidentally deleted at two o'clock in the morning. (I was a hero!)

I realized that Notre Dame was full of other students aiming at perfection too, so I continued to strive. I was accepted for the competitive Notre Dame in London semester study abroad program in my junior year and carefully followed the rules there too, attending every class and making only short trips on weekends, so I was able to check back into our flat with the rector on Sunday nights as we were required to do. I will confess, though, that I went to one (likely illegal, *shhh!*) after-hours rave in a London warehouse where people were blowing whistles to the music in a super annoying way, and I rode home that night on someone's lap in an overfilled and unlicensed taxi.

After college, I contemplated joining a year long residential community service program. (The manager from my summer job in a state of Oregon office who wrote a reference for me asked me why on earth I would want to do volunteer work—well, duh, I was trying to be perfect!) But, alas, instead I landed a job teaching conversational English in Japan. I lived there in my own apartment to be near Dustin, that loyal friend turned college romance, who was selling pacemakers for a Japanese company. He lived across the city in a *gaijin* share house—because I thought at the time that perfect girls don't live with their boyfriends if they aren't married.

The school where I taught was near a suburban Tokyo train station, and I went to work every day, even though I was sometimes sick with imposter syndrome, worried that the students would see the insecure, recent college grad hiding under the shoulder pads of my suit from Ann Taylor Loft.

I had signed a two year contract, though, so I kept up my end of the arrangement until I had a legitimate way out: after one year I could leave and the school would still pay for my flight home. As that exit approached,

Dustin and I discussed our future one night as we rode the Yamanote Line (a rail line that loops around Tokyo) back to Shinjuku station together, where we would catch our separate trains home. We were returning from having dinner with a lonely bachelor friend and began talking about how we didn't want to be alone like he was. Dustin spontaneously proposed marriage to me right there on the train—giving me my perfect excuse to leave my teaching job, as well as offering a path to a deeper commitment and a way to avoid a lifetime of loneliness, all in one. I flew home to Oregon to prepare for our wedding, which was, of course, perfect!

After our wedding, we returned to Japan together and Dustin continued selling pacemakers. I found a more comfortable part-time job editing business correspondence in English for Kiwi Japan, the shoe polish company. We worked for two more years there before it was time for a change, and Dustin applied to law school. We packed up and moved back to the Pacific Northwest, where I worked to pay the bills and the tuition for Dustin's studies at the University of Washington.

We bought a small house in Seattle, using savings from Japan as the down payment. We fixed up our home, planted flowers, and started our family in Dustin's third year of law school, when we had refilled our savings account and could afford a child—because that's what I thought perfect people did: planned things out and then followed through on their plans. Dustin and I were great partners in the pursuit of perfection, and Gabe, our firstborn, was the perfect baby.

We paid cash for a used 1997 Honda Civic and moved to Portland when Dustin (as a newly minted graduate) was hired by a law firm there. We bought a four-bedroom house and added two Oregonian kids within the next few years, Owen and Frances, so they could all grow up together as friends, and we would have a close family. We paid our credit card bills in full every month, careful not to live beyond our means. We made charitable and 529 contributions and filed our taxes on time. We reduced, reused, and recycled everything we could. We went to church together, and I stepped up to be president of the co-op preschool down the street from our house. I wrote thank you notes for any presents I received and taught my kids to do the same. We prayed for those less fortunate and practiced gratitude for all our blessings. It felt like we were doing everything right.

After the parent-run preschool, our kids attended the Japanese Magnet Program in the public school a few miles away from our home. This K-12 program seemed like the perfect fit for our family, as it kept us in the public school system, yet gave us a tight-knit peer group of parents deeply committed to making their children's education the best possible—through the lens of a culture Dustin and I already admired and wanted to share with our kids. Our experience with the Japanese language enabled us to help them with all their extra homework, and we opened our home to host many exchange students and student teachers from Japan, further immersing our children in the society and vernacular they were studying. That was pretty perfect.

During these years I was a stay-at-home mom, which gave me the flexibility to frequently volunteer in our kids' classrooms, hang out with them after school, and chauffeur them to all of their enrichment activities around the region—including music lessons, art camps, dance classes, computer coding workshops, and all the sports they wanted to try. I helped out as needed on the sidelines or backstage, packed healthy lunches, baked cookies constantly, raised money to save the elm trees at the elementary school, and ran the PTA. On weekends—between kids' sports and dance classes—I made plans for family hikes, beach trips, visits with their grandparents, and other "forced family fun," as my kids jokingly called it.

I wrote a funny (and not-too-braggy) Christmas letter every year that I sent out with a family photo to a long list of friends and family. Perfect! I baked biscotti and decorated Christmas cookies for the neighbors and helped the kids create homemade gifts for each other and their grandparents. Donating new and old toys for charity toy drives also became part of our perfect Christmas traditions.

I took everyone to the doctor, the dentist, the orthodontist, and the eye doctor. I even took Frances to the eye doctor, even though her vision was perfect. She failed the eye test at school on purpose because she really wanted to wear glasses like Gabe! I did mountains of laundry with eco-friendly detergent in cold water and cooked nourishing meals that my family all ate together at the dinner table. I went to the gym most mornings before everyone else woke up and later started taking tennis lessons while the kids were in school so I could stay healthy (and set a good example of learning something new as an adult). I let the kids get a dog and didn't even make them promise to pick up the dog poop. (I knew it would fall to me anyway and didn't want to feel bitter about it.)

Our kids went with me or Dustin on one-on-one visits to see Grandpa John (my dad) in New York City. They also got to see Mexico and Hawaii as guests of Nona on big family trips. Each of them traveled to Japan twice (in fifth and eighth grade) with their school classmates for cultural exchanges, and Dustin and I alternated as chaperones. I was a patient co-pilot when they were learning to drive. (I also absolutely rocked the difficult registration process for Driver's Ed classes for each of them, setting my alarm for the 5:00 a.m. opening of the website's portal!) I bravely let the boys risk concussions playing football and lacrosse in high school and let my daughter ruin her feet dancing *en pointe* in ballet.

When our oldest son, Gabe, went to college at Oregon State, I crocheted an afghan for his dorm room in the orange and black colors of his school—Go Beavs! Perfect! I made him watch a documentary on Netflix with me about the problem of sexual assaults on college campuses and talked with him about responsible partying and looking out for more vulnerable friends. He joined the marching band at school instead of a fraternity, and I felt like all his hard work (and my pursuit of perfection) was paying off. He was safely out of the nest!

When Owen graduated high school two years later, the documentary on sexual assaults had been removed from Netflix so we couldn't watch it together. Instead, we talked about consent, impaired judgment, the dangers of vaping, and the importance of making good choices. I was feeling pretty smug about how well Owen was prepared for college.

Owen got into the state university where his brother went and was offered a scholarship at the school he had visited in Montana—the one I thought was his #1 choice. That seemed perfect! But Owen surprised everyone by choosing to attend a smaller, Catholic school closer to home: the University of Portland, a sister school to Notre Dame. I was excited that he wanted to take this different path, though, as I knew it would challenge him academically, socially, and maybe even spiritually. It was only 20 minutes from our house, but Owen planned to live in a men's dorm alongside sophomores and juniors, with even a few seniors sprinkled around. I thought that would be so good for him, and I promised not to hover even when tempted by his close proximity.

So, you see, it seemed like things were still going along so perfectly. And then my world fell apart.

My world was shattered when Owen went missing. Perfect doesn't include your son's roommates calling you one morning to tell you he hadn't come back to his room the night before. It doesn't include a nightmarish two-week search for your kid and the beginning of an endless quest for answers to all the questions his disappearance unleashes. It usually doesn't include being confused and scared and in shock, just not knowing what to do. We were suddenly one of those sad, desperate families you see on the news pleading for any information that might help them. Our son's beautiful face was the one looking out from the missing person posters and billboards. It seemed terribly unfair that this was happening to me and my family, to Owen. I had lost a treasured piece of my heart, and I was humbled.

I realize now that striving to live my life so carefully, to make plans and believe that I could control the way things would turn out by doing everything in the "right" way was absolutely ridiculous. I was doing what I thought I had to do in order to be successful and happy. I think my upbringing in the Catholic church, my parents' expectations when I was younger (and my desire for their approval), and even my classical piano training all got me going down this path towards perfection and its hollow promises.

Despite my careful work toward building a loving, successful, happy family and leading a fulfilling life as a dedicated wife and a mom doing everything "right," I fell far short of this aspiration in one doozy of a measure: I lost a treasured child. Losing Owen in the way we did instantly connected me to all different types of grief and suffering that people around the world experience. I used to believe that following every rule—even the silly little ones like parking legally—could shield good people from bad things, loss, and heartbreak. I realize now that these are intrinsic parts of our experience as humans, and I shouldn't have expected to avoid them. I could probably have done with a less extreme "reset," but, wow, losing a beloved child really blew these pretenses away and left me in a profoundly new place. I'm surrendering to this new serious imperfection and learning to be OK with not being perfect, with not knowing what will happen to all of us, including the incredibly difficult reality of not knowing what happened to Owen.

Letters of Thanks and the Apple Club
March 2022

Photo of the Columbia River at sunrise. This peaceful image was taken in July 2022,
by the man who found Owen's body.

When he reached out to us in March of 2022, the man who found Owen told us he wished to remain anonymous, but since then he has given me permission to share his name: Anthony Kautz. In May of 2022, Dustin and I met Anthony for coffee and thanked him in person for finding Owen. I wrote this note when Anthony first contacted me and later sent it to him via Facebook Messenger. I also emailed it to the findowenk@gmail.com group and shared an excerpt of the letter on my More Owen Facebook page in October of 2022. We will forever be grateful to Anthony.

To the man who found Owen's body in the river: Until last night, you were just a name in the police report. A name and a phone number, surprisingly not redacted in that ridiculous report that wasn't helpful at all. I memorized your name and thought of calling many times, but who calls anyone on the phone these days? Especially out of the blue to ask about something like finding a body in the river? I couldn't do that, so I waited, telling other people how much I wanted to meet you and talk to you. And then last night you saw my post on the Facebook More Owen page and wrote to me. Thank you.

I had just posted the letter I sent to Owen's Japanese teacher before she died: A letter expressing my gratitude for the way she treated Owen with amusement and understanding in her classroom over the years, for the support she reluctantly gave to start the Apple Club which became such a silly and fun distraction for Owen and his friends. A letter singing praise for the compassion and care she showered on us when Owen went missing and in the months after he was found. A letter expressing awe for the way a tiny Japanese woman suffering from the side effects of cancer treatments anchored a community of students when they came unmoored and were trying to find Owen, and then hoping to find More Owen. A letter like I could have—and probably should have—written to hundreds of people who helped our family in ways big and small when Owen was missing, when Owen was found, when we knew Owen had died, and when we were raw and bloodied from the labor of birthing this fresh grief experience. It was a letter of thanks I could have written to you.

I was surprised you saw the post, or any of the posts. Sharing my grief on Facebook has been helpful but bizarre as I see how many people are moved by my words and pictures. While I grieve alone most days in my quiet house, I can read comments from strangers and close friends and know they are thinking about Owen. Somehow, I had not imagined you—the person who found Owen—would be among those followers, but I am so glad you found me. And I am beyond grateful that you found Owen.

In the weeks we were searching for him, I was completely breathless and almost paralyzed with the tightest back and neck muscles I have ever experienced. I could not eat. I could not sleep. Terrifying potential scenarios of what might have happened to him bloomed in my mind whenever I closed my eyes, and my thoughts could not stop racing through Owen's interactions with us, with his friends, with his new roommates, on social media or the internet, desperate for a clue we had missed. I do not think I could still be living and searching, striving, and straining to Find Owen without those sustained efforts having come at a great cost of their own. Your discovery helped shift us (painfully, unwillingly, reluctantly) into the next phase of this experience: knowing Owen was dead. These many months later, we still don't understand why or how it happened, and that anguish carries on, coming and going in waves and massive swings of the tide, but we found Owen. You found Owen.

I always loved the beautiful views of the Willamette River from Cathedral Park, but now I have a hard time going there. Sometimes I make myself drive by the river to see how much pain I can endure before completely losing it. I can barely breathe when I drive over the St. Johns Bridge or even over the lower level of the Fremont Bridge. I remember a fishing trip Owen and I took with my dad and Frances when the kids were younger. Skipping school to go fishing in the rain made us all feel light and free. I can still see Owen's proud smile when he caught a big salmon right under the Fremont Bridge. When I am close to the river, I think of that day and the day you found his body. All the moments of Owen's life and his death overlap and condense, fused together like incongruous layers of rock.

I have so many questions for you: Do you have kids? Did you know we were looking for Owen? When you saw a body in the water with long hair, did you think it was a woman? A homeless person? My son? Were you scared? Did you think about letting him sink back into the river and not calling anyone? After finding Owen's body, how do you feel when you are out on the water where you found him now? Could we go out on the water together some time to see the place where you found Owen?

Do you go to church? (I hope you don't mind me asking.) We used to, but it's been so hard since losing Owen and then the pandemic messed everything up. When I got your message, I thought of Mary, Jesus's mom.

(Is that weird for me to be basically comparing myself to the Mother of God? Sorry!) I imagined Mary drilling the women who found Jesus' tomb empty with questions: "What do you mean he wasn't there!? Where did he go!? Are you sure the rock was solidly in place when you buried him?" I wonder if talking to the eyewitnesses soothed her soul. Will it soothe mine?

I went to the Portland Grotto with a few friends from college last summer. I was a reluctant visitor, feeling abandoned by God and honestly extremely worried our car would get broken into in the parking lot, which was littered with broken auto glass and ringed by the debris of people camping just beyond the gates. "Who is the patron saint of grieving mothers?" I asked in the gift shop as we fondled the medals for the patron saints of taxi drivers, of health care workers, of travelers. My friends pointed to the ubiquitous images of Mary, "Our Lady of Sorrows," and I was humbled. How had I missed something so obvious? I started paying more attention after that, hoping to gain some insight into how to handle the weight of my grief from this mother.

Near the end of our tour, I saw a sculpture of Mary taking Jesus's body down from the cross and I lost it. That was a moment I did not get to have. I never got to hold Owen's body one more time, rocking him, cradling him, like the baby he was to me. I never got to feel the manly strength he had grown into, his long calves, his capable hands, his oddly sharp shoulder blades—maybe these were sharp since his birth as God was planning to give Owen angel wings! Mary would have had to deal with her son's dried blood, sweat, urine, sunburn, and more, I'm sure. But I imagine she also saw the beauty of her son and his sacrifice. Her sacrifice. I wish I had a moment like that, but I hope that at least I can have coffee with the person who found Owen's body and put an end to our search.

Thank you for finding Owen and for reaching out to me. When I see the river now, I will also think of you and the way the river flowing through our land and our lives connects us all.

With love,
Mary

* * * *

Below is the letter I referenced in my missive to Owen's finder. I emailed this to Owen's Japanese teacher, Kazuko Page, on February 19, 2022 when she was on medical leave from teaching. After she passed away later that month, I posted it on my More Owen Facebook page on March 16, 2022. (The man who found Owen in the river messaged me after seeing this post.)

Dear Page Sensei,

Well this sucks! I don't know if you want to read a message from the grieving mom of one of your past students, but I felt I had to write to you—and I have to talk about all the stuff that our polite society does not make room for. You can skip that part and just watch the old video I attached of Owen and his classmates doing their "Cook News" final for your class. We love watching this video where they make rice for their bento with umeboshi! I hope it brings you a smile.

I want you to know how much your support and outreach after Owen's death meant to our family. You had so much already going on but you took extra care to make space for the grief of the JMP students and to make sure that we knew Owen's spirit was being remembered and celebrated still in your classroom. We have all the origami cranes the students made with you when Owen was missing and will cherish them along with the notes from all the students.

I thank you for the photos and videos you shared of Owen singing in your classroom—especially his self-assigned solo. Our oldest son Gabe always reminds us that he did that solo first! We appreciate the story you shared at the Oya No Kai auction about the creation of Apple Club and how Owen wasn't really involved in the leadership, but would say that he was; how Owen's magnetic charm and contagious joy brought so many people to the club meetings that your room was dangerously full.

The story of how Owen would say "that's my name!" whenever you used the word "o-en" in class was very special. You took time to help me fill out the form for a memorial brick at Richmond's playground with this kanji. You also helped us look at different fonts for Dustin's future Owen kanji tattoo. (He is still trying to muster up some courage to get this tattoo! Dustin does not like needles—Owen didn't either!)

I love knowing that Gabe and Owen both had you as their teacher and especially Owen spent so much time in your classroom (at lunch and on flex days too!) Thank you, Page Sensei, for all of your energy and care. You showered the students of JMP with your attention and belief that they could learn.

We will do our best to continue to support Apple Club and we will always think of you when we eat apples, wrapped in our special apple club fleece blankets.

I don't know what happens to our energy or spirit—our souls—when we die, but I have found peace in imagining that Owen's energy and love are still here with us even if we can't see it or feel it, that his soul is still on a journey of discovery and love and learning. I hope that whatever you believe the next part of your journey is will be all that you have ever dreamed it could be and more. We will hold your energy in our already broken hearts.

With love,
Mary (and Dustin) Klinger

The story of Owen and the Apple Club as told by Kazuko Page Sensei in a speech delivered before a paddle raise for the Owen Klinger Scholarship at the Japanese Dual Language Immersion Program parent support group (Oya No Kai) auction in February 2020:

"O-en actually has a Japanese meaning, it means to cheer on, to help and push on others.

Hi my name is Kazuko Page and I am teaching Japanese at Grant High School. This is actually my 23rd year of teaching JMP students so I know most of you. It's very special drinking sake with my former kindergarten students. I had a great pleasure of teaching Owen during his 11th and 12th grade years. Many of you know Owen and his big smile and big infectious laughter. That's what he brought into my classroom every day. And I don't think he missed my class for these two years unless it was for his water polo meet days. So he always made other students laugh and we talked about his name in Japanese kanji that is O-en, that is to cheer or to support. He really made others laugh and he cheered for others when they were up for presentation. He would just clap his hands and laugh and say "yay! You did a good job!" He also laughed at my jokes, which made other students think that those were funny so we laughed a lot thanks to Owen and just his bright, kind personality. My classroom—his class especially—we just laughed all the time and we had a great time learning Japanese together.

So for this kanji, I believe I taught it to this group during his senior year. I said this is "to support one another and to cheer for others." Owen just raised his hand and said, "That's my name!" And I said, "That's true, isn't it? It's just perfect." And all the other students just nodded, "Yeah that is your name." Of course so every time this word came up in our readings or in a test or whatever he would just make sure that everyone knew that was his name "that's my name!" and the other students would say "yeah we know." and we would joke "but can you actually write it?"

So this is really truly the word that captured his spirit.

And he and his close friends, mostly JMP friends, loved hanging out in my classroom. In fact Owen and his friends ate lunch in my classroom for these two years and they would come to my classroom for every study hall. So I was kind of calculating and I think, on average, he was spending 2 hours a day in my classroom. So I really got to know him and his friends.

And those are the students who came up to me at the beginning of their senior year and said, "Sensei, we want to start Apple Club." And I said, "Well, I didn't know you were good at computers." And they said "No, the *fruit*! Apple club!" I said "What are you talking about? What are you going to do?" and they said "We're going to just bring apples and eat apples at lunchtime." I said, "that's what you already do so I don't get this. This must be something else." So I said, "No, I cannot be your advisor." But they kept coming back for about two weeks. We just kept going back and forth. I would say "No I cannot sign off on that. That would be embarrassing if I sign it and then you are doing something else. And I do not want to get into trouble. Anyways, after all they convinced me and I said "OK I will give you a chance." So I became Apple Club's advisor.

These students decided to meet every other week. Actually there were two students out of those who went around to get donations of apples from New Seasons and other places. They would get a different variety each time. And they would come up with Kahut quiz questions and have a prize (that was apple pie!) They would come and eat and rate apples. Really iffy rating system, and actually there were over 50 students coming into my classroom. It was a fire hazard and I was really concerned, but anyway you would think that one of the two students was Owen. But actually he was *not* one of the two students who worked really hard to make that happen. Owen, however, made sure that he was one of the leaders. He would say, "sensei, I'm in the Apple club leadership." And I would say "But Owen you don't go get apples. You're not doing anything. You aren't cutting apples. You are just coming here and eating apples." And so that was always a joke between me and Owen. "What are you doing for Apple club?" But then later I realized that *he* was the reason that so many students came to Apple club because he was such a fun person. And he would yell and laugh *so* hard and he would keep eating apples and rating apples *so* high it made it so fun. And they did a good job and we tried different varieties every other week for the whole year. And after one year I realized, "you *are* a leader because you are a cheerleader and you do support and cheer everyone all the time." So we needed Owen as an apple club leader. And so again that kanji for Owen is just perfect for him.

I shared this story of Apple club to my current students when we heard the sad news. And at that point there was no Apple club this year because they all graduated. But the sophomore boys came up to me after my talk and after I told them about Owen. They said "Sensei, do you think we can start apple club again?" and I said "Of course you can. That would be awesome!" So they started, but they are sophomore boys—sorry some of them are here waiting tables tonight!—and they just couldn't come up with free apples. So we met two times and then we stopped. And that's when Mary Klinger came to talk to me about other things about Owen. So we were talking and Mary asked "So how is apple club going?" And I said "Well, they cannot get apples so we aren't meeting. You know. It's a good lesson. They just need to figure this out." Mary said, "Hmmm would it be ok if I support them by giving them apples every other week?"

So now the Klinger family is the apple club sponsor this year. And thanks to them, we are eating great apples and having a great time, meeting, and laughing; eating and rating apples every time. So I was telling my students, "See this is like Owen is still supporting us? Isn't it?" I tell the apple club members this is a gift from Owen that is still coming and that is amazing. So today when I was asked to come to talk about Owen (and I'm sorry I was not going to come here tonight because I don't like driving at night and I don't drink and I love kids' art and I didn't want to spend too much money) and so anyways I wasn't going to come, but you know sharing memories about Owen is to continue to learn about him."–Kazuko Page

The Last Lacrosse Game

May 2022

From my journal on May 17, 2022:

I tuned in to the livestream of your high school lacrosse team's game last night, somehow expecting to see you there: #20 with your hair streaming out of your helmet, in the flow, throwing your heart into every play, giving every ounce of your strength and energy to your teammates on the field. But you weren't there. Some other tall boy with shorter hair and a longer pole wore #20. Had he known you? Did he know that was your number? The number that makes my breath catch in my throat when I see it anywhere. The uniforms were different too and I didn't recognize some of the coaches. Had they known you? And how you played the game with more grit and perseverance than you appeared to bring at first glance? How much being a part of the team meant to you? How the minutes you spent in the penalty box exponentially increased the love the team showered on you?

I looked for your cleats and ankle brace among the crowd of stutter-stepping legs in front of the goal. You weren't there. Your cleats are in your monogrammed bag up in your old bedroom closet and your ankle brace is gathering dust on the shelf. I remember that the original ankle brace we ordered for you was one of the only packages that had been porch-pirated from us that last Christmas you were with us. We laughed about how disappointed the thief must have been— or maybe it was just what they needed to put more spring in their step, to carry out more crimes.

When I watched the game last night, I didn't hear the announcers marveling at your speed and heroics. I didn't hear them exaggerate your statistics to intimidate the visiting crowd or call your name for scoring a goal. I wonder what goal was your last. How many of your lasts are things I didn't realize were your lasts until you were gone? And even now—two and a half years later—how many "lasts" are things I don't even know about? I know the last food you bought at the Pilot House, the last movie you watched that weekend on your computer, the last order you made from Amazon. But who was your last conversation with? One of your roommates? Sam? Someone you met while you were walking around St. Johns that night? What was the last song you listened to? The last song you sang?

When will I stop looking for you everywhere? When will I be able to breathe more easily at the high school tennis courts, finally accepting that I will not catch a glimpse of you on the fields below at football, soccer, or lacrosse practice, that you are not one of the boys laughing and running on the track or chatting with the girls on the bleachers by the baseball field? When will I stop looking for #20 and your long hair? Will we ever know what took you away from us? And will we learn how to keep you everywhere—in our conversations and rememberings, in our future days away from this house, this neighborhood, this school, these fields?

With every change in season, every year that goes by, I am struck by how there are already fewer and fewer people around who remember you. We can say "Never Forget" or "Always Remember" but is that possible? New kids join the team—kids who never knew you or Gabe. They don't know about #20, about your flow, your dogged devotion to the team. Your Japanese teacher—whose room you spent so much time in at lunch and during study hall for so many years, who was the advisor for the wacky "Apple Club" you and your friends started senior year—passed away last winter. She isn't there to tell the new students about you and the Apple Club, about the silly and enthusiastic solo you added to the "Umi No Koe" (Ocean Voice) song and all the energy and people you brought into her classroom or the way your friend Kent, who wasn't even taking Japanese that year, would come to class during his open period just to sit next to you and sing the songs and practice the language. Your workshop leader at UP graduated and will move out of Portland. She got to know so much about you in your few short weeks on campus and she was passionate about helping people remember you. One of your roommates transferred to a university in Australia, taking another part of you far away from campus.

The Hall Director also changed. Father Pat was on sabbatical to write his book, but he is supposed to come back to Christie Hall. Next year would be your senior year at UP. You never got to do so many college things—study abroad, parties, dances, sports, dates, silly late night pranks, snowball fights, internships, finals. I don't know what you would have missed most, but I know that I miss your sweaty self, excited after an exhilarating lacrosse/sports practice or game (win or lose), icing your ankle or proudly displaying the bruises on your legs. I'm only left with these questions and the bruises on my heart, trying to remember forever your last lacrosse game.

I Didn't Know

June 2022

I cringed when I heard a friend say, "That's the worst" while consoling a mutual friend whose dog just crossed the rainbow bridge. Yes, losing our beloved pets is so very sad, I thought, annoyed, but come on! We know they are not going to live as long as we do! You want to know what is *really* the worst? Losing your eighteen-year-old son who had just started college. I know I should have been glad that my friend didn't know pain worse than losing a dog— for her that *was* the worst. My reaction is just one of the many ways that losing Owen has forever changed me.

I do know about having to say goodbye to pets. Losing our ten-year-old beagle, Bella, in May 2022, was gloomy in its own right, but it also added to my maternal grief, as it was like losing yet another part of our connection to Owen. Bella had been special to him. He loved cuddling with her *in her dog bed* on the kitchen floor for a few minutes before school and he even shared his blanket, Fuzzy, with her sometimes (a rare honor). She was his most-frequent photographic subject, and he put the best of these photos in a 2017 calendar he made for Christmas. He practiced school speeches and trumpet parts before her soft ears and ever-wagging tail. Her presence in our family's lives after losing Owen was a soothing balm. Trying to process these losses together led me to think about how when we were spending our last moments with each of them, we didn't know they were the last moments, the very last times we would see either of them.

"I didn't know." I try to tell myself those three little words whenever I feel extreme sadness at not having taken advantage of those final occasions or guilt about things I did or didn't do when they were still with us. Telling myself "I didn't know" gives me an out, but it also doesn't really help at all. Still, I try to not only tell myself, but to tell those I've lost: "I'm sorry. I didn't know."

"I didn't know, Bella."

Dear Bella,

Dustin and I didn't know when we took you out on the beach during that crazy storm and you howled at the wind and sand buffeting your sweet face that you would pass away in your sleep and never walk on the beach with us again. I didn't know when I gave you your supper that it was your last supper. It was the same salmon and sweet potato food we always joked about feeding you—oh wait! It was actually some other food from the beach house grocery store. Was that a problem for your body? Is that why you died?!? Oh shit. I wish we had given you the salmon and sweet potato food that you loved. You loved it so much that you got Granny B's German Shepherd, Buddha, to open up a whole bag of it for you and you both had a royal feast that time when Dustin and I were at the gym. Are you with Buddha again? What about Duke, the first German shepherd you met? They are probably like "Oh nuts, here's that crazy beagle Granny B used to rope us to so she wouldn't run away." I hope they met you with tail wags and are letting you snuggle up with them if you are lonely.

Are you with Owen again? We brought you into our family because Owen was so lonely when Gabe went to Japan in eighth grade. I had always said no to a dog because I knew it would be extra work for me, that the kids most likely wouldn't help. But Gabe had just flown off on a two-week study trip so I got a glimpse of a lighter workload: I had one less person to drive around, feed, clothe, and nurture. I realized that with the kids growing up I had more time to do this extra work and that there might be some unconditional love and sweet doggy kisses in it for me so I said yes. The universe aligned and brought you to us very soon after we opened our hearts.

Do you remember when I first met you? You were so joyful and playful. The family you were part of at the time was surprised at the love and attention you showed me when we initially greeted each other. I think that made it a little easier for them to let you go. They had too much going on with their new baby and the two toddlers! We were so lucky to bring you into our home. You were a great dog for us.

I didn't realize this Christmas would be your last Christmas. I would have given you ten new lambies to chew up. Granny B would have let you get fat on treats from her cutting board and I would have let you chase squirrels at the park.

Bella's last Christmas

When we walked you around the neighborhood, so many people stopped us to tell stories of their beagles who had run away, and we were always so worried you were going to take off on a crazy scent-hunt, that we kept you tightly tethered. Would you have liked to run free?

What do you think about our new puppy, Almond? Sorry we couldn't wait for a more appropriate period of time to go by before replacing you, but you spoiled us with your generous tail wags and sweet couch cuddles. Are we totally crazy to take this on right now? How do you think we are doing? We didn't know you when you were a puppy, were you as nibbly with your teeth as Almond is? I hope she will grow out of it. And I can't wait until I can take her out on walks like you and I did. I miss walking with you. I'm sorry, Bella, I didn't know it was going to be our last walk. It was raining so hard we almost stayed inside, but I will always remember those moments we had together in the storm on the beach.

Love, Mary

"I didn't know, Owen."

After writing to Bella to ease my guilty conscience, I sat down to write the harder letter, to Owen.

Dear Owen,

I didn't know it would be the last time I dropped something off at your dorm when I brought you my guitar, the little bag of snacks, and fun cleaning supplies from Muji. I didn't know it would be the last time we talked about you writing a song for me since you had written one for Dad already. I didn't know it would be the last time we exchanged texts about something stupid like that Ford Pinto behind your dorm.

I didn't know I wouldn't get the chance to send you more mail and packages; to call you and chat; to drive you to Mary's house for yard work.

There are so many "last moments" that I didn't know about as they were happening in those final months you were alive. I didn't know it would be the last time you and Gabe would hang out together when he joined you at the food carts they had on campus during orientation. I didn't know the last restaurant we would eat at together would be the McMenamins St. Johns Pub. It doesn't seem like a special enough place for that distinction for someone with such a passion for food, but I know you loved their spicy tater tots and it was close to campus so you could eat with us and not miss the last of your freshman welcome events. Your

*grandmas didn't even get a chance to visit you at college. They didn't
know you wouldn't be there much longer.*

The last time Owen and Gabe were together–UP orientation August 2019

*Every single moment up until the moment we lost you now has the
potential for this identity of being a "last."*

I didn't know it would be the last time you drove Dad's car.

I didn't know it would be the last time I baked you cookies.

I didn't know it would be the last time I hugged you.

Or the last time I saw you.

*I didn't know it would be the last time you slept in your bed at home.
Was that the last time you made Frances laugh? When was the last time
you talked with Grandpa John and listened so kindly to his stories? I
know he saw you at UP when he stopped by campus to take you out for
dinner—maybe that was a good last time with him.*

*What was the last thing you wrote? The last song you sang? How was
the last shower you took? Did you sing in the shower—or did you cry? I
heard you had fun at the dance on that last Friday night. Was that the
last time you danced or kissed someone? Did you ever have sex? I know
you didn't talk about that with me and probably thought I wouldn't want*

to hear about it, but I hope you experienced this amazing connection of two people expressing love for each other.

When was the last time you were at Panther Creek? The beach house? When was the last fire you built? I wanted to see you cook more, bake more, work more, sing more, play more, dance more, laugh more, cry more, learn more, read more, travel more, mess up more, help more, be more. I wanted you to be more Owen. Have more fun, more days in the sun, more days in the rain, more days in the snow, more days in Hawaii, more days mowing the lawn, more days listening to records, or shopping for records with your friends, more days helping Granny B, more days visiting Nona, visiting Gabe at osu, *more dates, more video games! (I never thought I would be longing for you to have more time for video games, but that is where I am now.)*

I remember the last time you rode in my Mini Cooper, which was new to me that month you left for college. Not to add more drama, but it was Friday the 13th of September. Did we make any jokes about the bad luck associated with that date? You had fun playing with the lighting controls and exploring many of the car's unique features. I took you to the pediatrician's office for your last vaccination, and we laughed together about how much you hated getting shots. We didn't know that was the last time you would have to worry about seeing or feeling a needle. On the way back to campus, I didn't know it would be my last time to drive around with you. I would have wanted to keep driving, to always be joking and smiling with you in my little blue car. I keep your picture right next to me on the dashboard and think of you whenever I drive.

I'm sorry Owen, I just didn't know.

Love, Mom

Ticks Suck as Birthday Presents

June 2022

Frances, Gabe, Me, Dustin, and Almond slaying Scotch broom at Panther Creek in June 2022

Presents I received on my 52nd Birthday:
(a list from my journal dated June 4, 2022)

23 heart shaped rocks
2 free coffees
1 blueberry scone
A grief book from Goodwill (used grief?!)
2 boxes of Red Vines
Flowers
Glossier Birthday Cake lip balm
2 cupcakes
1½ slices of pizza
Time with two of my beautiful children, my mom, and my husband
2 ticks

"Ticks kind of suck as far as birthday presents go," my friend Jeanne said. She is absolutely right.

A little family posse went out to Panther Creek for my birthday this year—our crew included Dustin, Gabe, Frances, and even my mom. It was where I wanted to go, so Owen would feel a little closer on my special day.

We'd gone out for a short hike in the woods, and were relaxing on the cabin's deck playing the card game Golf. It had been a while since we had played this game (or *any* game) and I wasn't sure we were playing it right. Gabe kept peeking at the cards on the bottom of his pile, though I think you were only supposed to look at them once. He pulled up his phone's calculator to figure out the odds of how likely a certain card would next appear. I'm pretty sure you aren't supposed to use a calculator to win a friendly card game on your mom's birthday—aren't you supposed to let her win?—but I didn't say anything, letting Gabe win with his calculator-assisted cheatery while I savored tiny sips of sparkling wine from Grampy Bruce's old whiskey glass.

I felt a few light rain drops, but it wasn't enough to move us inside. I also felt a tiny tingle on my arm. It was just a little itch so I didn't explore it further. It was way up my bicep, past the tightly buttoned cuff, and down from the tailored shoulder of my new 50 UPF shirt. I wore it because I thought it would be good protection not only from the sun, but from ticks.

And then I felt the tiny itch again. There had been a very small tick on Gabe's shirt when we'd first come back from our hike, and he found one on his sock too, but I still wasn't thinking this was a tick on me. I was the birthday girl, after all! Only good things should happen on my day!

Dustin always told me that you don't feel it when a tick bites you because of the way they kind of anesthetize your skin while they're sucking out your blood. I was thinking this was something stinging me, which I also abhor, and I ripped open the snaps on my shirt and wriggled it off my shoulders. LO AND BEHOLD, THERE WAS A TICK ON MY ARM!

I freaked out and did what you probably are never supposed to do. I ripped the tick off my arm and threw it onto the deck—right by where Nona was sitting. She freaked out too, and tried to find it so she could squash it with her foot. I lost that round of the card game, and I spilled my glass of wine.

Why did we both freak out so much on account of that little tick on my arm, you might ask? Well, besides being aware (as good outdoorsy people are) of the diseases they carry, before we had gone hiking, Nona had told us a story about some pregnant moose that was found dead in the woods of Maine with more than **90,000 tick bites** and many live ticks still feeding on her. Needless to say, this was not a pleasant image, especially on one's birthday. And now one (or more?) had been on me! I needed a bigger glass for my wine. I needed to think about something other than ticks.

I turned my attention back to my mom as she chattered about food preparations for an upcoming trip she and I were taking with my brother John and his family to Sunriver Resort, at the edge of central Oregon's Cascade Mountains. "If I want to make those meatloaves, do I defrost the hamburger meat, make the loaves, and then refreeze them? Do you think that would work?" she was asking me. I didn't know the answer. I was supposed to learn stuff like that from her. I wasn't ready to be *her* mom.

As she talked, she was struggling to get her water bottle open in a way that concerned me, and I learned her eyes were still dilated from a recent visit to her eye doctor. She took off her glasses and opened her eyes wide to show Frances her huge pupils. I wondered aloud how she was able to drive from her home in Salem to the creek (about a two-hour drive) with her eyes like that. She said she had two pairs of sunglasses on in the car that she'd worn, one over the other, to protect them. I realized how grateful I was to be spending my birthday with my mom—horrifying tick story, meatloaf questions, crazy double sunglasses, and all—and I hoped there were no ticks on her. Oh shoot, I thought, there I was thinking about ticks again!

I let Frances have a taste of the wine from my glass as we put all the paper plates into the pizza box from our lunch, along with our cupcake wrappers and plastic salad forks. We'd left our fancy portable fire pit at home, and someone had stolen the one we had at the cabin, so we didn't linger when the rain started falling harder and the afternoon's warmth started to fade. I snapped my shirt back up and put on Owen's lacrosse jacket. I had a heart-shaped turquoise rock in my pocket, the best one I'd found all day. I was considering it my birthday gift from Owen.

In the car on the way home, as we came back into cell range, Gabe and Frances fussed with Snapchat in the back seat, sending me birthday Bitmojis that had them cracking up. I tried to use the special birthday filter on a few selfies, but I'm so clumsy with that app that I just gave them more things to laugh over together. I took off my baseball cap, the University of Portland trucker hat I like to wear to show everyone I had a student at UP: I am still Owen's mom. I was feeling peaceful and full, grateful to be making some new memories with my family.

I shook out my ponytail and ran my fingers through my hair, scratching along the scalp in a random attempt to make sure nothing was lurking there. I put my hair up in a twist and leaned my head back on the headrest, listening to the kids chattering without really hearing what they were saying. Then I felt a little itch, or tickle behind my left ear and I reached my hand up there. My fingers closed around something: a tick—bigger than the one that had been on my arm! In shock and disgust, I yanked it off my neck and threw it, not caring where. It landed on the top of Dustin's coffee cup—and even though he was piloting our vehicle down the curvy two-lane highway, he glanced over, grabbed the tick, said, "That's a big one!" and unceremoniously squished it with his thumbnail. Our car briefly rolled over the rumble strip as he did so, and then thankfully found its way back onto smooth pavement. We spent the rest of the ride in uneasy itchiness as we all tried to tune into the tiniest tingles and twinges of our bodies. Ticks make terrible birthday presents, it's true, but I had a memorable birthday celebration at Panther Creek. I wish Owen had been there.

A Big Old Truck and a Poem
about Grandpa John

June 2022

to: findowenk@gmail.com
date: June 20, 2022
subject: Father's Day 2022

Dear Friends,

Yes, we are still here. Still missing Owen, and still trying to figure out how to do this life without him. The school year didn't go as I thought it would. Frances started college the day after Hurricane Ida flooded many subways and streets of New York (an omen maybe?), but came back home in October and is taking some more time to prepare for that big leap into whatever is next for her. Gabe switched majors at OSU, further extending his journey towards an eventual bachelor's degree. I went back into my exhausting and unsustainable "vigil mode" of mothering. I stopped being able to quiet my mind, to make future plans, or to even breathe deeply. Every day was a challenge just to get up and get through; unproductive worry sucked up a lot of my energy. A large construction project deployed at the end of our block in an ironic physical display of the chaotic disruption of "normal life" I was experiencing. (Heavy earth-moving machines still clang an unmelodic chorus of backup beeps as I type this, and the kitchen floor is literally vibrating.) Neighbors made plans to move, children of friends graduated college, our special dog Bella died. I felt like I was being left behind in our house of grief as change happened all around us.

But even when I was macerating in the darkness, fiercely guarding my heart against letting in the light, some connections were still made and some joyful moments snuck in. Life goes on and we are limping along as best we can.

In February, I joined a 30-day grief writing group called "Write Your Grief Out!" led by Anne Gudger of Coffee and Grief and found that mindful writing helped me shift things around a little bit. It gave me somewhere to rest the heavy load of grief I was carrying, and I enjoyed spending time (on Zoom) with a supportive group of other grieving people. This experience made me want to continue sharing more about Owen, his life, and my grief journey; to let my words carry some of the heavy weight of my grief; and to use writing to help navigate through these experiences of loss that loving others inevitably brings into our lives.

Father's Day was quiet at our house this year. Dustin got up early to play golf with his buddies and then the two of us drove out to Panther Creek with our new puppy, Almond. We found a few heart rocks near the fast flowing water but didn't stay there too long. Even with the rushing sound of the creek, it was a little too quiet. We stopped by Dustin's mom's house on our way back home for a short visit. We were surprised to see two of Owen's friends there resurrecting an old diesel pickup truck Dustin had bought years ago for Panther Creek, a truck Owen had fun trying to drive on the property before he had his license. Seeing these young men in Granny B's driveway showed me that these connections made through Owen continue. With a lot of work, repairs to our broken trucks and our broken hearts can be made and we can still love each other.

Since yesterday was Father's Day, I wanted to share Owen's slam poem about his grandpa with you. All of the typos and grammatical errors are Owen's so I have left them as they were. We are still here and so is Owen.

With love,
Mary
#moreowen

Grandpa by Owen Klinger

My grandpa is kind like a humble monk
    Even after his heart surgery, he kept apologizing to
the nurses for
    "Being such a bother"
    The only thing he asked for from the hospital was a
burger,
    We had to sneak it in, he was worried and had my mom
close the door
    As soon as she brought it in
    Grandpa John loves taking his grandkids out to lunch
    He also loves to take us down to the shooting range that
always smells like lead
    He has a small arsenal at his house,

Each time we go out shooting he brings a fancy new gun with him

He is a man of few words

This may be due to his hearing being similar to that of my grandma's deaf dog

But once you can get a conversation going,

John's booming laugh will stuff the room with joy

He hasn't always had such a grand life style

His family was rather poor when he grew up and didn't always have clothes that fit him,

This is why he loves to take my siblings and I clothes shopping so we always have clothes that fit us

After becoming a doctor, he served in the korean war*

---

*Grandpa John isn't THAT old! He served as an Army doctor in Korea during the Vietnam war!

During his time in korea, my grandpa became a japanophile
Ever since, he has been addicted japanese culture
I have found memories of watching japanese samurai movies, eating sushi,
And just talking about japan in general.
Whenever we aren't seeing a movie or going to a museum,
We are devouring delicious meals
I am pretty sure that he preferres going out with my brother and I,
Because when he takes my Mom and sister to dinner,
They can't consume as much food as my brother and I can
When I visited him in his new York apartment, we joked about his lifestyle there,
The three M's we called it
Meals, Movies, and Museums
Grandpa John has also introduces my brother and I to some very wonderful steak
While visiting him there, my brother and I went to Keen's Steakhouse
They had the best darn steak I had ever tasted it was like heaven for taste buds.
I just hope that before my Grandpa goes on to a better place,
That he can see what wonderful things he has done, all of the people he has helped, and how many lives he has touched.

Missing My Tennis Drill

July 2022

Last Thursday, I missed my tennis drill. Some may think, "It's just tennis," but tennis for me is like therapy. I started learning tennis in 2009, when all three of my kids were in full-day school and I had time for something new in my life. I quickly became addicted to the mental, physical, and social aspects of the game. The focus needed to track the fast-paced movement of the ball and quickly adjust tactics and strategies on court gave me an almost meditative break from the worries of my daily life. It was better than yoga! Taking a group lesson twice a week and playing doubles on one women's team slowly developed into playing once or twice *a day* on six or more recreational teams throughout the year. I knew I would have more tennis in the coming days and weeks, but missing the drill rattled me and once again brought an unwelcome tsunami of emotion into my day.

It was a Thursday that felt like a Wednesday because Monday had been the Fourth of July and our family had been out of town at the beach and Sunriver before that, so this week I was really looking forward to some high-level tennis and a good workout with my city league teammates and our favorite pro, Wakana, at Portland Tennis Center (PTC). But I missed the drill. I didn't miss it because Thursday felt like a Wednesday, but it was just part of how out of sorts I was, not only emotionally but also when it came to being in control of the seemingly easier stuff, like appointments in my calendar. Grief has humbled me and wrecked my previously remarkable time-management skills.

That morning I had dressed in my neon orange striped top with a black skirt and jaunty pink and orange shoes. (My tennis clothes are some of my favorite things to wear! They make me feel strong and confident.) My hair was pulled up in a tight ponytail, ready for battle. I had a full water bottle and fresh sweatbands in my tennis bag. I was ready to go!

I showed up at 10:13 a.m., lucked out by scoring a tiny parking spot just right for my little car. As I got out, I noticed that the lines between the spaces looked like they had been spray painted by hand. That was typical for our budget-challenged public tennis facility, which had been going downhill lately. I snapped a photo for a friend who is entertained by evidence of PTC's numerous shortcomings. As I grabbed my bag, I glared at a soccer dad using a shaded corner parking spot as his office while his kid attended soccer camp behind the tennis center. His Tesla was parked right under the "Tennis center parking ONLY" sign. That was an ongoing battle I wasn't going to engage in today.

I felt self-satisfied as I entered the building, having not been there for a few weeks, but still feeling in many ways that it was my place, my home away from home. I saw my friends were already chatting on court with the teaching pro, so I skipped past the check-in desk and squeezed through the busy lobby (Who were all these people? I wondered briefly) and out onto court one. Then I realized my friends were chatting with the pro because the drill had just ended. They were dripping with sweat, their faces red with the efforts of playing hard points indoors on a warm summer morning. I had missed the entire exercise.

It always started at 10:15. If there was an empty court, we sometimes came earlier to warm up, but the real deal always started at 10:15. Until it didn't. Until the previous week—when I was out of town—when the time apparently had shifted to 9:15, and no one told me.

When I realized I had missed the action, tears sprang surprisingly from my eyes. I felt like I had failed, the day was ruined, and I was just a genuinely useless person who couldn't even make it to a simple appointment (one that I was truly looking forward to and very much needed, for my mental health as much as for the exercise). I was embarrassed that the tears came up so quickly, and then the pro felt bad and tried to offer me a spot in a drill session later that day. I passed; I'd probably miss that one somehow, too. My friends tried to console me, admitting they had been worried that I had the time wrong for the morning slot, but they didn't follow through on their impulse to shoot me a text reminder because I used to be so on top of things. Not this time. Not every time. Not anymore, even when I think I'm "doing better."

It's just tennis, but I was a wreck. I went to the desk then to try to explain what had happened and per the center's policy, to pay for my unused drill spot. My friend came with me and pointed out that there had been confusing language in the online signup page that still made it sound like the drill was at 10:15, even though the calendar now said it was at 9:15. I felt a tiny bit better when she complained about the confusion on my behalf, asking the teen behind the desk if someone could make the necessary edits so it would be clear in the future. I guess my tears scared the desk worker, and in the end he waved off the required payment for my "no show." I felt my spirits rise a little more.

Then I was struck with the sudden memory of a time when Frances missed a birthday party for a boy named Henry, her favorite friend in preschool, and how terrible we all felt about it for weeks and months afterwards. The mom had sent a handwritten invitation, but when the day of the party arrived and we went to Henry's house in our party clothes with a gift specially wrapped for him, his aunt said they weren't home and that the birthday party had been the day before! I felt helpless and sad—especially when I produced the invitation from the mom that had the day written incorrectly in her own handwriting! Henry's mom later said, "I thought it was so strange that you and Frances didn't come. I should have called to see if you forgot or something." It wasn't my fault, it wasn't Frances's fault, but we both ended up feeling really bad. Is it crazy that I remember this feeling fourteen years later?

In the wacky way, my emotions seem to be cross wired now, my extreme reaction to missing the drill at tennis felt strangely linked to the time we missed Henry's birthday party all those years ago. The sense of inadequacy I experienced with these rare calendar snafus that weren't even my fault seemed related to the debilitating sense of failure I suffered when we lost Owen.

What kind of parent loses a child? Especially while they are going to college in their own familiar hometown? People would ask me: Why didn't Owen have an iPhone you could track him with? Or why didn't he have his Google location settings turned on so you could see where he went? I was that person who had everything completely put together in my life. Or so I thought. *I can't believe I lost a child.* Is it my fault? If not, whose fault is it? As a parent, I had one job: to keep my kids safe as they grew and developed into adults. I failed to do that for Owen. Failing at these seemingly insignificant instances of calendar management reminds me of the unbearable failure of losing Owen.

Moss

September 2022

When Owen died, I imagined that the anniversary dates for his disappearance, the discovery of his body, and his birthday would be heavy, emotionally unbearable days. But I was surprised that the regular passing of days, months, seasons, and years also brought fresh waves of sadness and uncharted depths of grief. There is something so unjust about time ticking by, and the world moving on, when Owen isn't here. I wrote this poem at Panther Creek almost three years into his loss as summer was ending and fall, the time of year I miss Owen the most, was approaching.

> I lie down by the creek to feel closer to you
> And because sometimes standing up feels like too much.
> I lie down to let the earth hold me for a while.
>
> I don't know why I thought the moss would be soft
> Nothing feels soft anymore.
> The moss on the rocks scratches my cheek when I press my face
>   against it.
> It was green and lush just a few weeks ago.
> Now, at the end of summer, the green is tinged with brown and
> The once pliant fingers now crease and fracture under the pressure
>   of my heavy heart.

"I am from moss growing on river rocks in the spring," you wrote.
Now I am the moss dying on those same rocks
as the season of grief looms just around the bend of the creek.
The days grow shorter.
Mornings are chilly again.
The angle of the sun highlights your absence
And stings my eyes, or is it my tears?

Can I cling to this rock of life
Until the rain can refresh my soul, feed my roots
And give me strength to be green and alive again
Somehow
Without you?

Josh and Chelsea Found a House

July 2022

Josh and Chelsea, our neighbors two doors down, found a house. They put an offer in and it's been accepted. They are moving. They also got an offer on their house, and it looks like it's going to go through. So, for sure, they are moving. Their new house is on a double lot with a huge treehouse. We are still here.

Keenan and Farrah, who used to live behind us, already moved away—right after we lost Owen. After the neighborhood construction project was announced in 2019, Keenan said he grew up in the projects and didn't want his million dollar house to be across the street from the projects. We couldn't say that. And we couldn't sell the only house where Owen ever lived, the house that was sheltering all of us during the terrifying pandemic quarantine and period of mourning.

Bill and Susan, our neighbors across the street, are also going to be selling. They own their house, a duplex, *and* the lot between the two that they used as an extended side yard. They have been moving clutter out of their beautiful bungalow and even hired Frances to sell a load of their used books at Powell's. It's hard for her to see the change and people leaving the block where she has lived her whole life, the block her brother Gabe has lived most of his life. It's painful to watch people throwing away detritus from their years of living on the block her brother Owen lived his whole life on, the block Owen will never live on again, the block it might be too hard for us to leave. It feels like they are throwing away Owen.

As part of this pre-selling cleanup, Bill and Susan emptied out their storage shed at the duplex across from us. While I was in Spokane playing in a tennis tournament, they brought some boxes over to our house. I came home late on that Sunday after an exhausting weekend and a tense six-hour drive back while my little car's check engine light flashed on and off. It had been Dustin's birthday the day before; I had missed the celebration. Presents for him were waiting in my closet, and I wanted to dash upstairs to get them, but the boxes from Bill and Susan lurked in the middle of our living room, stopping me in my tracks and taking my breath away.

The boxes held posters, maps, and supplies from the time we were searching for Owen. I didn't even have to see Owen's face on them to know what they were: the background color and the font are burned in my mind from the dizzying sleepless days we plastered those signs all around Portland.

I steadied myself, left the boxes in the living room and went into the kitchen, trying to carry light and love in my greetings to Dustin, Frances, and our new puppy Almond (all of whom I'd missed deeply while I was away). But the boxes in the other room were like a radioactive cache pulsating and glowing with life-sucking toxins, fouling my mood and breaking down my being at the cellular level, lighting up all the grief particles of my mitochondria like something from a science fiction novella. I was drawn back to them. Dustin's birthday celebration had to wait.

My fingers traced familiar street names on the copies of search maps. Will I ever look at a map of Portland without seeing the grid overlay that Bill drew for our volunteer searchers? Shifting a pile of safety vests, I wondered, will I ever look at those vests as harmless tools of a trade, without thinking of all the sketchy places people who didn't even know Owen were willing to search, wearing a flimsy vest as a protective shield? The return of these boxes severed a connection to our old neighbors. They were moving on. Will we be able to stay on Holladay Street without people around us who knew Owen? Will we ever be able to live anywhere else?

* * * *

It's a few months later now and Bill and Susan have completed their move. They spent their first night in their new house last night and reported to me that they woke up this morning asking, "Are we on vacation?" Great. I'm so happy for them. Today Dustin and I were out on the lawn chatting with them while Almond chewed on a stick. They tried to figure out how to respond to my sudden tears—always ready to cascade down my face like our famous Multnomah Falls. I looked at the ground and plucked a few sprigs of clover from the grass. The dissonant chorus of beeps from heavy vehicles moving in reverse and the percussive hammering of the construction at the end of the block was ringing in my ears. Over the din I managed to mumble, "Don't forget us. We will be here. With this."

"We want to have everyone over for a party this summer," they replied. "In our new big backyard."

And I will be here hiding in my tiny, fly-filled backyard, I thought, with the thumping of dump trucks, and the sounds of saws and nail guns filling the air. With more new construction possibly looming across the street if Bill and Susan's lot sells to a developer. [Spoiler alert: it did!] I had to go back into the house. I couldn't stay out there anymore making polite small talk. I felt like screaming and tearing my hair out.

I'm not ready for more change, more disruption, more being left behind when I am still searching for More Owen. Our block is changing and I don't like it. I know Dustin and I have changed and are still changing, but I also feel that our grief handcuffs us in this situation. Where will we find the keys to break free?

(Grief is) Better at the Beach

August 2022

Bandon Beach, Oregon

The fog this afternoon, in the height of summer, was dense and I could barely see all the way across Siletz Bay along the central Oregon Coast when I went for a walk at low tide with Almond. We hiked on the trail to the end of Salishan Spit—which separates the bay from the Pacific Ocean—and emerged from wind-stunted trees onto the beach where the Siletz River cuts in to form the bay.

Across the water on the beach in front of Mo's restaurant, a popular local seafood spot, a summer crowd spread along the shoreline; they were picnicking, digging in the sand, beachcombing, and fishing. But Almond and I were alone on our beach as we dropped down toward the water's edge, following the river heading out to sea. Almond seemed spooked by the wall of sand that hovered above us on our left. She kept barking and pulling on her leash, whining to somehow exit this corridor we were traversing. The people across the water disappeared, and even the water was barely visible in the intensifying mist as we approached the ocean. It wasn't very cold and there wasn't any wind, so I didn't feel any danger. The waves were very gentle, sweeping elegantly onto just the edge of the sand at an angle because we were walking around the spit. Every once in a while Almond pounced playfully on a wet stringy pile of seaweed or a rock I tossed back into the retreating surf. There were seals in the water and gulls stalking our progress from the sand cliff above, but we were otherwise alone. The low tide had exposed lots of smooth sea pebbles. I quickly laid eyes on one of the most perfectly formed heart rocks I've ever found—and I have found hundreds, possibly thousands since losing Owen. It struck me that the beach is a perfect place to grieve. As we walked on, I continued to think of more reasons why the beach has been so good for me, and why it could be good for others.

For one, I hear fewer gunshots (or fireworks) at the beach. In the city, I've caught myself flinching and asking Dustin, "Gunshots or fireworks?" with increasing frequency in the last few years. Though Owen's death had nothing to do with gunshots, my nervous system is on high alert, and it's still traumatizing to hear that sound close to our home. It makes me think of the police and how they didn't do very much to help us find Owen—which makes me wonder how much help they are to anyone. It feels better to be in a place where I won't hear those triggering sounds of violence.

In Portland we live fairly close to a big hospital, just a few houses down from some major streets, and near a highway that runs through a sunken ravine. We are subjected to sirens from police vehicles, fire engines, and ambulances at any hour of the day or night. This can be incredibly disruptive—especially if I have had a hard time falling asleep (which now is often) or have woken up and can't get back to sleep (even more often). Sirens can signal help is on the way, but now to me they mostly indicate that someone in our community is in urgent distress, experiencing terrifying, life-changing events.

At Nona's beach house, I do occasionally hear ambulances passing on the main highway, but it's much less frequent and I can handle it better. When we are actually out on the beach, walking or just sitting by the water, I can't hear any sirens at all. The sound of the waves crashing in and pulling back out to sea is mesmerizing and oddly calming, even though the water can be strong and violent at times.

The sand on the beach reminds me of grief in the ways it can take so many different forms. It can be hard and cold, supporting you for a brisk walk near the water's edge, or soft and shifting, rolling your ankle or making it hard to trudge through. It absorbs water, causing your feet to sink into the unstable shoreline, or it can be dry and desert-like up in the dunes away from the water. It can be hot and soft, burning tender bare feet, or a gentle heating pad for wind-chilled legs if you lie down on the sand even on a cloudy beach day.

The Klinger kids at Gleneden Beach, Oregon

Sometimes the incoming tide churns up the sand and clouds the water, making the ocean look dirty and muddy. I've also seen sand shaped into artistic patterns by the action of the waves. It can appear bright white in the dazzling sunshine, or it can look almost black when the sky is dark and the sand is wet with rain. It can disappear overnight with the high tide. It can be washed back ashore the next day with another storm. It can hide shit (literally: I've seen dog owners bury their dog's poop in the sand instead of picking it up!) or treasure. It can be easily brushed away from a heart rock or off a blanket but can be hard to shake sometimes, clinging to your hands or anything you might try to eat at the beach. Tiny grains of sand can sting your skin like needles or knives when it's weaponized by the wind.

Grief can be like all these things for me too.

Storms on our coast wash huge driftwood logs onto the beach or out into the surf. Sometimes there are big awkward rocky steps you have to navigate to get down to the sand. Other times it's an easy ramp with nothing rocky or hard barring your way. Sometimes the beach access path is closed altogether due to erosion or dangerous surf conditions. I have been surprised to see islands of sand far out in the water or pools of ocean on the beach. The beach itself renews its look frequently through the seasons, with high tides swamping previously dry areas or very low tides exposing beds of previously buried rocks and agates. Gentle dunes that gradually slope towards the shoreline can be reshaped into unstable sand cliffs that crumble and slide underfoot high above the wet sand.

My grief moves through similar wide-ranging changes. Sweet ramps of happy memories of an adorable, smiling boy lead to tears of love and poignant sadness that he is no longer here making his friends laugh. Other times angry thoughts about the way searching for Owen was so frustrating and difficult, how we didn't know what to do, and how we still really don't know what happened with Owen, leave me feeling stranded like I'm at the top of a dangerous, rocky beach cliff, with the sand about to collapse from under me. My jags of ugly, violent crying feel like they echo the destabilizing erosion of an especially high tide.

I'm not responsible for all of my usual housework when I'm out at the beach. It's been hard for me to pull our home in Portland together in the way I used to before Owen's death. Even with a working husband, three kids, and a dog, I used to keep things pretty tidy and organized, with the help of a twice-monthly house cleaner. Now, in my grief, I can't handle having someone in the house where I am often crying or looking though

Owen's photos. We let our house cleaner go, and I've let the house go a bit, too. I used to love planning and preparing family dinners for everyone, but now cooking for a smaller family feels kind of empty, and my ability to efficiently plan menus just hasn't rebounded. If the down-sizing of our family had happened in a less traumatic way, maybe the change would be exciting and more approachable. With Owen ripped out of our emptying nest, cooking for a smaller family now reminds me how unfair it is that we lost him.

When I stay at the beach house during the week, I'm often all by myself, which further reduces my domestic responsibilities. Life is just simpler overall. I might just have wine and popcorn for dinner if I'm not very hungry, or cook something simple one day and eat it for several meals. The washer and dryer at the beach house are in the kitchen behind some accordion doors, where I can easily do one load a day. I don't have to dread schlepping heavy baskets of sheets, towels, and clothes up and down two flights of stairs as I do at our house in Portland. The electric dryer at the beach dries things so fast; folding hot, fluffy laundry actually feels kind of cozy in the chilly house there.

Owen's last visit to the Oregon Coast July 2019

Personal grooming is simple, too. The dress code at the Oregon coast is always casual and comfortable. I can wear baggy old clothes and I will be dressed just right. I love to wear Owen's lacrosse jacket or his high school football flannel pajama pants. The moisture in the air makes having good hair almost impossible, so I just let mine go. It's almost mandatory in our family to have your hair look a little like Hagrid's from the Harry Potter films after a walk on the beach. "Beach hair, don't care!" is real. There's also no need to wear makeup or worry if your eyes and nose are red from crying. Everyone else's are red from the cold and windblown sand stinging their face. I can wrap myself in a blanket—inside or outside—and no one will look at me oddly.

The foggy marine layer that comes ashore right along the coast in summer as I described earlier also matches my mood: grief makes me feel invisible, and being in a literal fog feels appropriate. You can also experience wind blowing through your soul with such force that all thoughts are temporarily erased. I haven't flown a kite for a long time, but I still remember watching four-year-old Frances lying on her back on the sand holding on to a kite with all of her strength. It was like she was simultaneously grounded and soaring in the sky; I want to feel that way; at the beach, I can.

There is uncertainty there, too. Beachgoers on the Oregon Coast are always warned to look out for sneaker waves and King Tides. Sneaker waves are extra large waves that can surprise you and suddenly crash ashore, surging up the beach much farther and faster than all of the other waves. This can unmoor the huge log you might have been sitting or standing on, causing a dangerous situation out of the blue on even the mildest of days. Grief can be like that, too. I never seem to know when seeing a new photo of Owen, running into one of his old friends, or just finding myself having a surprisingly good time will suddenly swamp me with pangs of sadness, anger, and guilt.

King Tides occur a few times a year when the gravitational pull of the moon lines up with the sun, creating higher than usual tides and some coastal flooding. People flock to see the dramatic waves they create crashing onshore, but if the water levels rise too drastically, visitors can be at risk on beaches or jetties, even in the parking lots. Some people have been tragically swept out to sea. Will my grief sweep me away to my death? I

Whiskey Run Beach, Oregon

feel like there are times of year—around Owen's birthday in the summer and in the fall when we lost him and searched for him—when my grief is definitely at "King Tide" levels. Though I need to honor Owen at those times and reflect on who he was and mourn how we don't have him here anymore, I need to avoid some "low-lying" places in order not to get pulled in too deep or be swept away by the King Tides of grief.

The beach is a place of light and comfort, too. There's a huge fireplace at Nona's beach house, and though I'm not very good at building fires, I love to sit and watch the flames. Owen loved building fires at the beach or in the fire pit at our cabin. (I also remember he was really good at—and liked!—cleaning out the fireplace.) Lighting a fire as darkness sets in, or as the familiar rain starts to drum against the windows and roof, brings comfort to my ravaged heart. This human ritual of gathering by a fire, chasing away darkness and creatures that might attack in the dark, seems rooted in primeval urges to seek light and warmth, to push out darkness and fear. Turning on the gas log fireplace at my home in the city, though it does bring warmth and light, does not feel as cathartic or fulfilling.

The experience of losing Owen, having my heart wrecked by the death of a precious son, has connected me to all these natural cycles of life and death, love and loss, that have been part of the human experience forever. Spending time in the raw, natural environment of the beach is a good fit for this episode of my life, when I am simultaneously feeling marooned on a deserted island of grief and cosmically linked to all the human suffering in the world. I feel like everyone grieving needs time alone by the seashore. Maybe I should start making needlepoint pillows with a new phrase, "Grief is better at the beach." I wonder: Would anyone buy one on Etsy?

Seeing the Big Apple with (and without) Owen

October 2022

Many of my friends took trips to Europe this summer to explore new countries and cultures, to taste different cuisines, to get out of their comfort zones. Dustin and I didn't. We went to Kentucky with Frances and my mom to visit my mom's brother and sister-in-law. We've traveled there before as a family of five for reunions; I believe spending time with family is important. I don't regret spending our summer vacation at this mini family reunion, but it got me thinking about places I traveled with Owen throughout his life. He never got to visit Europe (another loss to mourn), but he made it to Japan twice. He saw Kentucky and a dozen other states. I found myself especially grateful Owen had opportunities to see New York City and reflected on the different experiences we had in the Big Apple.

I was in college the first time I visited New York City. My dad's sister, my Aunt Phyllis, passed away, and my dad invited me to fly in from London (where I was studying abroad) for a small gathering of her friends and family in Manhattan, where she lived. My aunt was a college music professor who delighted in following and supporting my serious piano studies from afar, so my dad thought I should play something in her honor. My parents were separated at the time, so my mom stayed home in Oregon where my younger brother was a busy senior in high school. My older brother was working in California. I felt very important and cosmopolitan, flying in from London for the weekend. I should have remembered that the weekend wasn't about me.

I had traveled to other big cities—London obviously, Chicago, Boston, San Francisco, Los Angeles, Mexico City, and Seattle—but New York was something different entirely. I'm sure I gawked like a typical tourist seeing mile after mile of tall buildings and people of all shapes and sizes hurrying everywhere all at once. London, which had been blowing my socks off with history and art at every turn, seemed so calm and quiet, ordered and genteel compared to this city. I didn't have much time to explore New York during that short weekend trip, but I remember being shocked and thrilled when a waiter slipped me his phone number at the group dinner following the somber event.

I also visited the Ellis Island immigration museum with my grandparents, who were both children of immigrants. Bump and France (as we called them) were grieving the loss of their daughter, their precious eldest child who should not have passed away before them. I hadn't known my aunt very well, since I'd grown up in Oregon, a place she'd only visited occasionally, and I was distracted with my own life at college when my dad flew to New York a few times to visit my aunt during her cancer treatments. There is no way I could have understood what my dad and grandparents were going through when I was so caught up in the seeming importance of my own experiences. Now, I am grateful for the opportunity I had to be in New York with my grandparents during that vulnerable and scary time for them. They were playing the role of chaperones because I was a young, unmarried woman in the city, but in a way *I* was in charge of *them* as they stumbled through the unfamiliar city in their daze of fresh grief while my dad tackled my aunt's estate and cleaned out her apartment. After living their entire lives in Cleveland, Ohio and retiring to Salem, Oregon, they were finally seeing New York, the city where their daughter had lived her adult life, where she had passed away. How I wish I could hold their hands again, squeezing gently but not letting go too soon, so they would know that I know now how terrible it is to lose a child and how precious the moments we had together were. All of my New York memories from that time look different through the lens of my, and their, grief. And today I see a lot of Owen in New York.

My aunt had no children of her own and was divorced at the time of her death. Bump and France were settled in their cozy little house in Oregon, attending my younger brother's high school band concerts and track meets when they were not going rockhounding or polka dancing. They had no interest or energy to do anything with the small co-op studio apartment my aunt left to them. Though still living in Oregon and working full-time at his medical practice there, my dad ended up taking ownership of "the apartment" (that's what we always called it) in New York. With my dad's vision and help from some skilled cabinet-makers, the apartment became a very swanky pied-à-terre with cleverly designed storage and fold-out beds where we have been able to bring our kids for special trips to visit their grandpa in the city. (A few times we even sent them by themselves—and Dustin and I had a few trips of our own there, too.)

Owen was only seven years old when I took him to New York for the first time in the fall of 2008; it was a trip for just the two of us to visit Grandpa John and see the sights. The same city that was a sad and cold place for Bump and France was a very exciting destination for Owen. Even so, he surprised me with his particular thoughts about what he wanted to see and do in the city. Apparently he had been listening when I told stories of my family's "big city" trips, where the days were planned around what my older brother called the Three M's: meals, museums, and movies (or musicals). Owen's ideas for this first foray were impressive, and we let them guide our trip. Looking back I can't believe everything we did in just a few short days.

We flew out of PDX on a JetBlue red-eye and Owen "only slept one hour," or at least that's what he wrote in the photo album we made after our trip. Grandpa John met us at the airport, and Owen was so excited to show him what he had packed, Owen started taking stuff out of his bag on the subway platform while we waited for the train to take us into the city! Owen had brought his favorite stuffed dog, Otto, and lo and behold, our first stop was a restaurant with the same name as his dog: Otto Enoteca e Pizzeria, where we crunched on sesame breadsticks and devoured spaghetti carbonara and gelato. My dad was unaware of this coincidence when he chose the restaurant, but Owen (and Otto) thought it was pretty neat.

Owen was very interested in the apartment with fold-out beds, a tiny bathroom, and a TV that rose up out of a cabinet with the push of a button. I wonder now: Had he ever been in an apartment before? It's possible this was his first one. He had a disposable camera for the trip and took photos of everything. I also made him keep a writer's workshop journal since he was missing school. This was my favorite entry: "Grandpa John's apartment was squished together. Luckily, there were fold out beds."

Grampa John's apartment was scwisnt together Luckily, there were fold out beds.

We didn't stay in the apartment much, which was a good thing. Owen had a lot of energy and was burning to get out and explore New York. And he had an agenda to get to, after all! Owen's favorite artist at the time was Vincent van Gogh. Do most seven-year-olds have favorite artists? I don't think my other kids did, so I have no idea how that happened, but Owen knew exactly what he wanted to see when we visited the Metropolitan Museum of Art. We consulted the map to locate the van Gogh paintings, and he made a beeline for that room. Owen documented this pilgrimage by taking (unfortunately blurry) snapshots of the paintings he wanted to remember. He was also fascinated by the Met's display of arms and armor, so we have lots of blurry photos of that stuff, too. My dad took us to MOMA as well, where *The Starry Night* is part of the permanent collection. Owen didn't get a photo of that moment, but I know he cherished that experience forever, as he still had the van Gogh postcards he bought as souvenirs in the gift shop that day hanging on his bulletin board at home when he left for college. (My dad told me that he and Owen went back to MOMA together in 2018 and Owen saw *The Starry Night* again. Big sigh.)

There were pure kid things too. It wasn't exactly a museum, but Grandpa John took us to FAO Schwarz, which Owen wrote was the "best toy stor Iv evr sene." (Translation: "The best toy store I've ever seen.") Then we went to the gigantic Toys"R"Us in Times Square, where Owen was impressed with the Ferris wheel inside the store (a first for sure!). He used his own money to buy not one but two lightsabers because he thought it would be more fun if his big brother Gabe had one, too! What a great little brother. Owen also wanted to shop for art supplies in Chinatown—he had become interested in the Japanese sumi ink and brush painting at his Japanese immersion elementary school. I still keep the set he bought with my other art supplies.

The only time I ever rented a rowboat was with Owen in Central Park. He wasn't satisfied with just watching other people rent boats and row around, he wanted to be out on the water. I will admit this was a little out of my comfort zone, but my dad wasn't volunteering to take him, so I went for it. We had a great time; we didn't hit any other boaters or flip over! It was a unique opportunity to experience Central Park from a different perspective, and I am forever grateful that Owen's enthusiasm made it happen. This photo he took of me rowing the boat is one of my favorites.

We explored other parts of Central Park that day—Owen especially liked Belvedere Castle—and New York continued to deliver a steady stream of delights throughout our time there. Owen loved riding the subway, the Roosevelt Island Tram, and the Staten Island Ferry. He noshed on popovers on the Upper East Side, a giant pretzel in Times Square, clam chowder at the Oyster Bar in Grand Central Station, and soup dumplings at my dad's favorite restaurant in Chinatown. (Owen wrote in his journal that Grand Central Station was "really really really really heuooj" [huge].)

Owen's first New York Pretzel

He watched *The Lion King* on Broadway from the very edge of his seat, marveling at the animal costumes of the actors. He was enthralled by the view of city lights from the roof of the apartment building near Gramercy Park and arranged his Playmobil pirates and Otto into little scenes around the apartment whenever we took a little time to rest.

On the last day of our trip we went up to the top of the Empire State Building. Owen had been obsessed with it after reading the children's picture book, *Sky Boys: How They Built The Empire State Building* by Deborah Hopkinson and James E. Ransome. Riding up in the elevator with him that day I could feel excitement radiating out of him, yet he wasn't jumping around like the other young kids I saw. He was reverently soaking it in. Once we arrived at the Observation Deck, he showed uncharacteristic patience and reserve as we moved through the crowd. He waited his turn at the viewing binoculars and found space at the railing to gaze down at the city that had been his playground all week.

Owen at the Empire State Building

I feel incredibly lucky I was there to witness and be a part of Owen's inaugural trip. My dad was amazing to host us for the first of what turned into many NYC-area excursions for our family. A few years later I returned with Frances for a ballet-focused trip. Dustin took a trip with Gabe featuring an outing to a freezing cold NFL game at MetLife Stadium. Gabe and Owen visited together over Christmas break in high school, touring the United Nations complex and searching for the best tacos in the city. Owen flew out to meet Grandpa John for meals at the Culinary Institute of America and a workshop at the Orvis Wingshooting school outside Poughkeepsie, NY, during spring break of his junior year. Frances and Gabe went on a fashion- and skincare-themed shopping trip during winter break of 2018. Dustin and I used our time there to tour Teddy Roosevelt historic sites and watch tennis at the US Open.

The apartment in Union Square, originally the home of my aunt Phyllis, links all of these adventures together. My grandparents Bump and France never met Owen, but I think they would have been impressed by his appetite for New York City attractions, even though their only trip to the city was for such a different reason. My aunt loved living in the city and had filled the apartment with books, art, kimonos, and tchotchkes of all kinds. If they had met, I imagine she would have taken Owen to her favorite restaurant, the now-closed Sammy's Roumanian Steakhouse on the Lower East Side, with its pitchers of schmaltz and heaping portions of old-school Jewish foods. Owen would have loved it.

My dad is retired now and spends a few months in New York every year. Next time I am visiting him, staying at the apartment Owen was so enthralled by, I might go up in the Empire State Building again so I can look down on this special place that holds so many memories for all of us. Maybe I will even rent a rowboat for Owen.

Broken Auto Glass

December 2022

I stepped in a pile of shattered auto glass last night. Again. I had parked on the street by Portland Tennis Center (PTC) when the parking lot was full of soccer and tennis parents idling in their cars waiting to pick up their kids from the late afternoon practice sessions. I'm getting used to this routine: pull into the parking lot, find nowhere to park, struggle to turn around among all the waiting cars—even in my petite Mini Cooper!—and then find a spot out on the street, sometimes blocks away. What I am *not* getting used to is parking next to a pile of broken auto glass.

In Portland these days there is broken auto glass everywhere. Why doesn't anyone sweep it up? Is it left there as a warning to others? There are signs posted in parking lots: "Management is not responsible for loss or damage" or "LEAVE NO VALUABLES IN YOUR CAR." Is the glass just punctuation for those warning signs? An exclamation point after the implied warning: "...OR ELSE!" Maybe these sparkling chunks of broken auto glass that we park next to and step over (and in) on our way to try to live our lives are like loss and grief.

Since losing Owen, and being blindsided by ongoing and unpredictable surges of grief, I've felt like I should be helping prepare everyone for a traumatic loss like this. I want to warn people that suffering and loss is coming into all of our lives; we just don't know the day. "Management is not responsible for loss or damage"—thanks, God! I think of Chicken

Little calling out "The sky is falling!" in the childhood story, but no one wants to hear it.

Maybe no one *can* hear it until their own personal sky actually falls on them. Maybe this is a good thing. Earlier in my life, I had lost my grandparents, a beloved childhood pet, and my Aunt Phyllis in New York (who, although I didn't know her well, was an inspiration to me), but losing Owen the way we did opened my eyes to a world of sudden, unexpected, and seemingly endless suffering. If we knew how much it could hurt, would we ever knowingly enter into any close, loving relationships?

But how can we live fulfilling lives if we are constantly looking over our shoulders expecting the worst? How would we sleep at night or ever let our loved ones out of our sight? To love is to open ourselves up to potential pain so, yes, there is risk involved—but what amazing rewards we will reap if we can find a way to keep living and loving with abandon. If we get too worried about broken auto glass—things or people that might get stolen from us—we might limit our human experiences. To protect our hearts from being shattered, we could not fall in love, bond with our parents or siblings, or love our kids (probably best not to even have children in that case!). That is no way to live.

We have to find a way to carry on, to keep waking up, walking the dog, and breathing. I have to step over the broken glass and go into the tennis center, a place to play and officiate a sport I love. And I need to let my remaining kids leave the nest to find love and have their hearts broken. Should we sweep up the broken glass? So no one else sees the danger? No, I think we should leave it right there.

Christmas Volcano Rescue

December 2022

Owen, Gabe, and Frances in December of 2016 when a large tree branch
fell close to our house during a winter ice storm.

to: findowenk@gmail.com
date: December 24, 2022
subject: Christmas volcano rescue movie

Dear Friends,

I have been really trying to feel the spirit of Christmas this year and to reprise my role as the ringleader of Christmas magic for my family. It has been a lot of work and the jury is still out on how magical this holiday will feel for our healing hearts, but I am glad I challenged myself. To fuel my efforts, I listened to holiday music as I ran my errands and decked our halls inside and out and streamed Hallmark Christmas movies on my laptop while baking cookies. (I watched *Die Hard, White Christmas, It's A Wonderful Life, Miracle on 34th Street,* and *Love, Actually* too.) One day last week, Netflix suggested a different kind of movie for me: a documentary about people who had survived a volcanic eruption in New Zealand: *Volcano: Rescue from Whakaari.*

I used to love stories of dangerous storms, fatal mountaineering accidents, and shipwrecks. When we lost Owen in the traumatic and mysterious way that we did, my interest in stories where other people lost their lives or lost their loved ones dried up. I was surprised that Netflix remembered a part of me I had forgotten. I had a few more things to go in and out of the oven, so I clicked "play" and thought, "I can always switch back to a holiday movie if this sucks." But it was enthralling—I was riveted.

The New Zealand scenery was breathtaking. The exotic accents of the people interviewed kept my eyes glued to the captions on the screen and I found myself sitting down at my kitchen desk to take in this dramatic story of rescue and survival. The phone videos of the eruption and the interviews with survivors were haunting. When it was over, I actually felt relieved that I was in my kitchen in Portland, holding my singular vessel of grief over Owen's death, preparing for a feast with friends and family.

Our family has been rescued from a volcano of sorts, too. We have more rehab to go through as our scars heal, but we are still here. More than all the holiday prep I did, watching this documentary of nature's power (highlighting our powerlessness), the heroic rescue efforts, and the resiliency of the survivors fighting through difficult recovery from extensive burns and trauma gave me hope for Christmas. I am ready to eat cookies, play games, and gather around the table with everyone. Even if Owen isn't physically here with us. Maybe there is something about experiencing loss and grief—or escaping a volcanic eruption on your vacation—that primes us to seek deeper connection and joy when we can find it. Now if the weather would just cooperate and melt the ice so I don't have to eat all the cookies myself.

Wishing you all the joy of being rescued from a volcano this Christmas and #moreowen.

Love,
Mary

Do You Have a Graduate?

May 2023

Owen's high school graduation in 2019

Owen's posthumously awarded UP diploma
by his tree on campus in 2023

"**D**o you have a graduate?"

Why hadn't I anticipated that question? Dustin was out of town so I was sitting by myself at the University of Portland's Baccalaureate Mass for the class of 2023 when another family came to claim the seats next to me. "I don't have a *graduate*," I awkwardly answered, "but I am a parent of someone receiving a diploma this weekend. My son is Owen Klinger. He passed away in 2019." The family looked shocked, and I thought I had ruined their sweet celebratory mood, but then they quickly said their daughter had been in a freshman writing class with Owen. I'd made another surprise connection.

The Mass in the Chiles Center took me back to Owen's funeral Mass, when we also had a long line of priests standing at the altar, as there were on this day. My eyes scanned the rows of students seated in chairs on the arena floor during the opening hymn, but I didn't see any familiar faces. Owen wasn't there, of course, and both of his freshman year roommates had left the college. Owen hadn't been at school long enough to make many friends I would recognize. At least I knew some of the priests.

Father John Donato was the main presider, and I concentrated on keeping my breathing slow and even through his opening prayer. I wanted to lose myself in the meditative rhythm of the liturgy, but the memorized words of response stuck in my throat and tears in my eyes blurred the print in the program. "Lord have mercy." The dusky scent of the ceremonial incense seemed to fill the arena, making me feel lightheaded and evoking Owen's funeral Mass.

The homilist was Father Pat Hannon, the resident priest from Owen's dorm Christie Hall. Of all the priests standing before us, I thought, marveling at the coincidence, it had to be Father Pat. I sat up on the edge of my seat and imagined he was talking to Owen. When he said the graduates had spent 1,355 days "on the bluff," my heart sank as I started calculating Owen's time at UP: he didn't have 1,355 days there. How many did he have? Do I count the days Owen was missing too? Then Father Pat said, "In the heart of God, no one is ever forgotten. In the heart of God, we are always at home." I let my mind linger on these words as he continued. I really wanted to believe that no one is ever forgotten—that Owen is not forgotten. My focus came back as Father Pat quoted French philosopher Gabriel Marsell: "To say to someone 'I love you' is to say they will never be lost." Mic drop. Well, no, he didn't actually drop the microphone, but that was the last thing I heard him say. I let my tears flow as the Mass moved on. Owen will never be lost.

The university president read the prayers of the faithful and mentioned Owen as one of the "faithfully departed" members of the UP community. I was glad I was there to hear he is still remembered, and in my joy at hearing his name I actually snickered to myself thinking that Owen would find it funny to be described as "faithfully" departed, as if his death had been some kind of Christian martyr move. But then I kind of ambushed myself into remembering that we really don't know how Owen "departed." Did he pass away peacefully, or was he killed? Did he kill himself? Why do I keep doing that to myself?

More deep breaths got me through the rest of the Mass, and, when it ended, I walked with a fake smile on my face through the joyfully reuniting families to visit Owen's tree in the drizzle. No one else had come over that way from the arena, and the rainbow I saw over downtown while sitting at the bench there seemed to be shining just for me. "I love you, Owen," I thought. "You will not be forgotten." After a while, I gathered enough courage to make a brief appearance at a party for a graduate whose mom I'd met a few weeks before when we played each other at a tennis tournament in the Tri-Cities area of Washington state. I had been planning on ignoring that invitation, but the tiny world of UP and the strong connections I'd made there through Owen found me walking into Mass right next to my former tennis opponent and her family, so I changed my mind. I can be sad and missing Owen, I told myself, and still go to a party.

The graduate and her friends lived in a brown rental house on the corner of Willamette Boulevard right across the street from campus. I hadn't been inside any off-campus houses in the area, and as I waited for a break in the traffic to cross over to the house, I found myself wondering where Owen would have lived in his sophomore, junior, or senior years. Would he have stayed on campus in Christie Hall, maybe becoming an RA (resident assistant), like Dustin and I had done at Notre Dame? Would he have shared a well-loved party house with other lacrosse guys? Would he have moved back home to save money for graduate school or travel? Did he know the girl whose party I was on my way to? Did she know him? I know he went to some off-campus parties in his first semester; had he ever been inside this house? I was a mess by the time I made it across the street, and even though my new friend kindly welcomed me and introduced me to her daughter and the other students, I didn't stay long. My heart had too many questions, and no one at that party had the answers I was seeking.

The next day was commencement. UP had offered to present Owen a degree posthumously, so as hard as attending Baccalaureate Mass was, I went back up to "the bluff" for another helping. Dustin was still out of town and Frances and Gabe declined my invitation, but my mom and dad were with me, and I was ready with an answer in case anyone asked "Do you have a graduate?" It was a little easier, but still not easy by any means.

My heart squeezed with pain when the graduates were encouraged to thank their families for helping them get through the past four years, and I could only think "We *didn't* get Owen through this. He isn't here." I clapped along with everyone, but I couldn't feel my hands. The valedictorian was a transfer student who came to UP part way through her college journey. Throughout her well-prepared speech I couldn't help but think, "She wasn't here when Owen was—she didn't have to experience that traumatic search for him and the sad discovery of his body during her first semester like so many of his other classmates. Of course her grades were the highest." I was not feeling good.

The commencement speaker, National Public Radio's Ari Shapiro, appropriately encouraged the graduates to find success in the future by continuing to nurture the close relationships they have with family and friends. This stung like a slap in my face. Owen *had* close relationships with his family and friends. Why wasn't that enough? Somehow I am still here, and he is not. So I wanted to tell Ari Shapiro it wasn't enough, that we needed more: more advice, and, yeah, you knew it was coming: More Owen!

As the awarding of diplomas advanced alphabetically, the man who had been in charge of logistics for Owen's funeral skillfully slipped me into the line of gowned graduates without causing too much of a stir. I felt like I was in a bubble, isolating me and my grief from contaminating the surrounding joy. The students with last names starting with the letter K looked excited, yet seemed aware that having this mom in their midst was something unusual and awkward! When I reached the front of the line, the provost approached the microphone and silenced the robotic voices that had been reading out the graduates' names. "We pause to award a posthumous diploma to Owen Klinger." I couldn't focus on the rest of her words, but suddenly everyone was clapping and rising to their feet in a compassionate standing ovation. I hugged the university president and gestured with my hand over my heart to express my gratitude as I tried to keep moving across the stage and back to my seat, so the celebrating of actual living graduates could continue.

The people sitting in my row shrank quickly out of my way as I brushed past them clutching Owen's diploma. Was this because they didn't want to catch what I was suffering from? Or were they in awe that I was even still standing—let alone appearing in public—sharing my grieving heart? I can't tell you how many times I have heard friends of mine say, "I would just die if I lost one of my kids." Well, in many ways I *did* die, the person I was in the fall of 2019 (1,355 days before graduation!) is gone. I'm someone different now: I'm the mother of a posthumous college graduate.

I wish Owen had been there. He would have loved all the cheering, and there would have been a huge cake.

I'm Still Doing This

June 2023

From journal entries dated June 17–June 20, 2023

Dear Owen,

I'm still taking photos of pictures of you, messing up my mind's timeline and confusing myself with just when these events actually occurred. I thought I would be doing less of that—or that I would at least be better at it. They are still pretty bad sometimes, with lots of glare from overhead lights, shadows from the cell phone camera, etc.

There always seem to be more photos to view, to study. Whenever Google photos prompts me to "remember this day 8 years ago" or something like that I have to click on the memory. I have to see if there is More Owen hiding in the digital archives, even if I can't always get myself to open the physical photo albums that fill the bookshelves in our den. (I know there is more of you in those scrapbooks, but sometimes it's just too hard to start or to stop.)

Today the photos Google suggested surprised me because they weren't images of you, they were photos you had taken when you went with Ron on a trip to the coast to see the falcon nest and the lighthouse up close. One of these regularly shows up as a screensaver on this laptop—your laptop—but there were a few I hadn't seen lately, and I made note of one picture of a bird in flight which reminded me of your song, "Skydogs."

I'm still listening to those songs you wrote and sang with your friends. Forrest G. did some digital editing of the recordings you made at Panther Creek, and I saved them from his SoundCloud account to my Google drive. I am still trying to get up the courage to try to play your songs on your/my guitar (yes, sigh, it's mine again). Listening to these recordings over and over again helped me figure out what the lyrics in "Skydogs" actually are. I'm still wondering when exactly you wrote that song.

I'm still listening to your Spotify playlists, and some of your CDs. You put some good songs together. I know Gabe thought it was funny that you mostly put the songs you liked into a few really long play-lists instead of making new playlists all the time for different vibes, but I think the songs that you liked, you liked for a long time and not just for a hot second. Last night I heard "Sweet Home Alabama" playing at the golf course restaurant as Dad and I went in for dinner. It's catchy, but I can't figure out why you loved that song so much? Alabama? Really? Toto's "Africa" comes on the radio a lot too, and I love it, but it's sometimes agonizing to hear. I wish I had talked to you more about music and why you liked who you liked. I'm still trying to figure that out.

I'm also still trying to understand the last songs you were listening to on the night you left campus. "Sadly Beautiful"? "Surrender"? Was there something in those songs that you needed to hear that night? Was there something you heard in those songs that led to you leaving us? I'm still trying to understand what happened. I wish you could tell me. I wish I didn't need to wish that.

I'm still finding heart rocks whenever I'm walking at the beach or by Panther Creek. Honestly I find them almost everywhere: in parking lots, on sidewalks, and around the neighborhood. I'm still hoping that finding those rocks and keeping them, and passing some along, or doing something with them will help heal this huge hole in my heart. People have been sending me photos of heart-shaped rocks—and other things—they have found. It's a little obsessive, but I love it. They think of you, they think of me. (I've even taken my own pictures of heart-shaped potatoes in the kitchen or heart-shaped bits of butter melting on toast!) I'm still thinking these are all signs from you that you loved your life, that you loved us, that your love is still with us.

I'm still wearing your lacrosse jacket when I walk the dog on slightly chilly days. The Generals' bright blue color with your name on the back seems brave and nervy to me, like I am just daring the people who see me to pretend everything is OK. That it is normal for a mom to walk the dog wearing her dead son's jacket. I'm still wearing your football pajama pants, too, even though they are too big. I have added a few of your favorite clothes to my closet, and I've been wearing your golf glove—one Dad bought for you, hoping you would play more golf with him—at my golf lessons. It's starting to wear out, which makes me a little sad, but I feel good wearing it.

When the house gets steamy from someone taking a long shower or bath, I'm still here sniffing the air to see if I can smell your Old Spice Fiji body wash or shampoo. If you can believe it, I'm still using your body wash sometimes. I know you didn't like the 2-in-1 shampoo/conditioner because it wasn't great for your long, beautiful hair, but I still have it in the bathroom. (Frances is using your Fiji deodorant!) I still look to see when it's on sale at Freddy's. I'm remembering how much you liked to splash in the tub as a kid and how we had to briefly suspend your bathing privileges because there had been a few too many waves going over the sides of our new tub when we redid the upstairs bathroom. You used to sing in the shower, too. I miss that so much!

I'm still trying to find more of you wherever I am. At restaurants, I look at the menu to see what I want to order but I'm always looking to see if there is something that you would have liked. Philly cheesesteak? Deviled eggs? Kalua pork? When I'm shopping at thrift stores, I scan the racks for Pendleton shirts like your favorite one and jeans that might have fit your long legs and slim waist (I keep a pair of your jeans in my closet now) and cool T-shirts you would have liked.

Owen and Gabe touring the campus at the University of Washington

I'm still remembering your joy on Christmas mornings and your exuberant cry of "I 'mell bacon!" whenever bacon was on our breakfast

menu. I still picture you sweeping our driveway and whistling while you did it, during a study break, or after school before starting your homework. I'm still trying to do a careful job when I mow the lawn like you did. I'm still in awe of how patient and meticulous you were with the edging and sweeping up of the grass clippings, how lovingly you treated your tools when you put them away. I'm still using your snow shovel—and guarding it from being lost or damaged by others, hiding it away in the garage as soon as I'm finished with it so no one else would ask to borrow it. Kevin [a neighbor] borrowed it from Dad last year and just left it casually propped against the corner of their house for a few days before returning it. I was so worried it would walk away and be lost to us, like you walked away and were lost to us.

I'm still trying to figure out if you did this on purpose.

If it was an accident.

If something terrible happened.

I'm still holding my breath to see if Frances and Gabe will be OK. If Dad will be OK. If Dad and I will be OK together. If we will be more than OK. If your friends will be OK.

I am still here, trying to live with the bedroom you used to sleep in down the hall, to breathe in that room where there is still a pile of the things you took to college. I'm still seeing your fingerprints on door jambs and ceilings where you jumped to show off your physical abilities, or where you were just tall enough to stretch up and leave your mark. If I close my eyes, I am still seeing you and hearing you laughing in the basement, wearing your headphones while gaming with your friends, drinking can after can of LaCroix. I'm still trying to decide if I can live without your socks, your old T-shirts, your shoes. We have given a few of your lacrosse things to other players—some of your pads, an extra pair of cleats and a stick—but can I live without any of the rest? Not yet. I am still needing to keep it all close (even though it is still so very smelly!). I still have your graduation party tri-fold award and picture board set up next to my bed. I hadn't taken it apart after your summer grad party; when you went missing in October, how was I supposed to be able to take it apart then? Or next year? Or the year after that? Now four years later, it's still one of the last things I look at before I go to sleep, and one of the first I see when I wake up (I'm still having a hard time sleeping by the way—this is my new normal and I don't like it.)

I am still trying to imagine living somewhere else. Can we move away from this house where you were brought up? Where you slept almost every night for eighteen years? Where you and Gabe played basketball in the driveway? So many people have moved away from the block since we lost you because of the construction of the low-income housing nearby that I wonder if this makes it easier to leave or harder. Many of the new neighbors never knew you. I don't know if they even know about you. Have they seen me wearing your jacket and wondered? I ponder whether they think I am a snob because I don't socialize easily. I am still trying to figure out the best way to answer the questions "How many kids do you have?" or "How old are your kids?"

Sometimes I think it could be freeing to move somewhere else, away from all this stuff we are clinging to, away from the memory of the police coming to our house to tell us your body had been found in the river. The living room is haunted by that memory. Maybe I should paint and get new furniture for it, or try a different layout. But making changes like that is hard, and what if I lose something of you in the process? I couldn't bear it. We are getting a new patio in the backyard because the old deck was rotting and getting rather unsafe. It was my idea, but it was still hard to see the dirt and grass you played on, bled on, and mowed being scraped out of the yard and hauled away. It felt like I was being scraped up and thrown into the back of a truck for a journey into the unknown. The trees you and Frances climbed on are still there. Maybe I need to keep planting trees for you.

Maybe Dad and I should be figuring out where we are going to move, if we're ever going to do it. The fear of the unknown is big—bigger ,I think, than my fear of leaving this home, because I know you will be with me wherever I am. You will always be with us. Wherever we live, I will have my memories and all the pictures and videos of you (if I can ever bring myself to watch your vibrant, exuberant aliveness).

For now, I'm still here in Portland, holding my breath when I drive over the St. Johns Bridge. I visit UP every few weeks and walk the paths of the campus. I look up into your dorm room window at Christie Hall, and gaze over the edge of the bluff down to the beach below where you scrambled over railroad tracks and through a fence to hang out with your roommate soon before you were gone. I'm still trying to figure out what you talked about with him during that last weekend, and what was going on with his sexual assault charges? What was he asking you to say on his behalf as his support person?

I'm still here lighting candles at the grotto, remembering how I stood next to Father Poorman, UP's president, at the candlelight vigil when you went missing and said, "Oh, we are using up your entire candle budget!" and he said, "We are just getting started." He isn't at UP anymore, and I am still hoping that someone there will continue to light candles for you, to remember you. I'm still hoping that someone will come forward with more information about what happened to you. I'm still here wishing that your friend Sam had been able to say more about her last conversation with you—I think she was one of the last people on campus you spoke to. She was so sweet at what would have been your college graduation with her efforts to honor you and remember you. I saw her singing with the choir at commencement, and she gave me a little wave of recognition. On Instagram she posted some photos she took by your tree in her grad gown and told how she wrote your name on the ceiling at Mock Crest Tavern in the common UP grad tradition. You would have loved that. I'm still trying to figure out what happened between you two. I don't think you were dating, but did you have a crush on her? Did you love her?

I'm still trying to get up enough energy to put on real clothes—not just the leggings and sweatshirts I put on after tennis most days. Even though you know I am obsessed with tennis, sometimes I'm still hoping that rain will result in my matches being canceled so I can stay home.

I'm still here looking for #20 in every sporting event I watch, or to see your long hair flowing out the back of a lacrosse or football helmet whenever I'm by the field at Grant HS. I cheered for a player wearing #20 at the Portland Thorns soccer match the other day and was inspired to look up a little about her. She reminded me of you, Owen. She wasn't drafted onto a team after she graduated college, but she kept working hard and was eventually called up to be an alternate for the national women's team, then a full member of that team, then she was signed by the Thorns.

I'm still trying to imagine what you would have done athletically at UP and beyond. Would you have gone to more of the practices for the lacrosse team? (It's still puzzling, what happened that night you left, how your roommate said you told him you were going to practice but you didn't take your gear.) Would you have kept playing dorm rec soccer? Would you have gone on more long walks or hikes? Played basketball in the driveway with Gabe whenever you were both home together? Would you have taken your casual golf success any further with Dad's support? I would have cheered for you at any sport you tried to play. I'm still here cheering you on. Remember Frances used to call me the Last Person Clapping? That's me, still here clapping for you, even after everyone else has moved on.

I'm still digging around in your closet to see if any of your old sweatshirts or jackets retain any of your Owen-ness. I'm carefully unzipping your lacrosse bag every once in a while to smell your stinky gloves and pads. Who would have ever imagined that I would cherish that smell? But it is proof to me that you were here and that you were a real living boy who sweated and played your heart out for your team.

When no one else is home, I'm still here sitting in the used La-Z-Boy recliner that you bought with your lawn-mowing money. You were so proud of yourself that day, so excited when you found it in the store and realized you could afford it and it would fit in your room. It was fun for you to have it there when Gabe moved away to college and you had the room to yourself. I imagined that eventually you would move it to your own college apartment. How could I ever sell that chair, or give it away?

Maybe Gabe will put it in his apartment someday. For now, it's here for me to sneak away to, whenever I need to feel close to you. I thought about your chair a lot when I was having my ketamine sessions at Cascade Psychedelic Medicine. The chair in the room there is a big special recliner that tilts back and I felt so supported and held in that chair. Like you were holding me, like I was holding you, like the world was just holding us up with love. I usually write at my desk or at the kitchen table at the beach house, but maybe I will take my laptop—which is really your laptop—up to your room and write in your chair.

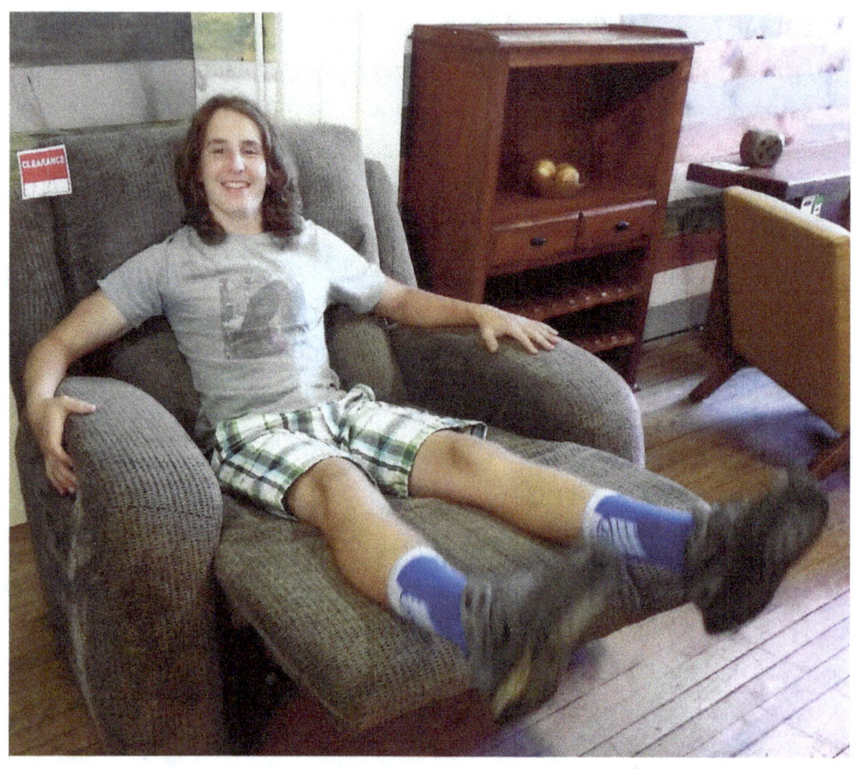

I am still buying Hot Pockets. Pepperoni is the easiest to find, but I do look for Philly cheesesteak. After you passed away, your buddy Everett and his mom, Carrie, came across that essay you wrote in the writing magazine from your high school freshman community and sent it to me. What a gift. You never showed it to me. I don't think I knew how much you idolized Hot Pockets. I would have bought them for you all

the time! I did know how much you liked the chocolate chip cookies I baked. I love knowing you packed them in your lunch on the first day of your senior year. I remember your excited high-pitched "OOH, cookies!" whenever I was baking them. I would have baked them for you at college and delivered them to your dorm. I don't bake them as much anymore, but I still do occasionally, and of course I think of you.

Owen packing his lunch with homemade chocolate chip cookies
on the first day of his senior year in 2018

I'm still seeing your face when I look in the mirror sometimes or see myself on the screen during a Zoom call. I just saw your face in Frances's when she made a German chocolate cake for Dad on Father's Day. I know that's why she changed her hair color after you were gone: she couldn't bear to look in the mirror and see you. She didn't want to hear people saying, "You look so much like your brother." I love that you looked like me, and I love hearing people say so. I wonder what you would have looked like when you were older. Would you have kept your hair long? Or would you have gone back to the shorter hair you had when you were a freshman in high school? Would you have lost your hair like my brothers and Grandpa John did?

I'm still trying to remember what it was like to hug you, to remember your laugh and your singing. I remember the last time I saw you, but I wonder when Dad saw you last. I know you came home mid-September to do some yard work for Mary R. and didn't want to stay for dinner so Dad took you back to campus. Maybe that was it? When they first bloomed, Mary cut some of the tulips you planted that day and brought a bouquet over to us. I loved seeing flowers that wouldn't have bloomed without your touch. (Mary and her family have moved away now, too, so no one else remembers that those tulips were planted by you.)

I know I picked you up and brought you to Broadway Medical Clinic for your last booster shot (something for meningitis?), and the nurse was so proud of you for your start at UP. They didn't get many college students at the pediatric clinic! I know Dr. Bengtson (the pediatrician) had given you his phone number so you had someone to call anytime if you needed help. I wish you would have called him when you were out walking around on October 6th. He left a voicemail for you when you were missing, offering support and urging you to come home to us. I wish you had gotten his message. (The doctor and nurses came to your funeral, too!)

When did we last talk on the phone? Is it stupid that I still pay $10/ month to keep your number? I wish we had your physical phone. Did you turn it off while you were out walking that night? Did someone take it, or did it fall into the river with you? I want to keep your number because it's linked to your Snapchat account. Maybe your number could be our home phone. We could keep my old cell phone with your number on it on the kitchen desk so it would be like a home phone...except our home doesn't feel like a home anymore without you here.

I'm still having a hard time going places where I might see people I haven't seen since you died. Seeing people again for that first time is one of the hardest things I've had to go through since losing you, and I never know where or when it will happen. Last month, Dad and I were traveling to Austin to visit Uncle Mike, and we saw your friend Sho working for the TSA at the Portland airport. I know he'd been in your class since kindergarten, but you guys weren't that close in high school. I wouldn't have recognized him, but he recognized us and said, "Long time, no see. I'm so sorry about Owen." It was shocking and hard, and of course I cried when he said your name. He told us right away that he always thinks of you when Snapchat memories come up on his phone. I'm still trying to go places and get out of the house, even though I know I might run into your old friends, or some of our old friends.

What's hard is that I also am struggling with going places where I might meet new people who don't know about you. A few times I have found myself longing to live somewhere where no one knows what our family used to be like when you were here in the middle of everything. When we do go somewhere new, though, it's not the stress-free situation I imagine. Will someone ask about how many kids we have? How will I answer? How will I explain about the ages of my kids now that Frances is older than you were when we lost you? (Does this mean you have a big sister now? Not a little sister?) Meeting people who don't know we lost you sucks. They don't know what we lost when we lost you because they didn't know you. They don't know what a beautiful happy family we used to be. I have a knot in my stomach wondering when it might come up, or that it won't come up, in conversation. I want everyone to know how special you are and how much it sucks that you aren't here anymore. I can't pretend that losing you doesn't affect everything I say or do now. I feel like I can't fake it, but as I reflect on how I'm still here doing my best to keep going, I think that essentially I am faking it a lot of the time. I'm living even though I don't always feel like carrying on without you.

I'm still here loving you.

The Oil Portrait

August 2023

Joanne Radmilovich Kollman, "#MoreOwen," 2023, oil on linen, 14" x 11", The Klinger Family.

The artist who made this striking portrait of Owen is a woman we didn't know, a stranger to us, but not a stranger to grief and tragic loss, having lost her husband when her two boys were very young. She is a stranger and yet, there are connections we didn't see at first glance: Gabe and Owen played in the same youth football league as her son, Tony, who was between them in age; they likely crossed paths playing basketball at the local community center; and Tony was a student at UP who sang in the choir at Owen's funeral Mass.

Joanne Radmillovich Kollman, a Portland artist and art teacher, had received a commission to paint a portrait of Jesus at the time that Owen went missing. As a mom, she got involved supporting her son as he and other students at Owen's college grappled with the loss of their classmate. When I turned the "Find Owen" Facebook page into "More Owen" and used that space to share photos and stories of Owen as we mourned his loss, Joanne was moved by Owen's story and the tremendous outpouring of community support. His "Where I'm From" poem gave her an insight into his essence, and Owen's long hair inspired her to use him as the starting point in paint studies for her Jesus commission.

I was touched when Joanne contacted me about using Owen as a study model for this commission. She shared with me a quick slide show of all of the images she had gathered from my posts. It was like seeing Owen's life flash before my eyes and I was in awe of how much preparation she was putting into this painting. The main photo she based the work on was Owen's senior photo for his water polo team taken by John Davenport. In this close-up, he looks serene and confident, but isn't smiling the big smile we see in so many of his other photos. The water polo ball he is holding covers his chin. Joanne did a deep dive into hundreds of photos of Owen to see if she could figure out what his jaw and chin looked like with this expression.

At some point while working on the study, she decided to make that painting a gift for our family, and I was truly humbled. Joanne had used her finest paints in the test portrait of Owen because she wanted to examine the paint quality for her commissioned piece. Now we have our own private, custom, museum-quality "Jesus portrait" of Owen hanging in our dining room! Owen would have loved knowing that his long hair helped the artist envision Jesus's hair. As his hair grew out, we teased

Owen about his resemblance to depictions of Jesus—especially when we ran out of bread and I liked to joke that he should just make some more appear so I wouldn't have to go to Fred Meyer.

In 2017, Dustin and I traveled to Washington, DC, with Owen to watch Gabe compete with the Grant High School Constitution team in nationals of the We The People competition. Looking back, it was unique that

Dustin and I spent several days alone with Owen, our middle child. (Gabe lodged in the team hotel and was absorbed in last-minute practice sessions; Frances was on a school research trip to Japan.) We took Owen to the museums he was interested in, went to restaurants serving the type of food he wanted to eat, and let him choose what to watch on TV in our hotel room. He didn't have to compromise with his siblings on anything! We thought we saw Owen in *Portrait of a Youth*, a portrait attributed to Sandro Botticelli, at the National Gallery of Art. It wasn't just Owen's hair; he had a long neck and long Jesus-like fingers, too. What do you think? I think Owen was beautiful and definitely worthy of being captured in a timeless oil painting, but I'm partial!

Sandro Botticelli, "Portrait of a Youth," 1482, tempera on panel, approx. 17" x 18", Andrew W. Mellon Collection, National Gallery of Art, Washington, D.C.

When her work was completed, Joanne submitted her Owen/Jesus painting to a juried show at the Oregon Society of Artists, where she teaches classes. The painting, fully titled *#MoreOwen University of Portland 2023*, was on display at the gallery during the Portland Rose Festival in

2023 and received an Honorable Mention. Dustin, Frances, and I went to the opening night reception and had to laugh when we overheard the Rose Festival Princesses chatting as they paused in front of Owen's portrait. "I'd love to paint a cute boy like that," one said. "I'd like to *meet* a cute boy like that," another answered. It was surreal and bittersweet—like so many experiences I've had since losing Owen.

I hope that more people can see this painting someday, though it hangs in our dining room for now. I am grateful for the interest Joanne took in Owen's story and for her artistic talent. In an interview about the piece for KBOO radio's *Art Focus*, she said, "Creativity helps people process other things going on in their lives."* I couldn't agree more: this is why I write about Owen.

---

* "Oregon Society of Artists," narrated by Joseph Gallivan, Art Focus, *KBOO Radio*, June 20, 2023, https://kboo.fm/media/116539-oregon-society-artists.

My Pink Shawl and the Emotional X-Ray Machine

October 2023

to: findowenk@gmail.com
date: October 20, 2023
subject: 4 years without Owen

Dear Friends,

I have been clinging to summer, dreading the descent into fall (formerly a favorite season of mine) and the change in light, shadow, and temperature. I have been anticipating the anxiety of releasing my precious daughter to college life again, reliving the trauma of the season we lost Owen.

I also haven't wanted the leaves to fall in our neighborhood—raking leaves and sweeping our driveway were some of Owen's favorite study breaks when he was in high school. Doing those seasonal chores without him is still so weighty. I'm worried that without the green cover of summer's leaves on the few trees that remain between our house and the newly constructed 127 units of very low-income housing, the large building will be revealed as an even bigger eyesore than we all dread it might be.

But this morning it is cool and misty. Fall is indeed here. It's past the hour that our neighborhood streets are busy with kids walking and biking to school. I put on my long down coat and zipped it all the way up. It felt good. I felt safe and held. I stepped outside to take my dog for a long walk.

Maybe there is something redeeming about this season after all: I have an excuse to walk around all wrapped up and insulated. My vulnerable self is protected from the outside as I hide in plain sight in my ordinary Columbia coat. I can pretend I'm like all the other people out walking their dogs this morning.

When we lost Owen, my friend Tami gave me a bright pink wool shawl, and I wore it everywhere for months. I was staying warm, yes, but also signaling to everyone who saw me after the traumatic experience of losing, searching for, and discovering Owen's body that my heart was bleeding. I needed swaddling, careful handling, and all the love. The shawl was my cocoon for the metamorphosis of grief. The voluminous draping of the oversized scarf and its bright, hard-to-ignore color signaled to others, "Something is going on with this person. Step closer to help or get out of her way!"

I know black garments are traditionally associated with mourning, but for me this pink shawl is the signature garment of that season of my grief. I wanted to wear it over my black dress at Owen's funeral, but felt it might be too much, so I switched it out at the last minute for a more modest blue and gray scarf. (I think of blue as one of Owen's favorite colors too.) But I should have worn the pink one.

I still have the pink wrap and cherish it (and try to protect it from the drifts of dog hair that have inundated our household since we adopted Almond last year), though I am finding that I don't walk around outside the house in it very much anymore. Maybe no one else knows what it means to me, but I would know and I feel like if someone noticed it, I might have to explain. After four years on this grief journey—and even though I am writing this book!—I don't feel like I should be hogging the grief spotlight or demanding attention. (Also, yes, I know I shouldn't be "should ing" on myself, but it still happens

occasionally!) Many fresher losses loom large: senseless deaths in conflicts around the world, beloved parents and grandparents succumbing to the end that awaits us all eventually, and the frightening degradation of our planet's climate.

It's complicated because I still want everyone to remember Owen, to smile about the funny things he said and did; I need everyone to recognize that Frances and Gabe are doing their best to navigate life without their anchoring (and occasionally annoying) middle brother, that Dustin and I carry on having lost a priceless son. I am trying not to judge my grief, not to frown impatiently at the stopwatch timing my pace as I slowly complete lap after lap of this life without Owen. Can I give myself permission to wear the pink shawl when I need to? I will work on it.

Wearing my long, protective coat I feel a little different today. I'm so tired, yet determined to continue walking (and living!), to remember Owen and to fiercely love Frances and Gabe even though my heart is scarred. I know more losses will come. This season of fall will sneak up on me at the end of every glorious summer. The anniversary of Owen's death will forever be indelibly stamped on my bones. (Maybe I don't need a tattoo for Owen—the season of grief is inked permanently on my soul.) A coat or a shawl really can't protect me, but it sometimes feels good, and I am trying to let myself lean in to what feels good when I can.

I had an idea the other day about how we need some kind of emotional x-ray machine to help us see the grief in others. I have no idea how it would work, but I imagine if we could see the struggles the people around us are carrying—without having to ask them to explain anything—we could know better how to support them, accept them, hold space for them, and be gentle with them. Most days we aren't even really seeing each other. It seems we are preoccupied with protecting our own vulnerabilities and projecting an image of what we feel is expected of us.

Even if we do try to see each other, not everyone is going to be wrapped in a bright blanket or shawl to signal a need for extra compassion. Most of the wounded are likely hiding inside those neutral colored, long, down Columbia (or Patagonia or Lands' End or fill-in-the-blank-sportswear-company) coats. We are trying not to take up too much space with our messy grief. We are trying to zip it up and keep it in and keep going. Since I don't have that emotional x-ray machine yet, after hugging the ones wearing pink shawls (or black funeral garments), I need to personally check in with others I see wearing these coats of comfort and invisibility. Maybe we can take a walk together with our grief.

Love,
Mary #moreowen

Natalie's Service

October 2023

The Facebook post said it was a service "celebrating the life of Natalie Liessler" on Monday, October 30, 2023, at River View Cemetery in Portland. This day, October 30th, is the last of my sad October anniversaries: the date of Owen's funeral. I was struck by the coincidence, and then thought one of my newer thoughts, "This is most likely not a coincidence." I knew I had to go. I knew it would be uncomfortable, but I wanted to be there for my friend.

Natalie's mom, who I'd known mostly as a tennis opponent, had come to my house when we were searching for Owen with a surprisingly large and glorious live orchid at a time when many other acquaintances and even close friends were staying away, not knowing what to say or do. She opened up to me about her daughter's struggles after becoming addicted to opioid painkillers prescribed after a serious car accident. Natalie never made it to college—she instead had spent the next six years living with her addiction: failing to hold down jobs, burning through relationships, and straining connections with her family. Sometimes Natalie slept on the streets or crashed with friends her family didn't know, so my friend had known the terror of a "missing" child. I was moved by this visit from a mom who knew some of what I was going through. The orchid rebloomed a few times as we went through the early years of grieving the loss of Owen (one of the reasons I like plants better than flowers as signs of sympathy) and still sits in my kitchen window, where I monitor it for signs of life while washing dishes.

Now Natalie's struggle was over, and another mother's heart was shattered. I arrived early and first went to the wrong side of the property. I drove into the parking lot for a chapel I had visited before, but now that part of the complex looked run-down, and I was saddened (dropping my dark mood even lower) to think of the families who had laid the cremains of their loved ones to rest in this place that was starting to look shabby and not at all well kept. Then I realized there was another chapel across the road in the middle of the cemetery. I drove over to the other parking lot and sat in my car for a few minutes, working up the courage to go inside.

I signed the guest book with just my name. I couldn't think of anything else to write and my name was at the top of a new page, so I couldn't see what others had written to copy their sentiments. I knew there were no magical words I could write. I hoped that by just seeing my name in the guest book my friend would know what it took for me to be there, how much I wanted to support her, how I knew what she was going through. As I entered the chapel, I saw my friend in front of the altar greeting family members. She was sobbing uncontrollably and appeared about to fall down. I found my mind turning back to the day of Owen's funeral, when Dustin and I reflexively raised our voices to sing the songs I helped choose, read the eulogy about Owen, and murmur thanks and greetings to the other mourners when the Mass was over. I cried some, but not like this. In the video of Owen's funeral, Dustin and I appeared to be composed and calm. I don't know how we did it—I know we weren't feeling any sense of peace about Owen's death—but that was how we got through that day. Then we came home and fell apart again. A few months later the whole *world* fell apart when the pandemic closed down schools, offices, and airports. All this falling apart flashed through my mind as I saw my friend falling apart, and I had a moment of doubt about my decision to attend the service.

Natalie's service felt like a scene in a movie, where the mom is given a sedative to get through the funeral, or taken into a dark, quiet room to lie down for a spell. My friend's husband rubbed her back, and her mom offered water from a paper cup. I knew it wasn't about me, and I felt ashamed that I couldn't help comparing myself during this hard time for my friend—maybe I didn't cry enough at Owen's funeral, wasn't sad enough?

I took a seat in the middle of the chapel, realizing as I sat down that the pews were all closed on the ends by walls and windows. There was only one way in and out of each row. I didn't like feeling penned in. Since losing Owen, I like to know I have an available exit in case I need to escape with my emotions.

After I sat down, I watched the slideshow of a lovely young girl. Natalie grew up before my eyes, but the end came too soon. I was struck by the brevity of her life—and then, of Owen's life. *There should be more,* I thought. *It should be a longer slideshow.* When the photo stream started over, I let my eyes move around the room, and then I realized that Natalie herself was there too. The small altar area held a beautiful white casket that was open, and Natalie was inside! People were going up to the casket and weeping at its side. I had never been to a memorial like this before. This was a celebration of Natalie's life, with Natalie's lifeless body right here, too. This is when I realized I should have had a clue when the chapel was on the *cemetery* side of the road—not the *mausoleum* side. My heart squeezed tighter and tears poured out. We have Owen's ashes in a beautiful cedar box on our living room mantel. I could not imagine that my friend was going to watch her baby girl's body be put in the ground, but then I knew that was why we were there. That was what was going to happen. A few other friends from tennis came in and sat in my row. They hugged and consoled me (they had been at Owen's funeral four years before), and I felt bad needing their support when we were all supposed to be there to support another mother.

The service was brief, but beautiful. The priest's chant had a catchy refrain about Natalie "who has fallen asleep" that I can still hear in my mind. There were many words I couldn't hear, as he was chanting very quickly, but that phrase stuck with me. He spoke about Natalie, openly discussing her addiction and how we are not our addictions, but we often use that to define and dismiss people. Again, it seemed short (maybe I'm used to Mass-length ceremonies) and like there was just not enough to it. I felt like my friend deserved more and Natalie deserved more.

The priest broke out of his chant to say that there would now be time to greet the family before moving to the graveside for the burial. About

50 people were tightly gathered in the small chapel. A line formed and I didn't join it. I just sat, watching my friend break down with hug after hug. It was excruciating. I decided I had to leave. I didn't know how I would be able to watch another mom coming to terms with the finality of the loss of her child.

I told my friends I would just be waiting outside, but once I reached the parking lot, I got in my car and began driving, navigating around and around the winding cemetery roads, looking for the way out. The only signs I could see pointed me back to the chapel, and I imagined my friends would soon come out to meet me—or the procession with Natalie's coffin would begin!—and I would still be driving up and down these twisty roads among the oak trees looking for an exit. My heart began beating faster, and I had a hard time catching my breath between the sobs that snuck up on me. Thankfully, I eventually found the way out.

I don't know if anyone else left early. A friend who stayed until the end later described how gut wrenching it was to see the family at the graveside. "It was too intimate," she said when she texted to check up on me. I know it is uncomfortable to witness such raw emotion. But I'm glad that there were people willing to stay with their discomfort that day—even if I wasn't one of them. We need people to witness our grief. Natalie's mom knows that even if I couldn't stay for the whole service—and I didn't have any words to write in Natalie's guest book—I will always be with her in this grief that we unfortunately share.

The Neighbors

November 2023

I hear our Portland neighbors in their driveway, going off to school and work. They laugh easily and call out "love you!" to their teenage son, who lumbers moodily down the driveway with a healthy, home-packed lunch tucked in his backpack, his hair wet from the shower yet still looking somehow like he just rolled out of bed. Their easy morning banter drifts over to me and echoes around in my quiet kitchen. Should I be glad that their family life hasn't been wrecked like ours was? I endeavor to try.

The neighbor mom is a lot like me, and we've lived side by side for eleven years, but we haven't been very close. We are both moms of three kids each, but our kids attended different grade schools and middle schools. We both studied music in college and sang in church choirs. I know she likes Hallmark movies as I do, because once her husband ordered her some Hallmark wine as a gift and it was delivered to our house by mistake. I got a little excited when I saw the box, but my heart fell when I saw her name on the package, not mine. I thought these shared interests could be the start of a deeper connection (or at least a shared glass of Hallmark wine!), but neither of us ever initiated anything more.

The dad next door has always seemed a little shy, but kind and well meaning. At the open house we hosted after Owen's funeral, I remember being surprised at his long conversation with my brother Mike, but then I remembered how much they would have in common, both of them being introverted engineers with experience at University of Illinois Champaign-Urbana.

During the bleary and blurry days of missing and losing Owen, we had many friends helping us, but I rarely knew who was doing what. My sister-in-law told me she spent an afternoon folding laundry with the neighbor mom in my basement, and I wonder if she had to fold Dusitn's underwear or my underwear! Mortifying! The oldest neighbor boy was still in high school then, just one year behind Owen, and I remember him coming in the house and talking to me at a time when a lot of adults were shying away. He stopped by on his way home from school to see if we needed anything. I asked him to return my library books. (I couldn't concentrate on reading anything at all during the terror-filled fortnight that Owen was missing and for a long time after.) It was a simple and small gesture on his part, but it meant a lot. He is mostly away at college these days, but the last time he saw me and Dustin working in our front yard, he stopped on the way to his car to let us know that he still thinks about Owen and that he learned a lot from him. It touches me that he can talk about Owen with us even a little, when so many others don't or can't, for fear they will make us cry.

The neighbors created a fun distraction for their family when they installed a hot tub in their backyard in early 2020, during that first spring of the pandemic. We were huddled with fear inside our home next door, our hearts still raw with the loss of Owen, worrying that someone we knew would also lose a loved one to this crazy mystery disease. It was hard to hear people enjoying their hot tub while we were drowning in an ocean of grief next door. I wondered if we would ever feel joy or laugh together as a family again. I tried to feel glad that they weren't experiencing pain like we were suffering with. (I also longed for an invitation to escape into the hot tub myself. Though knowing full well I probably wouldn't have joined in, as in those early pandemic days we were concerned about even sharing close outdoor space with others outside our family pod.)

During the first block party we had after the pandemic restrictions started to lift in September of 2021, Dustin and I sat spaced apart on our lawn with these neighbors, watching the neighborhood kids play in the street. The neighbor dad told us proudly about his daughter's college applications being filled out early and how excited he was about her essay. He said she had written about how difficult it was to move to

Oregon from Illinois when she was nine years old. I had to actually get up and leave because do you know what my daughter wrote about for her college applications? How hard it was to find out that her brother had gone missing from his dorm room and that after weeks of searching (with teams of people SHE helped coordinate from her high school-issued iPad), a stranger who wasn't even aware there was a search going on had found Owen's body floating in the Willamette River.

Frances wrote about the body of her closest sibling being found in the river. *That's* hard. I tried to tell myself to be grateful that the neighbor girl hasn't had to face something harder than the life-changing move that brought them to our block. But it's challenging to stay present and patient in what used to seem like normal conversations.

Then, in November 2023, the mom from next door shared a post on Facebook proclaiming she was done with her cancer treatments—what? She had cancer?—and reported that she was now "back at Orangetheory!" (a local gym, featuring intense group cardio workouts).

I was stunned. My neighbor noted that she had just gone through a series of radiation treatments (a ridiculous number of appointments that must have wreaked havoc with her work schedule and their family calendar), without ever mentioning it to anyone in our family. I guess it really is hard to ask for help, or to let other people know that you might need assistance or appreciate a little neighborly empathy.

Was she anxiously awaiting the results of diagnostic testing while she bonded with her family in the hot tub? Had she been getting ready for a chemo appointment when I overheard her happy "love you" sing song from the driveway? I'm chagrined to learn that the neighbors hadn't been sailing through this life as unscathed as I imagined. And now I find myself impressed by their resilience and quiet strength. She's back at Orangetheory, raising her heart rate to impressive levels and chasing exercise-induced endorphins, after beating cancer, after all!

Now that I know the mom next door was being treated for breast cancer these last few months, I feel like I should do something for her, or at least say something to acknowledge how scary that must have been for her, but I don't know what to do. Maybe the best I can do is try to squeeze the joy out of every moment *I* have with *my* loved ones, like the neighbors were doing in their hot tub. I can try.

Bridgetown

Owen was born in Bridgetown. Twelve bridges cross the Willamette River in the middle of Portland. Even more bridges span the Columbia River, linking Oregon to Washington state.

Crossing a bridge has been part of Dustin's daily commute in one way or another since we moved to Portland in 1999. When he worked for a few years in Vancouver, Washington, I made him keep an inflatable raft in the back of his car in case a big earthquake hit, damaging the bridges and preventing him from returning home. Someone later told me this was a bad plan due to the strong current of the Columbia River: Dustin would have better luck keeping a case of whiskey in his car that he could trade for a ride in a real boat!

Our family crosses the Columbia via an old toll bridge called the Bridge of the Gods when we head to our cabin at Panther Creek in Washington state. Dustin's car has an automated toll pass now, but for many years the ritual of rolling down the driver's window and passing $2 in cash over to the toll-taker before venturing forth onto the open grating high above the water was an important kickoff for family camping trips at the cabin. Going fifteen miles per hour on that narrow span (the same limit remains today, though the toll is now $3) was like going back in time, especially given that Dustin's great-grandpa Garfield Klinger worked on the bridge. Dustin's family stories tell how Garfield's crew removed the old wooden deck when the bridge had to be raised—so it wouldn't be submerged when water levels rose on account of a new dam, the Bonneville, that was built downstream in the 1930s. Some of the old creosote-soaked slabs of wood were subsequently used in the construction of the original Klinger cabin at Panther Creek. (Dustin told us his great-grandpa made more money off that old bridge project later, too: he straightened the nails and spikes he had salvaged, and resold them during World War II—when local supplies of metal building materials were scarce.) So, that one bridge alone provided many things for our family.

Grampy Bruce, who lived in the old Klinger cabin at Panther Creek, also worked on several bridges in the region, including one that crosses Panther Creek, linking two parcels of the family's timber property together, before he passed away in 2007. Our family jokes that he was probably still late to work, even though the jobsite was 100 feet from his bed, because he didn't like to get up early.

We put a lot of faith in bridges. We have to, or we would never be able to go anywhere around our town. What would happen if the bridges collapsed and parts of our city were cut off from each other? If Oregon was separated from Washington state? And what do we do if one of the bridges itself, the actual connecting link, was responsible for a tremendous rift or the loss of a life?

Owen's body was found in the water downstream from the iconic St. Johns Bridge. Was the bridge a factor in his death? How can we know if the bridge was at fault? How can we ensure that other bridges will be safe and not mortally dangerous? We need more than a life raft—or a case of whiskey—in the back of our car. Living in Bridgetown (actually one of Portland's nicknames), bridges appear in many of our happy and everyday family memories. Now that Owen's story ends near such a prominent one, I find myself reexamining our personal history with some of our bridges.

The Burnside Bridge

One summer, we had tickets to see a life-size Thomas the Tank Engine at a rail stop in scenic Hood River, east of Portland along the Columbia. Gabe was four and Owen was not quite two. Frances was just a few months old, a sweet sleepy weight strapped to my chest in the Baby Bjorn. The boys loved listening to stories about Thomas, playing elaborate imaginary games with their train set, and wearing matching Thomas sweatshirts. It seemed like wholesome family fun, an afternoon trip that everyone would enjoy. I didn't factor in a bridge lift.

Owen and Gabe with Thomas the Tank Engine 2003

A hastily drawn countdown calendar in our kitchen featured my rudimentary sketches of trains and tracked how long it was until we would meet this amazing talking train who played such a big part in our household. Ten days until Thomas the Tank Engine, then nine, then eight... Anticipation was building.

Finally the day arrived. At the time, Dustin was a young associate working long hours at his law firm downtown in the US Bank Tower, nicknamed "the Big Pink." He had taken the bus to work that day, so the rest of us drove downtown to pick him up before we headed east to Hood River. It was rare for Dustin to take off during the middle of the workday, so I'm sure we were cutting it close to give him the most time at work possible. The kids and I were almost downtown, cheerfully bumping along in our white Ford Windstar, when the Burnside Bridge (one of the dozen that cross Portland's Willamette River) went up.

Unlike some of Portland's spans, the Burnside is a drawbridge, and when it's opening, traffic isn't stopped until right before the edge where the bridge breaks and rises up, which is a third of the way across the river. This is where our car was when suddenly the bridge's red barrier lights started flashing and the gates came down right in front of us. It felt like we were stopped right over the middle of the river, but I thought it would be exciting (although also possibly disconcerting) for the kids to see how the drawbridge worked up close. However, when the road right in front of us slowly tilted up, up, up into the sky, it eclipsed our view of Dustin's skyscraper and downtown, and Owen started to cry! He had never seen the bridge open up, and he really wanted to get to his dad—and to get to meet Thomas the Tank Engine! Owen's hot, red face grew redder and his eyes squinted shut with the pain of his cries. His tiny little heart was shattered, and he let us know how upset he was about all of this. I loved how badly he wanted to share this adventure with his dad, but I didn't love his crying.

On any other day, this dramatic bridge lift would have been an amazing sight for Owen to witness, and he would have marveled at the seemingly miraculous way the bridge opened to allow tall ships to pass while keeping the cars safe above.

About ten minutes later, the bridge plate came back down and settled into place. The barrier gates lifted up and we were on our way again. We picked up Dustin, drove out to Hood River, and saw the bright blue train with giant googly eyes that blinked and winked at us. The rest of the day was a hot, sweaty, windy fulfillment of childhood fantasies. But what stands out in my memory—even twenty years later—is the agony Owen experienced when the bridge went up. Every time I'm stuck on the Burnside Bridge, I remember that when Owen saw the bridge open for the first time, it struck him as an obstacle rather than a connector.

Steel Bridge

We don't drive over this bridge very much, but it is the bridge that the MAX light rail uses to cross the Willamette into downtown, so Owen and our family would ride across it whenever we went downtown on the MAX together. Freight trains and Amtrak trains also use this bridge, and there is abundant bike and pedestrian traffic, too, since it connects the large Waterfront Park on the west side with the Eastbank Esplanade path on the east side of the Willamette. I remember our family walking across the Steel Bridge all together when we hosted middle school exchange students from Japan. The pedestrian path is just 26 feet above the water, but the bridge has two levels that can be raised, singly or together, to create as much as 164 feet of clearance for tall ships to pass underneath. It's a rare double deck vertical-lift bridge, which is kind of cool, and I love that both Gabe and Owen made replicas of this bridge for their mandatory third grade bridge study project*. I think they loved the little machine house that rested on top of the truss and how that went up and down whenever the top level of the bridge was raised or lowered. I smile when I see this bridge, remembering how Gabe and Owen used to talk about living in the little bridge house.

---

* "Steel Bridge" Wikipedia, Accessed, November 2, 2023, https://en.wikipedia.org/wiki/Steel_Bridge

Fremont Bridge

Cars are traveling at highway speeds on this bridge, so there's not much time to admire the scenery, but the view of the city is stunning when you are headed west across the Willamette on its top deck. It's dark and a little spooky, though, when you are driving east on the lower level. I like seeing the bridge, with its soaring arch, from other parts of the city. It helps me find my bearings in relation to downtown. And it holds some nice memories.

Owen skipped school one day in the fifth grade so he and I could go on a special guided fishing trip with Frances and Grandpa John, on the Willamette. The guide set the hooks and served us a delicious lunch while we waited for the fish to bite. Owen caught this huge salmon he could barely lift. He was so proud. That's the Fremont Bridge rising behind him. His dorm room at UP had a view of this bridge, too. I like to think he enjoyed that view. Maybe in those first weeks away from home, it even helped him get his bearings, like it did for me.

Hawthorne Bridge

The Hawthorne Bridge, originally built in 1910, scared my kids when they were learning how to drive. The lanes are very narrow, so depending on which lane you are in, you have to drive extremely close to either oncoming traffic or the immobile metal trusses. But it's a main thoroughfare here (one of Portland's busiest, for cars and bikes), so every driver needs to make peace with crossing it and add in a little extra travel time. It's the oldest vertical lift bridge still in operation in America, and bridge operators must lift and lower the center span at least once every eight hours to keep the bridge in top working order, resulting in many frustrating delays for motorists, cyclists, and pedestrians[*]. As with many of the bridges in Portland, its span and surroundings are also a place where people gather.

We aren't a family of avid cyclists, but when Barack Obama's Presidential campaign made a stop in Portland in spring 2008, it was time for us to

___

[*] "Hawthorne Bridge," Multnomah County Bridges, Accessed November 2, 2023, https://multco.us /info/hawthorne-bridge.

test out the bike lanes of the Hawthorne Bridge. Dustin led the way, Gabe rode our Trail-A-Bike attached to Dustin's, and Owen sat in the caboose: our Burley bike trailer. I stayed home with Frances so she could nap. The future President's campaign rally attracted over 75,000 people that day to the park at the foot of the Hawthorne Bridge*. Owen made his own tiny "I love Obama" sign that he brought along and waved from his trailer. The bridge was a spectacular backdrop for that memorable occasion.

The Waterfront Blues Festival is held every year over the Fourth of July weekend in that same spot. You can see the bridge in this image from 2017, when Dustin took Owen, who was starting to play guitar in a band with his friends and work with sound equipment at school, to the Blues Festival at the bridge's feet. When you look at pictures of Owen, he seems like a typical teen, wearing T-shirts or sweatshirts and jeans or shorts. What you might not realize is how he was pretty strategic in what shirt, sweatshirt, or hat he would wear. This day, since he was with Dustin, he chose a Notre Dame shirt from a family trip there in 2016. His hat is from Kapalua on Maui, a favorite golf resort of Dustin's.

---

* Larry Rohter, "Obama Draws Record Crowd in Oregon," *New York Times*, May 18, 2008. https://archive.nytimes.com/thecaucus.blogs.nytimes.com/2008/05/18/obama-draws-record-crowd-in-oregon/

He probably didn't even know that his picture would be taken that day, but Owen's seemingly meaningful clothing choices, combined with the hardworking Hawthorne Bridge in the background, created another image that's become part of the powerful bond that our family has forged with Bridgetown's vital arteries.

The St. Johns Bridge

The St. Johns Bridge is stunning. Photographers and artists love to feature its 400-foot-tall, light green towers popping against the dark evergreens of Forest Park, which anchors the west end of the bridge. It creates many powerful, dramatic images. But how much power do I let the bridge hold?

I don't know exactly what happened with Owen when he was lost to us and how (or even *if*) this bridge was involved, but to me now, this breathtaking span and the way it towers above the water where his body was found seems like a taunting defender standing over a vanquished opponent.

Did it have meaning for Owen? It's possible. One of his friends from UP told me Owen had gone on a run to the bridge early in the semester;

she thought it was a strange place to go because the bridge was so busy with fast-moving traffic. Owen's roommate told us that Owen was trying to quit smoking, and that at some point, he had gone up there and thrown his stash of marijuana over the edge of the bridge. (I didn't know he was smoking or vaping anything, let alone trying to quit! Dustin had an inkling about this since the time Owen and his friends set off the smoke detector in our basement. I wonder what else I missed.)

Does the bridge hold some of Owen's secrets? No credible witnesses came forward saying they saw Owen on the bridge after he left his dorm room that last night, and there aren't any cameras. Did Owen fall from the bridge? Did he jump? I really don't think so. I pored over the autopsy report, but it doesn't reveal the kind of injuries one might sustain falling from 200 feet above the water. The police showed us video footage of someone walking behind the St. Johns police station that night, a shadowy person walking *away* from the bridge and back toward campus. Was it him?

Sometime during the first year after we lost Owen, a kind neighbor gave me a chain with a pendant bearing the image of one of the iconic St. Johns Bridge towers. I was slightly horrified with this symbol that haunted my dreams, but I remember mumbling my thanks and stuffing the necklace into my pocket as questions I didn't feel strong enough to ask flooded my mind: Why was she giving me this? Did she believe Owen committed suicide at the bridge? Would wearing this show that I have power over the bridge, or that the bridge is central in his story? Talking about Owen and the bridge is difficult. Would wearing this help? "Oh, my pendant? It's the bridge where some people believe Owen committed suicide." I honestly don't know how to feel about this bridge, because I don't know what happened. Would it be creepy to have an image of it on my body and next to my skin, or would it just feel like a cool, crafty necklace? (Portland is a very crafty place, and we do love our bridges.) I have never worn it and I don't think I ever will, even though I think it's the most beautiful bridge in Portland.

On what would have been Owen's nineteenth birthday, July 23, 2020, we went to Cathedral Park, below the bridge, an aptly named location for a ritual of remembrance. The bridge structure loomed high above us as we released biodegradable paper lanterns into the river. They bobbed silently on the sparkling summer water before hidden currents swept them quickly downstream, through the bridge's eerie shadow. I imagined the same currents steering and secreting Owen's body while we searched for him. I felt like screaming. We haven't done this again, but I might need to revisit the park by myself to stand reverent in the bridge's presence and watch the river currents have their way with my St. Johns Bridge pendant.

I don't drive over the bridge very often anymore, but I try to not avoid it completely either. I don't want it to own my fear. Someday I hope it will feel like just another bridge in Bridgetown, connecting two sides of the river. Is there a bridge that will link me to Owen and to knowing more about what happened to him? I'd wear a pendant of that bridge any day.

Tennis as a Grief Sport

November 2023

Iwas explaining how I felt about tennis in my grief support group the other day and it struck me that not everyone is as obsessed with this sport as I am. I felt the need to elaborate on my theory of how tennis is such a good outlet for my emotions these days, and how I feel it can substitute for traditional talk therapy sometimes (but not always!).

The woman I was talking with in the group that day is a college professor of Japanese history. She was sharing about the difficulty in finding the right kind of support in her academic community for writing her second book, while grieving the loss of her young adult daughter and her mother, who both passed away around the same time. I learn so much from everyone I have met on this grief journey, and that day, I learned that there is a special problem with writing your second academic book: there is more pressure and anticipation for you to deliver something as equally profound as your first academic book, or even better. She also said that within the academic community, there is a culture of personal discipline and an emphasis on your personal control over the project and its success.

I was exhausted just listening to her talk about this, and I felt so sad for her lack of support. She mentioned how she wanted to try to create a more helpful and intellectually curious approach to writing projects in academia instead of having the pressure from colleagues continually asking, "How many pages have you written? When will you be done? When is it coming out?"

In a rough attempt to find some common ground, I suggested that maybe it would help if they all went outside and played some tennis.

Owen and Gabe playing tennis at Grant Park

Tennis helps. Or at least tennis helps me—and so I think it is a perfect grief sport.

Before I became a mom, I used to do yoga. Finding that zone where stress slipped off my shoulders for a few minutes felt so good. I loved how it could take me out of my head or even out of the drafty room in an old church where my teacher held class, and then gently bring me back to myself, leaving me somehow better prepared to carry on through my day.

As our family grew, eventually maxing out at three kids (at one point all were under age four!), finding that peaceful feeling eluded me. I couldn't get quiet or still; my mom brain was buzzing with worry about each of the kids, my to-do list, or our chaotic family calendar. I needed to try something different, so when my daughter entered kindergarten, I signed up for beginning tennis lessons at the public tennis center and started hitting the crap out of the little yellow ball.

I had so much to learn: the forehand, the backhand, volleys, lobs, overhead smashes, and serves. Time in my group lessons flew by. While I was on the court, I simply didn't have time to think about anything else. The amount of concentration required to not get hit by the rapidly fed balls in those early days gave me the same kind of respite from my daily stresses I had once found in yoga. There was no time to perseverate about anything but the ball. I loved it! I signed up for semi-private lessons.

Once I was able to generate some shots, I started playing against other people. I had to learn where to stand, when to move, where to move, and the nuances of singles and doubles strategy. I'm still learning new tactics fifteen years later, and I still find it just as absorbing. I have to focus on what's happening on court: every ball, every point. I joined a team. And then I joined another team. And now I play on nine or ten different teams over the course of a year. (Don't tell my husband. He knows I play a lot of tennis, but even I think ten teams might be a little too much.)

When we lost Owen, I couldn't do anything for weeks. I couldn't focus on anything but him. Closing my eyes to rest or to try to fall asleep just brought on waves of terrifying images of what might have happened to him. I couldn't watch anything on TV. I couldn't read even a single page of a novel—fiction didn't hold the appeal that it used to, now that my real life had turned into a nightmare. A few weeks after Owen's body was found, after the funeral with the thirteen priests and 2,000 mourners, when I had to start facing this new normal without him, a friend took me back to the tennis center to hit some balls.

It was hard at first, to even let myself go to do something that had brought me so much joy. I didn't feel like feeling good. It felt right that I felt wrecked and that my life as I knew it was over.

In one of the confusing dichotomies of grief, while I needed to see people to know I wasn't alone, I also didn't want to see a lot of people. Seeing someone for the first time after we lost Owen was always hard, as they didn't know what to say and I didn't know what to say to make them more comfortable.

In tennis—at least when you are playing singles—once you get started, you are alone on your own side of the net. Sure, someone is on the other side of the net, and you can come over to the bench between games and talk to your opponent or hitting partner, but mostly you are on your own. Sound echoes oddly in the tennis bubble where I was playing after losing Owen, and I was grateful that I didn't have to make small talk—or any kind of talk. I just had to hit the ball. And hitting the ball felt...good. Focusing on the ball helped me set my grief on the bench for a few minutes at a time. It didn't take away the pain of losing my son, but somehow these interludes made it more bearable.

I eased back into playing doubles with my close circle of tennis friends. No, that's not quite right. Nothing was "easy" about any of this, but I needed to play to get that slight separation from the heaviness of my grief, and my friends were very supportive about my rough emotional state. I remember the first team doubles match I played after losing Owen. My friend Tonya, a UP alum and crafty-minded mom of four, made temporary tattoos for the whole team to wear. They were simple purple hearts with the letter O in the middle for Owen. I was so touched and grateful that the whole team would put something (even temporarily) on their bodies for me and Owen.

Along with the focus that tennis required of me, I also found it gave me an opportunity for a new kind of emotional release. For the first time, I became the athlete who yelled out "C'mon!" like Serena Williams when I hit a clean winner. It is loud and a little obnoxious, but it really feels good!

After playing tennis matches in the first years after losing Owen—win or lose—I often ended up weeping uncontrollably on the bench. I don't think my friends really understood what was happening, maybe they just thought I was sad about how I played, but it was more than that. The tears sprang out of surprise that I could still function at any kind of competent level on the tennis court with Owen gone. I cried because once the intense focus playing the match required ended, the reality that Owen was still gone came slamming back. Sometimes I cried because I felt guilty that I was still able to laugh and play a game with my friends. I cried for everything I had lost, for things I might still lose, for the abundance of blessings in my life, and, yes, sometimes I cried because I played like shit. All that is to say I was a mess, and it was OK. It was a totally appropriate time for me to let everything flow out. No one cared, or at least no one told me they cared. I believe that being able to shift the heavy weight of grief around for a little while was healthy and healing for me, even if the pain came flooding back in after the match ended.

Having not been a competitive athlete until I was almost 40 years old, the opportunity to play at the National Tennis Center in Orlando is something I never thought I would experience. But in 2023, one of my mixed doubles teams placed first in our city and then beat the other teams in our region to advance to the USTA 18+ 9.0 Mixed Doubles Nationals, a competition for teams of players eighteen years or older with combined individual ratings of 9.0. (USTA player ratings range from beginners at 1.5 to internationally ranked players at 7.0; yes, it is a funky numbering system!) Over my years of practice, I have moved up to a rating of 4.0; players rated above me are usually former college players or work as tennis coaches. My main partner for the season was Marco Pineda, a strong 5.0-rated player whom I had also taken some lessons from over the years. It made me extremely nervous to be paired with a tennis pro. I didn't want to screw up and do the wrong thing, but he was a great partner, coaching me about what returns to hit and where to position myself on court. We were undefeated at nationals, though the rest of our team was not. I cried many tears of gratitude, pride, exhaustion, and grief.

I wonder if perhaps my grief was my secret superpower, propelling me through the intense weekend of competition. I inked Owen's initials ("OK") on my shoes and felt like his spirit carried me at times, giving me a little more energy when I was tired and helping me believe in myself when I felt like an imposter among the talented athletes. Dustin traveled with me that weekend too, another angel on my team. He schlepped my heavy tennis bag, filled my water bottles, and brought me ice towels when I was overheating. Focusing on tennis was good for both of us; since then, Dustin began taking tennis lessons. It's nice to have him involved a little more in something I'm so passionate about.

Me on court with Marco Pineda at USTA Sectionals August 2023

I cried again when Nationals ended—tears of sadness that the dream was over—but I told myself at the time, you never know when my team might qualify again. And, happy update: my team qualified for the 40+ 9.0 mixed doubles in 2024. I didn't get to play with Marco again, since he was still under age 40, but my team finished sixth in the country and I cried fewer tears this time! I remembered my grieving friend and her angst over writing her second academic book after a strong first showing. On my second trip to nationals, I wasn't as intimidated by the immense facility (98 courts!), the humidity, or the elite athletes on the other side of the net. I felt Owen's spirit cheering me on, and I knew that, win or lose, my team was grateful for the opportunity to compete at the national level. I wish my grief group friends could experience the immersive focus of a tennis match that eclipses grief for a short time or the cathartic release of hitting a winning shot and being a tennis superstar.

Hot Pockets Will
Always Be There for You

November 2023

2017 Thanksgiving at Nona's beach house

to: findowenk@gmail.com
date: November 23, 2023
subject: Hot Pockets Will Always Be There for You

Dear friends,

It's Thanksgiving. I've prepped the potatoes and stuffing we will take to our friends' house in Corvallis later today. I made the cranberry sauce with apricots and orange liqueur that my family has every year. Because our friends are vegan and won't be cooking turkey, I baked a turkey breast in my instant pot last night, blasting aromas of the holiday main dish all around the kitchen when I released the pressure valve. Owen really would have liked the instant pot. Sometimes I think it is so strange how food can hold our memories. It's just food! We cook it (or someone prepares it for us) and it nourishes us. We buy a bag of chips or munch on an apple without thinking a lot of the time, but at other times just seeing, smelling, or tasting a food we associate with someone we are missing can flood our senses with thoughts and feelings in a really amazing way.

Owen was a hungry boy who loved the hearty family meals I used to make every day. Owen wolfed down homemade mac and cheese, Japanese curry rice with beef or chicken, Philly cheesesteaks, spaghetti carbonara, pizza with handmade crust, and grilled salmon or steaks. Believe it or not, he loved broccoli, dipping the florets into mayonnaise to pack in extra calories. He was also a big fan of all the cookies I baked, the big apple puffed pancake we made for special breakfasts, and anything with bacon.

In September of 2023, it was my turn to host my cooking group. This group of eight women has been gathering and cooking together monthly for over 20 years with a rotating schedule of hosts, cooking teams, annual couples meals, and summer family picnics. Losing Owen and going through Covid disrupted our group for quite a while, but we were getting back on track and it was my turn to step up. However, fall is a hard season for me, with huge waves of grief to navigate. As we approached the fourth anniversary of losing Owen, I worried about how I was going to plan a menu and host a dinner even for these dear friends in my current mental state, but my friend Laura, who also knows about deep grief from the sudden loss of her husband, came to the rescue suggesting a menu of comfort foods. She asked, "What were Owen's favorite comfort foods?" The first thing that came to mind was bacon.

The menu came together easily from there. We had mind-blowingly delicious bacon baked on crackers as an appetizer. We also shared the tomato soup Owen and I used to make together and enjoyed small portions of homemade mac and cheese with bacon for the main course. Dessert was a decadent chocolate chip pie, because I remembered how much Owen loved the cowboy chocolate chip cookie baked in a cast iron skillet he and I shared during a lacrosse tournament on his fifteenth birthday. There were memories in every mouthful. It was heavier than our usual type of meal—with fewer vegetables (I should have served broccoli and mayonnaise!)—but it was comforting to sit around my cozy table with friends and feel Owen with us.

I wonder what he would have liked to cook for himself if he was still here? Would Owen be making these "family favorites" or trying out new TikTok recipes? Who am I kidding? It's more likely that he wouldn't be cooking at all: ice cream and junk food were probably some of his most favorite things to eat!

I hope that today you find yourself at a table surrounded by friends and loved ones, feasting on foods that hold special memories. If that is not what you are experiencing, no worries. There is still hope and you will be OK (or "more than OK" which is my new goal). Owen wrote a persuasive essay when he was a freshman in high school and wants you to know that "Hot Pockets will always be there for you." He put an asterisk after his claim that "the flavors are endless," but there is no accompanying footnote; we will never know what he was going to say about the flavors. Again, any typos are courtesy of Owen.

Love,
Mary and #moreowen

Owen Klinger
Per.1
16 May 2016

Hot Pockets, The Food of the Gods

I sincerely recommend that you try hot pockets. If you already have, then you are ahead of the game! In this essay I will present an opinion that reinforces the eating of hot pockets.

There are over 23 different flavors of hot pockets available to the everyday consumer. That means you can eat a hot pocket everyday for 23 days and never eat the same flavor!!! Now that's what you call variety. Some people may worry "But aren't hot pockets bad for you?". I assure you that is not the case.

Here are some cold hard facts about hot pocket nutrition: hot pockets have zero grams trans fat and some have up to 14 grams of protein in them! These tasty treats will also give you 10% of your daily value of Calcium and Iron. Yum! If you are trying to slim down, you can always give Lean Pockets© a try. These low-fat snacks are an amazing way to stay trim while still enjoying that classic hot pocket flavor. Don't think that hot pockets are a lunch and dinner thing only! There are over 6 varieties of the Breakfast Hot Pocket©. From hickory ham egg and cheese, which is made with real ham and cheese, to applewood bacon egg and cheese which contains smoked bacon that is actually smoked! The flavors are endless*! If you get tired of eating hot pockets in their usual form, be not afraid! The new Hot Pocket Bites© are here! Instead of having to peel back the gooey wrapper every time you want to take a bite, try nuking up a bunch of bites and just popping em' as fast as you can! Critics are calling the new Hot Pocket Bites© "The most efficient way to eat hot pockets since the hot pocket"! To further your satisfaction, the cooking time on these babies has been cut in half! It now only takes 1 minute to prepare yourself some delicious Hot Pocket Bites©! Now some cold-hearted critical thinkers out there may be thinking, "This is too good to be true! I bet you can only get them in Alaska or something!". Actually, all hot pocket products are available to you online or in a store near you! As a matter of fact, they are available at Fred Meyer's a mere 5 minutes away! My personal favorite is the Philly Steak with seasoned crust. I would definitely recommend it to anyone and everyone who likes or loves philly cheese steak. It is literally heaven for your tastebuds. In my opinion, the Nacho Bites are the 2nd best. It is almost of Taco Bell© quality by which these Nacho Bites are made. I hope that this informative and factual paper has provided you with a little more knowledge on the topic of hot pocket products. Who knows, maybe someday you just feel like you need a hot hearty snack. Hot pockets will always be there for you.

Mary, Did You Know?

December 2023

As a kid named Mary, I was teased around Christmas when our elementary school music teacher had us sing songs like "Mary Had a Baby Yes, Lord." At my neighborhood public school, I was the only girl named Mary (this would radically change when I went to college at Notre Dame). My shy, introverted self did not appreciate this extra attention. I used to look at the floor through my glasses and mouth the words because I didn't want anyone around me to hear me saying that I had "had a baby" and "named him Jesus" and "laid him in a manger," etc. I didn't want to give the rumor any ground to stand on. Kids really can be cruel, but at least it was only seasonal snickering I had to endure.

In middle school, I got contact lenses and some more confidence and joined the jazz choir. The teasing at Christmastime either stopped or I didn't notice it anymore. There were bigger issues at play (as you might imagine, lots of teenage drama about boys, friends, hair, and clothes). I continued to sing in choirs through high school, college, and beyond, eventually joining a small contemporary music group at our Catholic church in Portland. Singing Christmas songs about Mary got easier—until one day when it was again too hard for me.

I don't remember listening to Christmas music that first holiday season after we lost Owen, but how is it possible that I still sang with the choir at Christmas Eve Mass? I did! I was even the lead soloist. I was doing things on autopilot, trying to keep going when I didn't feel like carrying on in this life without my sweet middle child. I don't remember much from those early months of paralyzing, numbing grief, and I don't remember anything from that Mass.

I know friends from my book club stepped in to help fill Christmas stockings for me and my family that first year. There was an evening of gift wrapping where several members of my tennis teams came over and made an assembly line to wrap and decorate the paltry presents I had gathered to put under the tree. It seemed futile to give each other presents that we knew were not what we really wanted, which was to have Owen with us again. But with the help of my friends, I tried. Other friends came and baked holiday cookies with my family recipes. They didn't taste the same, but nothing tasted good in those early months of our bitter loss. It was such a sweet effort to help us connect to our past traditions in this radically different world we'd suddenly found ourselves living in.

Soon after that first Christmas, I stopped singing at church. Choking on the words, "Lord, have mercy" as I led the congregation from the front of the church was just not good for me or anyone. I didn't feel connected to the words I was singing as I had before. I was angry at God and felt like a fraud standing up and singing hymns of praise. (And I have already told you that I'm not good with anger.)

In December 2023, I heard the song "Mary, Did You Know," written by Buddy Greene and Mark Lowry, a Christmas song addressed to Mary, mother of Jesus. I was a big fan of the 2015 *The Voice* winner Jordan Smith, and it was his beautiful voice singing a dramatic rendering of the song, with sweeping strings and stunning high notes and dynamic changes, that came on while I was sitting in my car outside the library. I just completely lost it. I cried in my car for a long time after the song ended, and then I drove home. I didn't go into the library that day.

The song stirred up other questions I have for Mary, as the most famous "bereaved mother" I know, and inspired my version of "Mary, Did You Know."

Mary, did you know Jesus was going to die before you? Would you still have gone through with becoming a mom if you knew it would end with losing your child? How did you cope with the anxiety and worry during those days he was persecuted and hanging on the cross? Could you sleep at all? I could barely sleep while Owen was missing. Every time I closed my eyes, I imagined terrible things happening to him. My throat was so tight, all I could handle was soup or tea. Did you eat anything that whole week Jesus was dying?

What did you feel when you held his body for the last time when they took him down from the cross? Did that give you any closure? I didn't get to hold or even see Owen's body after he died. Were you numb? Did you feel like you were unable to carry on? Or did holding him help you in some way?

What about after Jesus reappeared to his disciples? That was pretty wild. Were you upset that he didn't appear to you? Maybe he did and that story just didn't get out. Did you see your son in your dreams after he was gone? I've seen Owen in my dreams, but I really wish it happened more, that I could remember more, that he would say more and hug me more. I got some Facebook messages from a woman (a stranger who didn't know

Owen or me) telling me *she* was having very vivid dreams about Owen. I was glad she told me about them, but I was jealous and angry that he wasn't appearing the same way to me.

Did you ever think you saw your son in a crowded market or on the street? What about when you were looking at water moving in a stream? Or sunlight dancing in the leaves of the trees? Did you know it was him? Did you get signs that he was still around? Did you question whether you were just wishing that these were signs from him? Or did you feel it in your gut?

Did you have other kids? I really can't believe that I don't know this about you. I guess I think Jesus didn't have any brothers or sisters because I would have remembered reading about them in the Bible, but my two other kids aren't super keen on being written about, so I get it if they didn't want their grieving to be part of the story. How did you find the strength to carry on for them? Or did you?

Since losing Owen, many people have shared with me the way their own loss of a sibling was accompanied by the loss of their parents too, as their parents were never the same after losing a child. I don't know how much longer you lived after Jesus died. Did the heavy weight on your heart ever lift? Or was it grief that held you down so you couldn't breathe? I have felt that way and I know I will never be the same mom I was.

Were you angry at God? At Jesus's friends? I have found myself mad at God—even questioning my faith in the whole system of belief that everyone said they were so glad I had to lean on in these dark times. I get mad at Owen's friends and roommates for not being able to tell us more about what happened with him, and then I remember that they were just other bumbling young people, trying to figure out how to balance the challenges of growing up and "adulting." They weren't all making the best choices, but it must have been hard for them to lose their friend. I was so proud of Owen for choosing to go to a college where he would be making new friends, but now I wish he had gone to the school where his good friends were. He could have been their roommate and might have avoided this tragedy. (Would you believe me if I told you his two best friends ended up rooming with another Owen?!) Did you think that if Jesus had been with different friends, this wouldn't have happened to him? Did you see his friends often after he was gone?

What about Joseph? How did he handle this loss? Did it pull you apart or make you closer? I am so afraid that losing Owen has put me and Dustin on separate journeys; as united as we are in our love for Owen, we are different in the ways we miss him, search for more of him, and shepherd our other kids. So many families fall apart when there is a loss that leaves such a gaping hole in a parent's heart. The loss of a child is a deep laceration with jagged edges that can't be easily bandaged or tidily sewn. It feels like it will be hemorrhaging forever. Parts of my heart are just gone, and there are painful bits of memory and longing and not-knowing that fester in the wound, keeping it from healing. I wonder if you and Joseph felt that way too.

Owen's baptism 2001

What happened to you after the gospel chapters and verses were written? There is no "Book of Mary" in the Bible. I know I would love to read the "First Letter of Mary to the People who Killed Jesus." Did you write any letters like that? I wish I knew who I could write to about Owen. We still don't really know what happened—whether this was an accident or self-intended or if anyone else was involved. Did knowing how and why Jesus died make his loss easier to bear? I wonder if I would feel better if we knew what happened to Owen, if I could identify someone or something that took his life? He would still be gone and we would still be here without him, trying to remember his laugh, and what he sounded like when he sang in the shower. Our hearts would still be shattered. (Did Jesus sing while he bathed with a bucket or in a stream?)

What did you do to keep going? Did you know that images of you holding your baby or you holding the body of your dead son would be so revered? Could you have imagined that your life would be so scrutinized by millions of people for so many years after your son passed away? Did everyone you know find out about Jesus dying before you had to tell them? Telling people Owen died was hard, though as his disappearance and search was so public, a lot of people already knew. Did having everyone know make it easier to bear? Or did you find yourself wishing you could move somewhere new where no one knew that you had lost a child? Where no one knew how you used to be or what you were once capable of doing before grief trampled your hopes and dreams?

Did you ever come to a place of acceptance and peace? You look so peaceful in all the artist renderings I have seen of you, but most of those are from when you still had the gift of Jesus in your life. I'm trying to look for lessons in the loss of Owen, to be grateful for the connections the crazy search for and discovery of his body revealed and all the changes I have gone through since he died. As the song asks, "Did you know that your baby boy has come to make you new? And this child that you've delivered would soon deliver you?"

Oh Mary, did you know? Because I didn't.

Flowers from the Killers

January 2024

I did not count how many floral arrangements were delivered to our house when Owen was missing, when Owen's body was found, or when we were preparing for his funeral. Honestly, I think there were too many to count.

My favorite came in a square glass vase; it wasn't tippy like some of the others. It stood out for its simplicity. I didn't take a picture, but I remember there were pure white hydrangeas and sturdy green leaves. It made me think of a wedding bouquet.

The tiny card that came with the flowers said, "You're in our thoughts—the killers."

WHO?

The Killers are our pest control company. They are not the people responsible for Owen's demise.

When the kids were little and I was a stay-at-home mom who really was home most of the time, the same sweet, socially awkward agent from the pest control company came to our house every few months and spent hours chatting to us—not exactly *with* us—as he carried out the inspection and treatments around our home. I was too polite to cut the conversations short; I had the feeling the man was a little lonely and didn't get to talk to many people. The Killers sent us flowers when we lost Owen.

These beautiful flowers with this simple card made me cry. (To be honest, everything made me cry during that time, but this card brought forth fresh tears.) I found myself wishing that the card really had been from people who had killed Owen. I had a brief "cozy mystery" moment, imagining we could trace the delivery back to the flower shop, find out who had purchased the flowers, and hunt down the stupid and heartless criminals who had killed Owen and then sent us sympathy flowers. We would solve the mystery *and* I would know which florist was responsible for my favorite arrangement.

After that dream passed, I cried again, realizing I was now someone who the pest control people—the unenviable people who kill mice and rats, cockroaches and carpenter ants—felt sorry for.

Eventually it made me laugh. It is funny and kind of ridiculous that I had thought this flower delivery was a clue to the mystery of Owen! I did not save all the cards that came with the flowers we received, but I saved this card and I look at it often. It reminds me that I can laugh.

Sometimes we have to cry before we can laugh, or we might laugh so we don't cry, but we will laugh again.

Heart-Shaped Rocks

March 2024

I have been collecting rocks for a long time. Family time at the beach when the kids were growing up almost always included searching for unique rocks. Mostly we hunted for agates, which are common in the Pacific Northwest. Big ones were the special finds, but even on windy winter days, we hunkered down out of the wind, close to the sun-warmed sand, and combed through the swirls of rocks left behind by tides and waves for what we called "teeny, tiny, shiny" stones that glowed like miniature gems. We displayed these treasures in glass bottles back at the beach house, or left them in our pockets to be rediscovered in the bottom of the washing machine after the next laundry day. Many of them are likely still hidden in the cracks and crevices of our old minivan.

We prized rocks of unusual smoothness or color, marveling at the rare ones with stripes! We even had a little game we played after some of these rock hunting sessions (my secret mom-way of keeping the kids safely away from the water, where unpredictable waves crept up the slanted beach) called Trading Post. We would each find a large flat rock to set up as our display and arrange our special rocks on it for trading with the others. "Who is coming to my trading post? My trading post? My trading post? Who is coming to my trading post? No–bo–dy" were the lyrics to a little nonsense song I made up to sing while we crawled around from post to post, haggling and trading a smooth black rock for a tiny, translucent agate, or a rusty red triangle for a two-toned, perfectly shaped oval.

Rocks played a part in our family time at Panther Creek too, but mostly we were looking for rocks to throw into the creek. (Why were we so obsessed with doing this?) A large rock with a hole in the top rose above the water in the center of the creek. Dustin told the kids he called this rock "Mermaid Island" when he was little. Standing on the shore and tossing rocks towards the hole in Mermaid Island occupied us for hours during our family camping trips. We marveled at the bright turquoise color of many of the rocks there. The volcanic provenance of the creek rocks rendered them strikingly different from rocks we found at the coast.

In the background, like operating software that keeps things moving but you don't actively think about it until there is an alert for an update, we were always searching for heart rocks. Over the many years of family beach trips, we had found a few—maybe one or two a year—and we proudly lined them up on the windowsill in the funky master bathroom with the sunken bathtub at the beach house. Those "first finds" are still there, gathering dust and occasional cobwebs, their value as rare finds now eclipsed by the abundance of heart rocks I have encountered since 2019.

I wish I had paid attention to the first one I found after we lost Owen. I don't know which one it was, or exactly when that was. After Owen's body was found, I spent a lot of time meditatively walking at the beach where our family had made so many special memories. I also found solace by the waters of Panther Creek. I wrote in my journal on July 9, 2020, after a few days at the beach, "I have never found so many heart-shaped rocks." My collection grew from dozens to dozens of dozens, to hundreds, and now I have lost count. Some are a little wonky, some are astonishingly close to perfect, and I see each one as a special gift from Owen.

A few discoveries in particular stand out. In 2020, I remember sitting around over Labor Day weekend at Panther Creek in the spot where we usually read or have a drink by the water. When our dear friends Michelle and Kevin joined us for a picnic on the holiday, I looked down at my feet and a heart-shaped rock was suddenly right there, lying on the moss in plain sight. I gave it to Michelle, who later made it into a necklace for me.

Another was on Owen's birthday in July 2021. Our family had been planning a big outdoor picnic and celebration at the creek in 2020 to thank the friends and family who had helped us search for him when he went missing. Covid restrictions forced us to scrap our plans that year; we imagined that by 2021 we would be able to gather safely. Now I don't remember if it was still restricted or if our hearts had shifted and we didn't feel like throwing a big party, but in the summer of 2021, Dustin and I went out to Panther Creek by ourselves and invited just a few visitors to stop by separately to spend time with us in Owen's favorite place. Looking down at the creek from the bridge Grampy Bruce helped build, on what would have been Owen's twentieth birthday, I suddenly spied a huge rock on the creek bed that was three or four feet in diameter, shaped like a heart. Father John from UP had come out to visit us that day, and we took him up on the bridge to look down into the creek. I feared he thought we were going a little crazy in our grief, desperately searching for signs of Owen, but he too saw the heart-shaped rock, and he believed, as we did, that it must have some deeper or spiritual meaning. This is a rock that has been there for a very, very long time. But Dustin and I never saw that it was in the shape of a heart until that weekend, with the thoughts of Owen, our beautiful, soulful son who we were missing so very much.

I wish I had started counting even from *that* day, but the truth is I don't know how many heart-shaped rocks I have found since we lost Owen. I can go on a walk at the same beach today, where we used to find one or two a year, and find fifteen or twenty in an hour! An afternoon at Panther Creek dipping my toes into the bracing water can yield a dozen or more. I've made some of them into #moreowen keychains that I gave away to friends and family one Christmas. I've pressed them into the hands of other grieving moms I've met, and I've left them on the bench by the tree planted in Owen's honor on the UP campus. I've passed them out at my book club, in my cooking group, and to friends from tennis. I have placed a few dozen in our backyard, where they are frequently washed with the rain, covered with falling leaves, or baked in the summer sun. It's here that I have begun to see how these heart rocks can shift and change—how their heart-shaped magic is sometimes fleeting.

Some of these rocks have broken or split apart due to changes in temperature or by fluctuating moisture levels. Broken hearts. The shiniest rocks—special speckled rocks from the beach that sparkle and twinkle in the sun—have completely shattered, leaving a pile of pieces that I can imagine would be softened by the action of the waves over time and eventually turned into grains of sand themselves. How miraculous that when I encountered these bits of sand and sediment they had been pressed and formed by nature into this shape that we (and Hallmark) associate with love. This makes these heart rocks even more special to me, the fact that they were in my path when I was thinking about Owen and yearning for ways of knowing that his love was real.

The shattering of the sparkly heart rocks reinforces my thought that it's often the most amazing, brightest spirits who are taken from us "before their time." Owen was certainly that bright spirit in our family. Laughing, making music, moving his body, loving his friends and family and beagle harder, faster, and with more passion than many. Maybe he knew he wouldn't be here as long as the rest of us. I know now I can't leave these special rocks that have caught my eye out in the elements if I want them to stay the same. I have to keep them safely on the shelf or in a jar so I can easily see and preserve their special shape.

But they are so beautiful out in the open, sparkling in the sun and darkening with the rain. Change is an inevitable and integral part of our lives—even in the life of a heart-shaped rock. Maybe I need to leave those rocks—and my own sparkly heart—out in the open and surrender to being changed by the experience of loving and living.

Her Freckles (a Poem)

May 2024

After the disruptive trauma of losing her brother, and then the chaos of the pandemic, Frances, Owen's little sister—and our family's baby—graduated from high school in 2021. She spent a few weeks that fall in New York at her first-choice school, Sarah Lawrence College, before deciding it wasn't the right time for her to be there and returning to our home in Portland. Dustin and I hovered and worried about her, probably more than was healthy for any of us, while she contemplated her next steps.

A few years later, she enrolled in Oregon State University and moved into a dorm in Corvallis, Oregon. It was terrifying for me to let her go again, to let her fly or flounder on her own, when all I wanted to do was keep her safe. But Dustin and I knew it was time for this, that she was ready. We limited our text exchanges and disciplined ourselves to just one FaceTime call per week. I wrote this poem in May of 2024 after one of these calls, where she showed me her freckles were back after an afternoon in the spring sunshine.

> I can't see much of her face at first.
> The lighting above her bunk is dim.
> I glimpse pale skin and dark eyes—brown like my eyes, like his eyes.
> My heart starts to beat faster.
> My breath catches in my throat.

My eyes strain at the small screen, trying to divine
Whether she is OK
Whether she will be OK
Whether *we* will ever be OK without him, without Owen.

This girl, now a woman, once grew inside me.
A marvel and the most precious gift of a child.
Now she is someone separate.
Someone different in ways I don't completely understand,
 yet familiar and lovable and messy in ways that secretly delight me.
The chaos of the last few seasons of trauma
And loss
And grief
Bleeds into the scene and leads my heart to the edge.
Then she leans close to the camera
And says, my freckles are back.

Her smile is beautiful
Revealing the tooth shortened after she chipped it in fifth grade.
She is all there and so are her freckles.
I see them as evidence of healing
Proof that she has been outside
Laughing in the sunshine.
A new constellation rising
Connecting the girl of the past
With the woman she is becoming
With the return of her freckles.

Footloose and Hamilton: Grief Musicals

June 2024

Do you think it's appropriate to describe a dad grieving the death of his daughter as someone who is "down on his luck?" I think luck has nothing to do with child loss, yet that is how Fox Searchlight Pictures describes the coach in its 2023 movie *Next Goal Wins*. Dustin and I streamed this movie one night after it was suggested to us on Hulu. We enjoyed the series *Ted Lasso* (Apple TV) and *Welcome to Wrexham* (Hulu) so we thought another soccer show—this one based on true events—would be fun.

We were astonishingly ambushed when it was revealed (spoiler alert!) that the out-of-work coach hired to help turn the team around is actually a dad grieving the death of his college-aged, soccer-playing daughter in a car accident and the subsequent collapse of his marriage! We were drawn in by this part of the story, of course, our hearts cracking along their familiar fault lines. For a movie using the dad's loss as a hook for viewers, however, it lost our respect when out of nowhere, a new recruit for the soccer team is run over by a bus in a cartoon-style killing, which is supposed to be funny. What?!? It's all wrong and made me so very mad, but I made myself watch the whole thing. It brought to mind other movies we have watched in which we are surprised by grief or child loss, and why isn't that mentioned when these films are tagged with other warning labels?

Like many parents, we enjoyed introducing our kids to movies from our youth. It turns out that some of those we remember liking as kids weren't very kid-friendly (intensely scary characters, underage drinking with alcoholic adults, etc.) and, oops, we inadvertently showed them to our kids at inappropriate ages. Does this sound familiar? I know now—too late!—that there are in-depth warnings online about movies to help parents make informed decisions about what is appropriate for their kids to watch. (Commonsensemedia.org is one.) So, terrific, there are now warnings about violence, nudity, explicit language, or depictions of substance abuse—but have you ever seen a movie label warning you about a shocking and traumatic loss of a child? Or that characters in the movie might act like zombies because they are reeling from grief?

Maybe movies should come with a "grief advisory." Several times since losing Owen, I have been blindsided by cinematic portrayals of sudden child loss or grieving parents. Grief is a ubiquitous human experience, so it shouldn't be surprising that it's part of a character's backstory, but often flashy plot elements eclipse the internal struggle and pain of grief, so it isn't remembered or remarked upon in movie reviews.

Now that child loss is a defining element in my own story, I am much more attuned to the way this is portrayed in the movies. I can't see past it anymore. I'm not easily distracted by a big musical number or a feel-good finale. A few times I haven't been able to finish watching movies that I know I enjoyed in the time before we lost Owen. Other times I force myself to watch all the way through, in case some special secret to coping is revealed. For me, grieving parents stand out as if highlighted in every scene they are in—even if they aren't doing anything—sometimes especially when they seem incapable of doing anything.

Do you remember *Footloose* from 1984 with Kevin Bacon and Lori Singer? There was a remake in 2011 that I didn't see, but Dustin and I remembered the fun music and dancing from the original movie and the basic premise of teens not being allowed to do the (risky) teenage things they wanted to do because a preacher was too uptight. In the fall of 2020 as we sheltered in place and tried to keep everyone safe from Covid, still struggling as we were with the loss of Owen, I thought this could be a fun movie to watch with Frances.

What had **not** been something I remembered—nor had we been warned about as we started watching the film—was **why** the preacher dad in the PG-rated movie was so uptight: his son died in a car accident after a night of teenage drinking and dancing. Seeing this film as a grieving parent, I found myself more understanding of the dad's rigid strictness about dancing. He was just trying to keep everyone else from experiencing the kind of loss he had felt and was attempting to regain control of a world which had greatly spun out of his control. I sat on the couch with tears running down my face as this powerful, but overlooked, plot line emerged. Of course this dad would do anything he could—even imposing stern restrictions—to keep his other child safe!

After the dad's motives were exposed, I tried to watch the *mom* closely to see how a fictional mother survives child loss without smothering her other children or taking her own life. I came away thinking there wasn't enough of her in the movie—but (gulp!) maybe there wasn't much of her left after she lost her firstborn child in a tragic accident. She does try to influence her husband, telling him he can't be everyone's father and that he isn't being much of a father even to his own daughter. I pondered how she got to that place of grace and wisdom. How was she able to swallow the fear of losing another child, a fear that still chokes me and catches in my throat?

The movie didn't show us that (too bad—I could always use more grief role models), and we didn't discuss it as a family afterward, but I thought there might have been some takeaways for each of us. Maybe having Frances watch it showed her a little about how hard the loss of a child is on a parent. Or maybe she was busy observing the daughter in the movie, to learn how *she* was able to process the loss of her older brother and still want to fall in love and dance?

It's not just old movies that ambush me. Sometimes it's newer movies or shows that I just forgot had references to child loss—because I saw them first in the "before times." Before losing Owen. For example, Dustin, Frances and I saw *Hamilton* on stage in Portland when the production first toured here in March of 2018. I was obsessed with Lin-Manuel Miranda's soundtrack and studied the lyrics before we went to see the show, wanting not to miss anything. The energy in the theater was electric, and the talented actors blew us away with their singing and dancing. We left the theater in high spirits, bouncing to the rhythms of the catchy songs.

In 2020, we watched the filmed version of *Hamilton* on Disney+, remembering we had loved it when we saw it live, and anticipating a lively distraction for our heavy hearts. This movie version of the musical is rated PG-13, but there was no warning that this might be difficult for anyone who has lost an adult child in a traumatic way. Somehow I had forgotten about the part where Alexander's nineteen-year-old son is (another spoiler alert!) killed in a duel.

The song "It's Quiet Uptown" flattened me; it really captured the experiences of both Hamilton and his wife as they coped with the death of their son, alone and together. Lin-Manuel Miranda's poignant lyrics conveyed the loneliness and emptiness they felt moving through regular routines after their loss, and the surprising ways their lives had changed. They *like* the quiet now, and Hamilton actually prays in church. "They are going through the unimaginable," the song tells us. Though lyrically softer and slower paced than much of the music in the show, this song for me remains one of the musical's most powerful songs. At the end of the movie, I was crying on the couch, curled up next to Dustin, my heart breaking again for the loss of our young son.

Maybe it's good that we aren't warned about these depictions of grieving parents. The death of a child at any age is a traumatic shock to any parent. The jarring distress I experience when I discover the loss a character has experienced seems fitting. This is how it was sprung on us, and we too have to learn to live with the unimaginable.

Sadly Beautiful

June 2024

I just returned home from traveling to the funeral for my aunt Cathy, my mom's sister-in-law, who passed away from pancreatic cancer in Muhlenberg County, Kentucky (the setting for "Paradise," a favorite song of Owen's). This 67-year-old vibrant, always smiling, light of a person was cold and shrunken in the open casket at the front of the little Catholic church. (My second open casket situation!) Her waxy lips were posed in a soft smirk, not the usual toothy grin I'd seen in the hundreds of photos my mom and I had been poring over with my uncle the night before the service. She looked terrible and also strikingly beautiful.

Especially in America—where we idolize straight, white teeth—it seems that we feel we need to smile big to show our beauty to others. But maybe those wide, cheesy smiles are actually hiding our true, inner beauty: beauty that comes from experiencing grief and sadness and still finding a way to carry on. Maybe we don't always have to smile.

In this humble church, pink roses from some of the largest arrangements I'd ever seen surrounded a statue of the Virgin Mary and dripped over the communion rail. There weren't many people there for the pre-Mass viewing, but as more people came in out of the rain (we had awoken to a frighteningly loud clap of thunder at six that morning) and filled up the church, the air closed in around me. I was relieved when they closed the casket and covered it with a white cloth for the Mass. I imagined Aunt

Cathy also being able to relax now that she wasn't "on stage" for everyone to see; she had been a generous "hostess with the mostest," even through challenging parts of her cancer fight, and she would no longer have to smile if she wasn't feeling like smiling.

Outside the church, as we gathered for the caravan to the cemetery, I hugged my aunt's son, my cousin Charlie, who I hadn't seen since we were teenagers. Now in his early 50s like me, he looked much, much older. (I had seen him sitting next to my uncle, his stepdad, at the church and wondered who he was!) Weathering the stress of his mom's illness had weathered his soul.

The next moment I was introduced to Kent, Charlie's husband, who drew in an exaggerated breath of surprise and exclaimed, "You are stunning. Just gorgeous! God, look at you!" I tried to shush him (we were heading to the cemetery!) and shrug off his compliment, making sure to credit my mom standing nearby for my good genes. But Kent doubled down and said, "Oh, your mom has always been gorgeous—but you! Stunning!" I didn't get to talk to him at the reception because whenever he would see me he would wave his hand across his face and blurt out, "I can't look at you! You are too gorgeous! I can't stand it."

The first time I remember someone other than my parents telling me I looked beautiful, I was crying. I was in Mexico on my eighth grade Spanish Club trip, and our last night in Puerto Vallarta was being cut short. I don't remember all the details, but for some reason, the teacher was not going to allow my friend and me to walk on the beach at night with the local boys we had met that afternoon. I was devastated. (Looking back as an adult, I'm sure that the teacher had several very good reasons to keep us in the hotel that night! Thank you, Ms. Shirley, for keeping us safe!) We were able to meet up with the boys briefly in the lobby to say goodbye, and that's where one of them, Eric, told me, "You look beautiful when you cry."

Maybe that boy was onto something. After I met Dustin at the University of Notre Dame ("ND" to many of us alums) in 1988, he mentioned three things about me to his mom: my name was Mary (a very common name at ND!); I was from Oregon (surprising and cool, as he was from Washington state); and there was something sad about me. My parents had just separated the summer before I left for college, and I had flown to the Midwest by myself. I was feeling a little abandoned and alone on that first day of freshman orientation, as almost everyone else had their parents and siblings helping them schlep their stuff across campus. Even in all my excitement to be starting college at my first choice, I *was* sad, and Dustin saw that as something attractive and interesting about me. Was sadness a kind of beauty?

In our search for clues when Owen went missing, we looked at the songs he was listening to the night he walked off campus. "Surrender" by Cheap Trick and "Sadly Beautiful" by the Replacements were some of the last songs he played. "Sadly Beautiful" is a song I have always liked—I didn't know Owen liked it, too. Had he met someone sadly beautiful at UP? Was HE feeling sad? Or was he just enjoying listening to music on a walk to unwind before midterms?

I do appreciate when those I love can see my sadness and still see beauty. I've been in a book club with the same women for 25 years. When we were mothers of younger kids, this was often one of my only social evenings. I would usually primp a little before our monthly gatherings, wearing a new pair of earrings, my cutest shoes, and most flattering outfit. We have gone through a lot of different phases in that group and seen each other through difficult times. This group of women were critical support for me and my family when Owen was missing and through those early months of grieving. Going through this loss with these women brought us closer, but it sometimes also left me feeling farther apart. As our meetups began to return to their old rhythm after the disruption of Owen's loss and the pandemic, normal chitchat was hard for me to stomach. I needed these women in my life and so I didn't want to stay home, but I also found it very hard to listen to my friends talking about their kids going back to school, struggling with normal teenage problems, getting summer jobs, and breaking up with (or getting together with) boyfriends or girlfriends.

At one book club evening in the summer of 2023, I tried to comment a little and nod along, offering knowing smiles when my friends shared their current struggles (we really *do* talk about books at book club, but that part took a little longer to be reestablished after the pandemic). I was in my friend Tami's beautiful backyard, with candles on the patio table shining their soft, flattering light on the faces of some of my favorite people in the world, but I felt like I was on an island of grief by myself. My friends were an arm's length away, but an ocean apart from where I was sitting with my feelings of loss and sadness. I took my hair out of the weird twist I had put it in to keep it dry in the post-tennis shower I took before book club. It had suddenly felt too tight, and I wanted to shake up my focus and bring myself back into the circle of friendship, so I shook my hair loose and settled more comfortably in my chair. Tami noticed and saw me.

The next day, Tami texted me to check in and see how I was. She could tell that I wasn't feeling super into the group the night before, that something was bothering me. She wrote, "I hope you felt okay at book club last night. When you put your hair down I was like 'Wow she is beautiful' so thought I'd at least share that."

She continued, "I see you in your being and the depth of emotional work you've had to do. That's what I saw in your beauty last night but didn't get to say."

Tami saw my grief that night at book club. It made me feel better and OK with being invisible in other places. It made me wonder whether we didn't see enough of Owen, and this is one of the reasons I am always looking for "More Owen!" It makes me want to find the sad beauty we all carry.

Owen Klinger? He's My Guy!

June 2024

They're remodeling my husband's office, and for a few weeks his law firm will be operating out of recently vacated space one floor below. Knowing we're always willing to pitch in, Dustin volunteered me and Frances to help move some boxes and artwork.

Dustin has worked at this law firm for a while now—about nine years—and I know most of his office staff pretty well. They were with us through the ordeal of searching for Owen and mourned his loss with us. I don't see them often, but I feel comfortable going in there because I know I won't have to answer any of those terrifying "How many kids do you have?" or "How old are your kids now?" questions. My friend Lisa from my cooking group had recently joined the firm and I was excited to see her in her new role. Frances was looking forward to seeing the people she worked with last summer again and catching up with Gunnar, Lisa's son, who was also coming to help with the move.

There was another young man helping that we didn't know. As we hugged Gunnar hello, he introduced us to Sam, who we learned had graduated from Grant High School, like Gabe and Owen. Dustin said he remembered Sam from football, and I asked what year he graduated. Sam told us it was 2019; surprised, I exclaimed, "Oh, that was Owen's class. Did you know Owen?"

"Owen Klinger? He's my guy!" Sam replied. He said it in such a cheerful, happy way, I got the immediate impression he did *not* know Owen was dead. I was afraid to break the spell of what felt like an alternate universe and avoided making eye contact with Dustin or Frances. It felt exciting and daring to imagine Owen as alive. I don't remember if we said we were Owen's parents, but I don't think we did. I know Frances didn't say Owen was her brother. Gunnar had introduced us with only our first names. But there we were, all making a lovely connection through knowing and appreciating Owen.

And then we were swept into our work packing up boxes, taking down artwork, and relocating a few tables and chairs. Time passed quickly, and since we were all moving around in different areas between the two floors, we didn't have any more time to talk. The whole time I was working, though, I kept thinking about Sam's face lighting up as he said Owen's name—and how it sounded like he used the present tense: "He IS my guy" not "He WAS my guy." I thought of Sam as a time traveler from a different, happier era when our family was whole. I wanted to be like Sam and exist in a time when Owen was still vibrantly alive, too.

And for a little while, I let myself pretend. Moving stuff like we were doing was exactly the kind of project Owen would have jumped into, making it fun and working harder than all of us. He would have been whistling the whole time, flexing his muscles by lifting the heaviest stuff, and using his keen spatial awareness to fit more boxes onto every cartload.

The setting aided in my time-travel fantasy because the office space Dustin's firm was borrowing had been the home of his previous law firm! We were moving all of his current files and photos down to areas where he'd spent many hours working as a new lawyer, when all three of our kids were curious and excited visitors to Dad's first downtown office in the Big Pink. These were windows I hadn't looked out of as a grieving mom; could I see the surrounding world as I used to, before I lost my son?

I sat alone for a minute in Dustin's "new old office," looking out at a view of Northwest Portland and the Willamette River. In the distance was the Bluff, with the University of Portland, Owen's college. I also spied the St. Johns Bridge, its distinctive bright green color a stark contrast to the dark forest beyond. Could I gaze at that part of the city where we searched for Owen, punctuated by the river—and especially that bridge—without the stabbing pain of terror and loss? No, I couldn't fool myself, and the happy bubble of illusion popped. I went back to moving boxes.

When we were done, Frances and I walked out to my car together. My heart leapt when I saw our old minivan parked on the same floor of the garage—maybe I really had traveled back somehow to the "before" times, and Owen was still here! Then I remembered that Gunnar drives my van now—we sold it to his mom last year. I noticed that Grant Lacrosse and OSU stickers still adorn the back window, but Gunnar has added a few, and Frances pointed these out right away, laughing at his "I suck at fly fishing" bumper sticker. I shook my head and smiled at the power of my imagination. I was glad to see Gunnar had kept the Grant stickers as a tribute to Owen, even though he'd gone to a different high school.

As we drove home over the Burnside Bridge that spans the Willamette River a few miles upstream from where Owen's body was found, I asked Frances if she'd caught what Sam had said about Owen. It turns out she had the same reaction I did: that Owen seemed alive for Sam! She was glad I didn't feel it was necessary to tell Sam that Owen had passed away—she was definitely not going to bring it up. We agreed it was actually weirdly nice to meet someone who lives in a world where Owen still exists, continuing to live his best life being funny, cool, and kind. I didn't tell her about how I tried to let myself really imagine a universe that still had Owen physically with us.

I spend a lot of time trying to feel a connection with Owen's spirit. Sometimes he just seems really gone and not here at all. Other times, in the middle of the night, or when I have been meditating quietly, I can close my eyes and see moving bands and waves of light (like aurora borealis) that I feel are Owen's love and spirit right in front of me and all around me. The heart-shaped rocks I find everywhere seem like signs from Owen, and they bring Owen closer to me. And yet I ache for more. I would love to be able to easily tap into the joy Owen brought to my life—to all of our lives—like Sam did, breezily proclaiming, "Owen Klinger? He's my guy!"

Flow

June 2024

Owen's flow by Sylvia Jiminez

Lacrosse stick in your hands
You run effortlessly down the field
With fluid strides and
Well-timed changes of direction
A master class of control

Scooping up a dropped ball
Without missing a beat

Always in the flow
And bringing the flow
With your hair flying behind you

I see you flowing off the field too
Your easy way with friends
Your quick wit
And infectious delight

Who knocked your stick away?
What made you lose a step and falter?
How did you get here?
Your hair floating in the water
Instead of flowing behind you

I see you now
In the currents of the river
And in the wind moving through tall trees
In the slow way the earth shifts under the night sky
Forever in the flow now
And flowing through me.

The Photographers

June 2024

I didn't think about the photographers before. Does anyone think about them? The ones whose images of our family and friends we rely on to remind us of times enjoyed together and unique moments we will never experience again?

I didn't think about the photographers when Owen was still here with us, full of life, making memories and being captured in family snapshots almost every day. We had reams of photos of him chasing his dreams, teasing his sister, and laughing with his brother—a gallery of images I was sure would continue to grow in the days and decades to come.

The photographers just blended into the background of our busy family days. They scuttled up and down the sidelines of basketball, soccer, and football games; they sweated at sunny lacrosse tournaments and steamy indoor water polo matches. They set up team photo shoots for the sports programs, took special shots of seniors on each team, and advertised their businesses in the school yearbook. I assumed there would always be more of them in our lives—the photographers *and* the images they captured of Owen. I took their presence for granted until Owen was gone, and I realized that there were going to be empty pages in our family scrapbooks and huge Owen-shaped holes in our hearts. It was then that I really saw the photographers and what they had been doing the entire time.

Have you ever tried to hold your hands steady and take an action shot in a crowded school gymnasium with crummy fluorescent lighting? Or on the sidelines of a lacrosse field in a freezing downpour? Dustin and I always tried during our kids' sporting events, in order to mark the occasion and remember the jump balls or the free throws, but our efforts consistently failed. The poor lighting, the quick-moving kids, and our own modest photography skills combined to produce dismal, dark, blurry photos. And yet because that's all we had, these fill many pages of the early years of our family scrapbooks. Eventually we learned to take our pics when the kids were at rest after the game or on the sidelines during a break in the action.

I have some shots of Owen from the sidelines of his lacrosse games. The action shots still eluded me, but I captured a sweaty and exhausted Owen napping on a blanket between games at a tournament in central Oregon, and a jubilant and sweaty Owen wrapping his arms around his teammates after an exciting win.

We have some great action shots of Owen playing youth soccer and basketball from my mom's ex-boyfriend, Ron Cooper. He also provided us with priceless images of Owen's first few years of football, when the shoulder pads dwarfed his small physique and his passion for the game was unstoppable. These are treasured photos. My mom and Ron separated when Owen was partway through high school, so we didn't have the benefit of his expertise when Owen was thriving at lacrosse and challenging himself with water polo. (Nor, needless to say, shots of him graduating and going off to college.)

When we lost Owen, I started scouring our family albums and digital photo libraries to soak in all that he had done, who he had been, who we were with him, and to get clues about who we might become—who we might still be—without him.

Oh, I saw thousands of photos, which was great and wonderful and sad and terrible. Worse, I also found some large gaps, which was heart-wrenching and frustrating. We had a family phone and PC crash in 2014 before cloud back-ups were the norm and when we were novices at photo stream sharing with our Apple iPhones. So, sadly, the Klinger family record of 2014 lacks depth and context. There are just a handful of random photos from a few events and occasions over that year. I thought I had cried all my tears out when we lost Owen, but I cried again over those lost photos. (Who am I kidding? I am still crying about Owen five years after he died. My tears keep replenishing—like a basket of tortilla chips at a Mexican restaurant.)

#20 in 2016 photo by John Davenport

There were other gaps I noticed, too: action shots of Owen in his prime that we had been too inept to capture ourselves. (Or that I had missed when I was busy driving another kid to another game or practice across town. It seems Dustin and I were always missing one child's shining moment because of the schedule of our other two kids.) When I pulled photos and certificates of achievement together for the tri-fold at Owen's graduation party just a few months before he went missing, I found some small posed football team shots and individual "mug" shots in the seasonal high school sports programs. I cut out the little pictures and included them on the display which I stashed away next to my bed after the party (it stayed there for years after we lost Owen—how was I going to be able to take that down?). When I was searching for more Owen, specifically more *photos* of Owen, I thought I should look to see if I could get prints of those photos. This led me to the websites of two talented photographers who had been hiding in plain sight! John Davenport and Jeff Day had been quietly documenting the agony and the ecstasy of Grant High School sports competitions during my kids' time there. They had captured several images of Owen, casually throwing his heart (and mine) around on all the sports fields he played on.

Owen chasing the quarterback by John Davenport

I was able to see many collections of images these photographers had shared online. There were photos of Owen playing lacrosse, standing on the sidelines next to Gabe at football, making tackles, looking scrawny, looking tough, running down the field in lacrosse WITH THE BALL! (a rare thing), knocking an opponent aside with his stick, and jumping out of the water to block a shot on goal at water polo. There was More Owen in every folder I clicked on.

One of the photographers had even taken shots at the Japanese language immersion program graduation ceremony, so there were pics of Owen, all spiffed up, with his best friends since kindergarten, proudly accepting a special certificate and the seal of biliteracy he achieved after thirteen years of studying Japanese. My heart melted. I immediately ordered prints and digital downloads of every shot I could find of Owen. And then I wrote messages of heartfelt thanks to each of the photographers. My notes to them follow.

#20 with the ball by John Davenport

John, I just want to say thank you for taking all these beautiful photos of precious young athletes putting their hearts into the game and their teams. Our son recently passed away, and it has been amazing to discover him again in your water polo, lacrosse, and football galleries and archives. You do a special job for our community. Thank you so very much.

Hi Jeff, I just want to send you a thank you for these beautiful photos of Grant HS athletes playing with their hearts on the line for their school and their teams. Our son, Owen Klinger, GHS '19, recently passed away, and it has been so amazing to see him in these archived photo galleries. I also discovered some previously unseen photos of our older son, Gabe '17. You make a special contribution to the community by documenting these young people. Please keep it up and know how much you are appreciated.

John wrote back, "As a photographer, I never conceived that my work would be viewed in the context that you are now...I am so extremely grateful that my work may have brought some small bit of peace." He has stayed connected with our family and continues to share his time and talent with us, taking photos every year at our annual Owen Klinger Memorial Game, where Owen's former lacrosse teammates reunite to play current Grant High School lacrosse players in a friendly scrimmage where everyone wears #20, Owen's last jersey number.

Everyone wears #20 at the Owen Klinger Memorial Game (OKMG) in 2023 John Davenport

Jeff actually called me on the phone at a time when not many people were calling, not knowing what to say to a freshly grieving mom and not wanting to say the wrong thing. He was very emotional in telling me that he had recently been feeling particularly *unappreciated* and questioning why he was even doing this work since no one seemed to care. My message to him came at a vital time and helped him renew his faith in his work and how important it was to the community. He sent my family a beautiful Thanksgiving floral centerpiece to express his condolences and his thanks for my thanks.

Just about everyone can take their own videos and photos with their phones, and this is great. But at games, recitals, and dance performances now, I see an audience full of parents holding up said phones, watching their kids perform on the tiny screen instead of the larger stage (or field or swimming pool). I have been there too, but I also really like knowing that Jeff and John—and others in different communities—are there in the wings documenting our kids not only to fill the gaps in our shared history, but so we can be present and watch their hearts soar. I am so very grateful for the photographers.

Hanging Out in His Inbox

June 2024

We never found Owen's phone. As I've said before, he had a Google Pixel phone, not an iPhone, so we couldn't trace it through the "Find My iPhone" feature, and he had his location tracking turned off, as was his habit to save battery life and because he and his brother Gabe had talked at length about the data phones could track and sell without your knowledge. Because Owen's phone was part of our family plan, Dustin and I were able to see a list of the apps he had downloaded on his phone, recent outgoing and incoming calls, some of the text message numbers (though none of the content of these messages), and sometimes when there had been group messages (again no details about these group messages).

We didn't know—and still don't know—what happened to Owen. If he had taken his own life or if he had walked away to go live somewhere else; if someone he met had forced him to go somewhere or do something dangerous; or if he was just out for a walk and a smoke and had an accident.

We looked everywhere for clues. When Owen left his dorm room on that Sunday evening in October, his laptop was powered up and unlocked on his desk. His roommates peeked in it the next morning and saw that his grades had been good. (He wasn't flunking out of college!) When Dustin and I went to the dorm, we looked at what Owen had been browsing on Amazon (his last purchase was a blue Carhartt hoodie sweatshirt). We saw that he had been streaming episodes of *Suits* and movies including

Good Will Hunting and *Into the Wild*. His YouTube channel subscriptions covered a wide range of interests and included videos of train hopping. We gave all this information to the police. This briefly led the police to think that Owen had hopped a train to Alaska; I wish that was where Owen had gone, but he hadn't actually watched any of the train-hopping videos. We were able to look at all of his emails, but none of them ultimately held any clues about the mystery of his disappearance.

I spent a lot of time then combing through his Gmail account—and even more after Owen's body was recovered from the river and we realized he wasn't coming home, that no one was going to be able to tell us what happened to him. Years later, I still log in every few months to poke around, clean out spam, and look for a little More Owen. The emails haven't given me any insight into what compelled Owen to leave his dorm room that October evening, but they show me that I really did know a lot about him and what he was interested in. They also reveal how he was starting to find his own path into the world through work and college.

Owen loved playing online computer games with his friends in high school. Almost every night after he got home from his sports practice and did his homework (or skipped his homework!), he would be down in the basement chatting with his friends on Discord while they played games together on Steam. (Gabe did a lot of this, too.) From that time until now, Owen's email account has received thousands of messages from Steam letting him know when games on his wish list were on sale. I never thought I would be longing for Owen to have more time to play computer games, but when I see these messages and photos like this one, that is indeed on *my* wish list. I've kept those emails.

In the summer of 2019, Owen and Dustin enjoyed watching the *Longmire* series on Netflix together. It was about a Wyoming sheriff who drove an old Ford Bronco. After watching that show, Owen set up an email alert for used Ford Broncos on Craigslist. This was something the police thought was suspicious; they briefly moved away from their conviction that it was suicide to entertain the idea that Owen had bought a Bronco and driven away somewhere. I wish to God that's what happened: that he was still alive somewhere, having driven off into the night in the used car of his dreams to have an adventure from which he would eventually return to us. Now that's just something else Owen didn't get to do. Nevertheless, I love looking through the listings of vintage Broncos in his inbox knowing that Owen let himself dream about owning one someday. His actual online purchases were more modest that summer: Longmire novel *As the Crow Flies* by Craig Johnson and a Weezer album.

There are many references to Weezer in Owen's inbox, as it was one of his favorite bands. I saw he purchased a few of their albums from Barnes & Noble, which surprised me. Owen usually bought music from Music

Millennium, an amazing independent record store just down the street from our house, but I think he had received a B&N gift card as a graduation gift and maybe he had more than enough books already! Owen got to see Weezer live with his two best friends when they were touring the Pacific Northwest in 2018 with the Pixies, another band Owen followed. There were emails in October of 2019 announcing the Weezer 2020 summer tour (which ended up being thwarted by the Covid-19 pandemic). I like to think Owen and his friends would have gone to another Weezer show together and that he would have had the time of his life. Owen had their poster hanging in his dorm room. It's one of the few things of his that Gabe expressed interest in keeping, but it's still just rolling around in the closet of the boys' old bedroom upstairs. Maybe someday, when these reminders of Owen might not be so painful, Gabe will hang it in his apartment. I can't bring myself to unsubscribe Owen from Weezer's email list, so I keep checking in on what they are up to. When I saw an email announcing the release of an album in 2021 called *OK Human*, I got goosebumps. Anytime I see "O" followed by "K" I think "Owen Klinger" (OK!), and what a great human being he was!

Owen had also subscribed to emails from country-folk musician John Prine and his record label, Oh Boy Records. We knew that Owen liked "Paradise," set in Muhlenberg County, Kentucky, and after we lost Owen, his UP workshop leader in the school of business, Kaylee, told me he claimed this song as his *favorite* in an icebreaker activity. Our whole family knew the song because Dustin's dad had written a parody of it, about Panther Creek's Skamania County, and because we had all actually visited my uncle and aunt's lake house in Muhlenberg County! What I didn't know was that Owen had listened to other songs from John Prine, who wrote many poignant and humorous songs about everyday Americans, and that he followed that singer's news. Owen was an old soul. On October 7, 2020—a year after Owen disappeared—an email came in celebrating and honoring John Prine on what would have been his 74th birthday. (The singer had passed away from Covid complications in April of 2020.) I was extra emotional that October day: missing Owen on the anniversary of his disappearance, still searching for answers as to what had happened, and struggling to figure out what we were supposed to do without him, so I opened the email and listened to a song called "I Remember Everything." I cried through the entire song and wondered, "Do I remember everything? Can I keep remembering everything about Owen?" That might not be possible, but Owen's email can continue to connect me to new things in the world and open me up to different ways of knowing my son.

Emails about the job interviews he had for the position he landed for the summer of 2019 setting up rentals for Peter Corvallis Productions reminded me how Owen hustled to score an interview for this job at a school career fair during his senior year of high school. After Owen's death, his friends told us Owen thought it was a particularly good fit because some of the other guys he worked with that summer also liked to smoke weed—great! But still, it was a real job that he got without parental assistance, and I know he was proud of every long shift and paycheck. He was even kind of excited about filing taxes for the first time.

I reached out to his boss a few months after Owen was gone to ask if I could meet her and see where Owen had spent so much of his last summer. When I visited the warehouse, everyone I met had kind things to say about Owen and what a hard worker he was. The boss told me a story about how Owen had actually *called* a client who was a little particular about things and arranged for his crew to do their delivery and set up a little earlier than they had planned because they were surprisingly ahead of schedule. She was so impressed that a young person would take such initiative—using the phone!—and how Owen handled the prickly client with confidence and respect. Her words brought forth a torrent of fresh tears; I loved hearing this story, but I felt the pain of losing him surge through me anew.

In his Gmail history, there is a sprinkling of emails about his lacrosse refereeing gigs at youth tournaments around our area. This was sporadic employment, and the communication about each assignment was often sketchy on details. "LAX bros," a nickname for the young coaches who organize these youth leagues and events, are enthusiastic about their sport, but they are not universally gifted organizers. Owen was flexible and pretty responsive in these instances. He loved making money doing something fun and enjoyed the free food that often accompanied these paid gigs. I like seeing evidence that he thrived in all kinds of work environments, but it cultivates a sadness that his productive presence is forever gone, leaving a lot of work undone. I guess there is the potential for us all to step up, contribute, and work hard ourselves, because he can't work anywhere ever again, but sometimes it's very difficult to motivate myself without his gregarious example.

Owen didn't send me many emails, but the summer before he left for college, we were communicating daily about all of the things he would need to pack for life on campus. My younger brother's wife worked for Yeti outdoor goods in Austin, Texas, and our family had received many Yeti products as gifts over the years. In the summer of 2019, Yeti released a new color: Peak Purple. Owen was going to UP that fall, and the school color is purple. Perfect! He emailed me a gift request: "Birthday? It's ok if you already got me other stuff. I like the water bottle with the screw on top with the handle." We got it for him, of course, monogrammed with his "O.K." He had this water bottle with him the night he left the dorm for the last time. We still haven't found it.

A reminder from Yeti came to his email on 10/3/2019, just a few days before he went missing, that he shouldn't forget about the items in his shopping cart as they were selling fast! He was thinking about buying 10-ounce stackable cups. I wish he had been able to buy them, even if they were just for him to take down to the river for a campfire/drinking party. He was loyal to his family and proud of his aunt's affiliation with a quality product.

During Owen's high school senior year, his inbox was flooded with emails from peppy college admissions officers at schools Owen was interested in. Montana State University, University of Portland, University of Idaho, Tulane University, and Oregon State University are the colleges he applied to, but there were also messages from the University of Kentucky, Penn State, Creighton, the University of Notre Dame, Columbia, Arizona State, University of Oregon, University of Montana, Washington State, Western Washington, Georgetown, University of San Diego, and the University of Vermont. Many of these were schools he didn't seriously consider, but some were schools he had toured and decided not to apply to.

Owen and I took a road trip with Frances in the summer of 2018 to visit WSU, MSU, U of I, and University of Montana Western. Montana State was the only survivor of that tour, as it turned out the small rural towns didn't appeal to Owen. The visit to Western was especially insightful: Owen was one of only a few kids touring the school that week, and we had a personal tour with a girl from Dillon, Montana, who was super stoked about the new frozen yogurt machine and the indoor rodeo arena. Even though he apparently liked John Prine's songs about the simple things in life, Owen did not apply to a school where he would live amongst them.

I recently did a deep dive in this mess of school messages because Dustin and I couldn't remember what had happened with Owen's Tulane application. Tulane is where my dad went for medical school, so Owen was curious about it and had applied in November of his senior year. The following March, there is a message directing him to log into his "Green Wave portal" account to learn about the decision on his application. Of course I didn't know Owen's portal password, but with access to his email account I was able to reset the password and log in to see that his application…was not accepted. I don't even remember him announcing this to us—or us asking about it. Dustin remembered thinking Owen had been waitlisted. I wonder if Owen was really disappointed about this, or if it wasn't a big deal. He had never toured the school, but in a strange twist he did get to take that trip with his grandma to visit its home base of New Orleans right after high school graduation. (I mean literally *right* after—we took him from the all-night graduation party to the airport to fly off with his Nona!) I think he liked his choice of UP, but if he hadn't liked it, his inbox still continues to receive offers from schools he could have transferred to every month.

I laughed out loud when I saw that Owen was getting emails about lawn care from the Scotts lawn care company! He even had downloaded their app at one point! This is solid proof of his passion for yard work. Mowing the lawn myself after his death—or seeing our neighbors hire others to do this work—has been agonizing. When I first went into the garage to get out our mower in the spring of 2020, I saw how carefully Owen had put it away after the last time he took care of our lawn, and I didn't want to touch it. I miss seeing him carefully edging at the end of the block or sweeping up the last loose clippings in the neighbor's driveway. At least I have the ongoing advice from Scotts to help me keep my lawn in good shape every summer in Owen's honor!

I also saw invitations for Owen to participate in ivy removal events with Portland Parks and Recreation. His lacrosse team did this one spring as a pre-season team building activity, and I bet that Owen was in his element.

He loved working hard like that. And a chance to do it with all of his friends would have been extra special for him. Perhaps his excitement over how fulfilling that activity was explains why he forgot to call or text me to tell me he was getting a ride home with the Morales family! I drove all the way out to the forested park on the west side of Portland where they had been working to pick him up, only to see that everyone was already gone.

Owen's lawnmower, power cord, and gloves after his last use in 2019

Now, at home without Owen for real, I wonder: should I unsubscribe from messages like this since they bring up these memories? Or should I keep looking at them BECAUSE they bring up these memories and More Owen?

Owen also had a few other Gmail addresses that I originally didn't know about. Google sends occasional reminders that these inactive accounts are linked to Owen's main account. One of these accounts I looked at once and saw a few messages from pornographic websites. I closed that window. No need to go there, I thought—though I would like to be able to tell the police about this now. They thought it was weird that Owen didn't have any porn on his computer, and they speculated briefly that he was maybe conflicted about his sexuality and didn't want to face telling us he was gay. After the tiny glance at this stuff that I can't unsee, I can tell you it doesn't look like Owen was gay, but thanks for jumping to conclusions, Portland Police! What else have you got?

For now, I will keep logging into Owen's main inbox. I hope he doesn't mind. I hope that maybe he might at least like that I'm keeping it active for him, taking in all the newsy tidbits about Weezer, John Prine, Scotts, and ivy removal parties (but not the porn, sorry). Maybe I'll find more courage to delve into the other addresses before my access to them evaporates. It's comforting that this collection of messages and junk mail reveals more about his typical young adult male interests and brings funny memories of Owen's personality to the surface, but it's also complicated when something unexpected pops up.

How can I ever abandon this archive of Owen's interests and portal to the world as Owen was experiencing it: as a young man just starting to explore everything around him, on his own? For now I'm still using his laptop, so it's easy to keep it in the background; we'll see what happens when I switch computers and am no longer using the one that has all his passwords memorized. For now, I strive to "remember everything" about Owen, and this is another way to do that.

It's Good to See You

July 2024

When we were still searching for Owen in the fall of 2019, Dustin and I held a press conference in our living room. Reporters from several local TV stations set up cameras next to my grand piano and we sat in chairs in front of our fireplace. We were average people who had never done anything like this before—but who desperately needed information, and quickly—doing our best to update everyone on the search efforts and answer questions from the media.

One of the sound techs clipped a microphone on my sweater and ran the wire down my back to a power pack in my jeans pocket. It felt awkward to have that cable inside my shirt, and the TV people saw me fiddling with it and shifting around in my seat.

Someone kindly asked, "Are you comfortable?" I looked up from where I was fussing, saw the surreal semi-famous faces of local news reporters in my living room and said, "I don't think I will ever be comfortable again." That honest reply, more than my answers to their questions during the press conference, seemed to have a big impact on the people in the room. One person shuffling through papers looked up at me with surprise, and a few other folks tilted their heads with concern. Maybe they were expecting me to say "It's OK. I'm fine." Well, I wasn't fine. I'm still not fine. This unimaginable experience has made me see that in order to better connect, or to help others who are not fine, we need to ask better questions.

Though we reflexively ask each other, "How are you?" most of the time we really don't want to hear how someone is doing on a deeper level—and likewise we might not be in a place to tell them how we are doing on that level. Losing Owen helped me realize this—and to recognize how our standard greeting can be a minefield for anyone carrying something heavy.

"How are you?" The words seem innocuous.

But when confronted with them now, my mind reels. How *am* I? How am I supposed to answer that? How do you think I am? Because the answer is sometimes pretty dark. I'm not good, but thanks for asking. I mean, what do you think I can say? My son died. At age eighteen. I'm not doing great. Do you want to hear about it? It was an effort just to get out of bed today. And yesterday. And the day before that.

You may laugh and say, "I am so tired, too." But my wounded spirit has to question that. Really, *you* are tired? I am EXHAUSTED. Sleeping is something I dream about doing—oh, but since I'm not really sleeping, I am not really dreaming, either! When I close my eyes, I still see Owen in the river, floating cold and lonely until he was found by that tugboat worker who had been in Alaska and didn't even know we were looking for our son. My brain loops through potential scenarios of how he might have gotten there, then takes off running through long lists of Owen's friends who might know something more than what they told us, other places we could look for clues to what happened, or how we could have done something different to change this outcome. Then the thought cycle starts over.

"Mary! How are you?"

"Well, if you really want to hear," I imagine saying, "let me tell you that it was heroic of me to even get dressed and get to the grocery store with my wallet *and* a reusable shopping bag so I could run into you and have to lie to your face because you can't handle the truth. You wouldn't understand. But you know what? I am glad you have no idea how hard it is for me to keep showing up, to keep going. Because I don't wish that on any friend, acquaintance, or just any good person. I'm glad it doesn't occur to you that life can really suck and be so painful, that every moment I am here reminds me of how Owen isn't here—even moments that have hints of joy and resurrection in them (sometimes it's *especially* those moments that sting). You wouldn't—couldn't—understand how the grocery store is a minefield of memories for me: of family lunches and dinners I shopped for, of Owen's favorite snacks, and the chocolate milk he loved so much he bought it for himself on the daily."

How about I say, "I'm OK," which I'm not—but that's hard, too. As I've said before, "OK" always makes me think "Owen Klinger," because those are his initials.

I could say, "I'm hanging in there. People have been amazing." That answer might be a bit closer to my current state without being too uncomfortable for most people. But even that's probably too rosy, because in truth I'm barely, just barely, hanging on.

Should I just default to, "Fine. How are you?"

The answer is there is no easy answer to this habitual question. Maybe instead we need to change our social patterns.

To be fair, I used to be someone who always started a conversation with "How's it going?" or "How are you?" I was blessed not to have known how hard that question can be to answer, or how hard it could be to just be here, existing, day to day.

After Owen's death, whenever I see someone I know at the tennis courts, or in the store, or even when I go over to a friend's house for book club, I try to greet them with, "It's good to see you" or "I'm glad you're here." It starts us out in a place of acceptance and support. Nothing is being asked of the person I am greeting—they only have to be there however they can show up at that moment. They don't have to pretend to be fine or even ask me back the dreaded, "How are you?" It's something small, but small mercies are sometimes all it takes to help us get through a day, through this life.

I hope others don't mind a simple request, then: can you try saying "I'm glad you're here" next time you see me? And who knows, by then I might be able to say, "It's good to see you, too."

A Season of Water Polo

July 2024

Owen decided not to play football in the fall of 2018, his senior year in high school. I was fine with that but reminded him of our general family rule: "you have to do *something*." I didn't want him just playing video games in the basement after school every day. Dustin suggested he go out for cross country, but Owen, my child who loved so many sports, did not love running. Eventually, he was gently persuaded (mostly by me) to join many of his lacrosse friends in the pool and try water polo.

Like all my kids, Owen had taken swim lessons for many summers at Grant Pool, steadily moving up through the proficiency levels: Penguin, Otter, Seal, Polar Bear, Sea Lion. He knew the basics and loved splashing and having fun in the water, but swimming laps wasn't his jam; Owen didn't know what he was getting into with water polo. At the first practice, the warm-up alone consisted of more sustained swimming than he had done in his entire life! Coach Damon, a lacrosse dad, didn't think Owen would return after that first workout, when he'd showed up wearing board shorts with his long hair hanging down his shoulders. But Owen did come back the next day—even after he finished last in that long warm-up swim—with his hair tied back and wearing a slightly shorter pair of swim trunks. It took him a while to work up to a Speedo, and he needed lots of help learning how to get all of his hair to stay inside the water polo cap, but he stuck with it.

The Grant High School men's and women's water polo teams practiced together, resulting in a relaxed coed JV team that played games or scrimmaged before the varsity men's or women's matches. Water polo isn't very popular in our area, so most of the pools they played in were pools made for other water activities, with one end that was shallower than the other. (Water polo is traditionally played in a pool of uniform six-to-seven foot depth.) The goalie at the shallow end is allowed to stand on the pool bottom, but all the other players and the goalie in the deep end have to tread water the whole time. Owen had experience as a goalie in soccer, futsal, and lacrosse, so shallow-end goalie was his first position on JV.

It took great courage for Owen to get in the pool with such amazing athletes. Owen knew a lot of the varsity water polo guys from his lacrosse team, but he was intimidated by their swimming skills and experience. I remember early on—when he was still on the fence about committing to the team—he joked about drowning at practice. I told him not to worry about that because most of his teammates were certified lifeguards who would save him. Owen worked hard just to stay above water but was not afraid of water polo's aggressive physical contact.

At some point during the season, Coach Damon had players write down what they saw as their strength, as well as something they were trying to improve on. Owen wrote, "The thing I'm good at is anticipating shots. I can work on my eggbeater and endurance." The coach tucked these scraps of paper away and was able to find Owen's note to give to us the next year, after we lost him. Owen's handwriting was ridiculously terrible, but I treasure this note.

Owen did work on his eggbeater kick (the leg stroke for treading water) and got better at swimming. He was a tenacious defender and eventually got some playing time on varsity. At one of the matches late in the season, Dustin and I overheard the coaches talking about Owen. One asked, "How many steals does he have?" The other coach replied, "I don't know, about a million." We loved hearing that exaggeration. I know that Owen did not have a million steals, but we do know that Owen loved being a part of the water polo team.

At the end-of-season banquet, Coach Damon said he would rather have a player like Owen who wasn't afraid of contact but needed to work on swimming than a good swimmer who had to learn to get physical in the water. I am so proud of Owen's effort learning to play what some people call the hardest sport. I am grateful to Owen's water polo teammates and coaches for making room for a novice senior in the midst of their well-regarded program. At the banquet, he was literally in the middle of the group of seniors who were honored that night. I love that he was wearing the sweatshirt from his first water polo tournament and smiling his beautiful smile.

Fall isn't football season for us anymore, nor is it water polo season. It's the season when we think heavily about the loss of Owen and do our best to keep going, one day at a time. It's a time I remember Owen's courage to play a swimming-based sport in a tiny swimsuit during his senior year. He was often alone in the goal, treading water once they moved him to the more challenging end of the pool, on alert for action that might come his way. I think of his confidence and strength in the water and wonder what went wrong.

Since 2019, I have gone to a few Grant Water Polo games. The first time I went back, I went to the wrong pool, just like I used to when Owen was playing! (The schedule often changed after it was published, leading to many last-minute detours.) Arriving late to the real venue, I felt lonely even sitting by a friend. I missed seeing Owen's hair sticking out of his cap, his long arms blocking a shot. I was moved to tears by the beautiful, fearless play of the athletes in the pool, and as I joined in the cheering it came to me that I am still part of the team. On my way out, I bought some apples for their fundraiser and got myself a new Grant Water Polo sweatshirt. (Owen would be jealous—he LOVED the softness of new sweatshirts. He didn't realize they started out so fuzzy until fifth grade, when he first got a new one that wasn't a hand-me-down from Gabe!) On the hard and lonely days, I try to remember that I am not alone in missing Owen, or in grieving his loss. The fuzzy sweatshirt is a balm, and when I wear it, I feel like I'm part of a team.

Knowing it would be hard (why I torture myself I don't know!), I decided to wear my water polo sweatshirt to another game the following year. The farther away we get from Owen's time at Grant, and Owen's time with us, the fewer people on the team or in the stands remember him or what happened to him. Sometimes this makes it easier; sometimes this makes it much harder.

In advance, I had asked a friend with a current player about the upcoming schedule, and when the day came I headed out in my still-fuzzy sweatshirt, preparing myself for the waves of emotion I imagined awaited me at the pool.

It was an outdoor match.

At a pool I hadn't been to before.

And none of my friends were coming.

Other than the sweatshirt, I had dressed lightly, anticipating the warm humidity of an indoor pool area. Luckily I had a blanket in my car, so I wrapped myself up, took several deep breaths, and settled in with the sprinkling of parents huddled in the cold cement stands to witness something mundane but miraculous: young people throwing their hearts and bodies around a pool, playing a game they loved on an unremarkable Thursday night in October.

I found myself wanting to talk to Owen, and this is the conversation I had with him in my head:

Owen,

I should have watched more of your water polo. What did I have going on those nights I didn't make it to the pool in time for tip-off? I wish I had always arrived early enough to see you splashing around in the warmups, reveling in your body's youthful strength and power. Practicing those stretching leaps out of the water, racing your friends, talking and laughing. I wish I had seen you trying to get all your long hair tucked into your swim cap every single time. I don't see anyone with long hair like you had in the pool tonight.

I would give anything to have another chance to see your body playing the game you challenged yourself to learn or even just see you sitting on the sidelines cheering for your friends.

I never really understood all the rules and I am so impressed that you could so easily learn something new as a senior. (Also I don't know how the referees can see what is going on as the evening gets darker and darker and the lights glare off the water in front of the goal! What are they missing?)

I forgot how very small Speedo swimsuits are. I love remembering how your confidence grew as you got in increasingly better shape with the rigorous workouts through the season. You were so strong and yet so casual about the grace and power you were capable of.

I love to hear the goalies calling out instructions to their teammates. I remember you doing that too. Even with all this time that has gone by since we lost you—or maybe because of it—I continue to marvel at the humble, easy way you moved through your life when you were doing really remarkable, hard things. Losing you has helped me see the strength and beauty that Gabe and Frances bring to their days. I'm trying to appreciate what I still have while fiercely missing you. I hope the other parents here tonight can see and appreciate the remarkable things their kids are doing. I hope I can have even a little of your courage, Owen, to try new things and to keep coming out to watch this amazing sport.

Things Seen on a Jumbotron

July 2024

Owen with one of his many foam fingers in 2007

S pirited pep band horn swings
Crazy shirtless fans
Radiant cheerleaders
Silly mascot antics
Sweet marriage proposals
Cute birthday wishes
Hilarious kiss cam interactions
Dazzling replays of slam dunks
Sad slideshow of pictures at Owen's funeral

As I described earlier, Owen's funeral was held on October 30, 2019, for almost 2,000 people at the University of Portland's Chiles Center, a large basketball and indoor track venue. This Mass, presided over by thirteen priests—including Oregon's auxiliary archbishop and the president of the university—was one of the last large-scale public events we and many of our friends attended before the restrictions of the coronavirus pandemic changed our lives in 2020.

I know it isn't really how it went, but in my mind, Owen's death seemed to lead directly to the shutdown; as if the world had to go into social hibernation to mourn the loss of such a special young person. My imagination had the slideshow of Owen's photos playing on a loop in the empty arena while we stayed home to save more lives: a huge cosmic mic drop.

The slideshow was a generous donation from our friend Ron Cooper, the retired professional photojournalist who inspired Owen's interest in photography and acted as an unofficial grandpa to my kids in the years he was dating my mom.

The moments Ron captured of Owen's life are unique and special to us, but they are also universal memories in a way, as they show my kids doing things that kids around the world do every day as they are growing up. Ron took photos of Owen sliding down slides and swinging on swings, feeding the ducks, listening to bedtime stories, jumping into swimming pools, playing soccer with untied cleats, raking leaves, stomping in mud puddles, eating watermelon, throwing rocks in the creek, performing at school assemblies, blowing out birthday candles, learning how to ride a bike, and digging in the sand at the beach. These beautiful photographs of unremarkable moments capture Owen's tremendous joy and delight at simple pleasures, his ability to concentrate when he was working hard, and the love he felt for his family and friends.

For a long time, it made me really sad that Owen's time on the jumbotron came after his death and not during some exciting sporting event.

It was another loss I was grieving. He was such a talented athlete, capable of dynamic defensive plays in football, lacrosse, and water polo. His youth basketball years were full of replay-worthy steals and blocked shots—and also lots of fouls! Highlights of his athletic feats will never be replayed in slow-motion for everyone to marvel at. What a loss for all of us! He was an enthusiastic fan at many sporting events, and he left behind an impressive collection of foam fingers. Now I know Owen will never be that crazy fan with a painted letter on his bare chest supporting his favorite team or the nervous date of someone he had to kiss on camera in front of a cheering crowd of people. So many experiences he will never get to have.

Scrutinizing Owen's life in the months and years after his funeral, to look for signs of what happened, to memorize the moles on his face, to remember all the silly ways he made us laugh over the years, helped me see that even the ordinary moments of Owen's life were jumbotron-worthy moments. Friends came forward with stories of how his small acts of kindness made a difference for them at critical times. I started thinking that Owen really did some impressive living on and off the sports field, and I realized I wanted to be more like him.

In February 2024, Dustin and I attended a men's basketball game at UP. At first I kept my eyes down on the floor of the arena, watching the players and avoiding the giant screen looming above us. It was hard to be in the Chiles Center again, under that jumbotron where Owen's slideshow had played. I didn't know how it would feel to see other images up there, but it turns out it was OK. There was a good crowd, and everyone was happily eating "walking tacos" and sipping the newly available-for-purchase "Pilot Lager" beer, made by a brewer from Skamania County (home to our Panther Creek cabin). I was glad to see students playing sports in front of a crowd again, and others cheering for them or sitting back and acting cool while the team lost badly to a more talented squad.

I looked up and saw the pep band on the screen playing their hearts out while two students in faceless full body suits danced in front of them, and I thought Owen would have loved the passion they were pouring into the moment. Not everyone gets a chance to be on the jumbotron, but we can all try to live as if we will be featured up there—even if it might not be until our funeral.

His Favorite Pendleton Shirt

July 2024

Owen's favorite Pendleton shirt

Every once in a while I get the question, "Did you make a T-shirt quilt?" "Um, no," I reply, "but what a nice idea. Thanks for asking."

I have received the suggestion to preserve the memory of Owen with this popular craft from several different friends (Portland is so very crafty!), but I'm not there yet—and I'm not sure I will ever get there.

I just haven't felt like I could cut up any of Owen's clothes, knowing there won't be any more concert T-shirts from his favorite bands or sweatshirts from teams he played on. Everything we have is "limited edition" and too special to disassemble. (I can hear Owen's silly voice imitating Johnny 5, the robot in one of our family's favorite movies, *Short Circuit*, "No Disassemble!")

One of the most revered items, because Owen loved it so much and wore it so many times, is his brown Pendleton shirt. Owen received this shirt for Christmas in 2016 from Dustin's mom, Granny B, who lives not too far from the historic Pendleton Woolen Mills building in Washougal, Washington. It quickly became Owen's favorite shirt.

The Pendleton company is a Northwest classic. It's named for the northeastern Oregon town (originally a trading post) that sits a bit inland from the Columbia River, where its first mill was established. Owen, like many people who enjoy and appreciate Pendleton's quality wool shirts, wore his everywhere. He donned it for his last parent-teacher conferences, several of his sister's ballet performances, and his only time on stage performing his original song "Panther Creek" at the high school. He wore it for a fancy dress-up auction, college visits in Montana, and many dinners out. He chose it for his senior photos—the photos we ended up using for his search poster, the funeral Mass program, and his memorial card.

It has Western styling with pearly snaps and pointy pocket flaps. One of Owen's friends described him as "the guy who always looked like he was dressed for going camping," and this shirt was a key piece in that casual, outdoorsy look. Owen's "Where I'm From" poem mentions Pendleton sweaters—and he did have a nice gray one of those, also a gift from Granny B—but it will be this Pendleton shirt that we forever think of when we remember Owen.

If I ever do make a quilt or a blanket from some of Owen's clothes, it's this shirt that I would think of honoring with prime placement in the design, but how could I ever cut it up? Even though I don't do anything but look at it now and occasionally run my fingers over the rough wool and the smooth pearlized snaps, it's priceless.

I had an idea that maybe I could find another shirt made with the same Pendleton wool and then we could honor Owen with that shirt by wearing it, sharing it with his friends (if I could find a few of them), or making it part of a memorial quilt. We could then keep his original shirt untouched in the Owen "museum" that my son Gabe teases me I have created in their old bedroom.

When pandemic restrictions were easing, and going shopping seemed like something acceptable and safe to do again, I decided to look for a copy of Owen's shirt at some of the Pendleton outlets in the region—we have several! Even though browsing in stores was a "normal" activity, it was surprisingly distressing. It had been uncomfortable to go into the local Carhartt store soon after Owen's death in 2019 to look for another sweatshirt like the one he had bought for himself, but I think I was still numb and a little unhinged back then. Now, I was feeling all the feels. I had to work up some courage to go into the store. First I would just drive by and look at the familiar Pendleton logo on the sign. I could feel my heart beating a little faster and noticed my throat tightening up: my body communicating that it wasn't yet ready for this search to find more Owen. A few times I was able to pull into the parking lot, where I turned the car off and sat there for a while, feeling sick to my stomach, before thinking up an excuse for why I couldn't go in that day.

Eventually I made it into the store and tried to casually shuffle over to the clearance racks, waving off the sales clerk's perky, "Can I help you find anything?" with what I hoped sounded like a casual reply: "Oh, I'm just looking, thanks." As soon as I started browsing, I realized it was going to be more complicated than I had thought. Who knew there were so many different styles and such a dizzying array of plaids? How could I ever find one that matched Owen's? I realized I needed to ask for help, but I wasn't quite ready yet.

One day in 2023 with Frances as my steadying accomplice, I went into the Pendleton Woolen Mill Store in Southeast Portland. This is a place that sells wool fabric as well as some of the shirts, so I thought it could be a good place to get help. Maybe I would be able to buy a yard or two of the fabric used in Owen's shirt. It was raining heavily that day, and we had a hard time even getting into the parking lot from the flooded road, but we finally found a spot that would let us both get out of the car without stepping into huge puddles. I grabbed Owen's memorial card that I keep next to the steering wheel of my Mini Cooper, and we made the dash to the front door of the store. It was a huge warehouse type of building, with sparse displays and not many shoppers. A few employees were huddled together, deep in conversation, and we almost decided to leave, but when a clerk made eye contact with me, I tried to be brave and seize this chance.

Owen P. Klinger

July 23, 2001 – October 20, 2019

Eternal rest grant unto him, O Lord, and
let perpetual light shine upon him.

My hand was shaking as I extended the card with the picture of Owen wearing the shirt we were looking for. His birthdate and the date his body was found are clearly visible below his name. It's obvious what it is with a cross and the italic text, "Eternal rest grant unto him, O Lord, and let perpetual light shine upon him" right below the dates: a memorial card from a funeral. It's definitely a conversation stopper, but maybe it could be a conversation *starter*. The young associate looked a little panicked when she realized what she was holding. I began to explain that we were looking to match my son's favorite shirt: to hopefully find more shirts like this or some of the identical fabric. She wasn't able to help us much in her hurry to separate from our awkward, grief-fueled mission, but she directed us to the back wall of the store, where large rolls of plaid fabrics filled a few aisles; she also pointed to a bin of remnants we could dig through.

We weren't successful that day, but I didn't want to give up. So during one of my solo beach weekends, I braved the Lincoln City outlet mall and shyly asked the woman working the deserted Pendleton store there if she had any shirts like Owen's. She told me she was a mom, too, and seemed to instantly understand how hard it must be for me to even still be living and breathing after my child's death, let alone to be searching for precious reminders of a beautiful boy whose life was cut too short. She spent half an hour with me hunting through densely packed sale racks in case a shirt was hiding in plain sight, and then she scoured the back room to make sure there wasn't anything we had missed. No luck, but she sold me a beautiful wool blanket (the beach house is very cold in the winter!) and suggested I visit the Pendleton Mills store in Washougal, Washington (where Owen's shirt was originally from!). She said the oldest items end up there for final clearance. She also helpfully mentioned that bringing Owen's actual shirt to the store could aid the search efforts.

In the summer of 2023, Dustin and I stopped in Washougal on our way to Panther Creek for the Fourth of July (always one of Owen's favorite holidays). The store was busy, with many customers out on the wide front porch, perusing the racks of bright beach towels and pastel short-sleeve dress shirts. We had Owen's shirt with us so we could find an exact match. We browsed by ourselves for a while, seeing a few things that looked kind-of like Owen's shirt, but that, sadly, weren't Owen's shirt. Eventually a sales clerk wandered our way and asked, "Can I help you find anything?"

I opened up the plastic bag and pulled out the shirt, still wrinkled from being stuffed into a duffel bag in the mad dash to empty Owen's dorm room when he died. I told her a little about what we were trying to do, and she jumped right in to help us.

She led us to an empty register where I laid Owen's shirt out on the counter. Her hands carefully and reverently moved around the shirt, as she looked inside, searching for labels that could identify the style and fabric. Why didn't I think of that? Unfortunately, Owen had cut those tags out. Not helpful, Owen! She asked when Owen had received the shirt. At the time, dates were fuzzy and I wasn't quite sure. The first picture I have of him wearing it was from January 2017, when he was having burgers at McMenamins Kennedy School with Dustin after a day of skiing. So, I guessed, "Christmas of 2016?" This helped her narrow down when the shirt would have been in the catalog, when it would have been in the stores, and when remainders would have been on sale at the outlet where Granny B bought it for Owen.

She called for the help of her manager, a smiling woman named Katie, and the two of them pulled out thick binders filled with catalogs detailing every season's designs. They flipped confidently through the pages, stopping occasionally to bend their heads together in conference before shaking their heads and moving on. Eventually they were able to identify the name of the colorway featured in Owen's shirt: "Brown/Tan Ombre" and its corresponding number of 31902. Just this little bit of information was exciting to discover. She told us that the style of Owen's shirt was called "Canyon" and gave us the corresponding number for that design: DA085. So now we knew what we had and what we were looking for. Pendleton also made Board shirts (#AA022) and Trail shirts (#AA032) in Brown/Tan Ombre that year, but a system-wide computer search revealed there were not *any* #31902 shirts in their inventory. I felt like I was on a roller coaster of emotions, being lifted dizzyingly high as the specific codes were revealed, opening up the possibility that we would really be able to find a matching shirt, only to feel our hopes sickeningly plummet when they came up with nothing.

Who knew that such a neutral-colored shirt would completely sell out?! Compared to some of the Pendleton plaids, this one is pretty quiet. It really is just brown and tan morphing slowly into each other and then out again. There is no line of green or blue to add interest or a punch of pizzazz. I have never seen anyone wearing another shirt just like Owen's, and I wondered about the other people who had chosen this classic wool shirt, colored in the soft tones of wood and sand. I would think about those people a lot more because that was the Pendleton manager's last suggestion to us: that we reach out to Pendleton Owners Club on Facebook or search for used shirts on eBay.

Several months passed before I finally dipped into eBay. I think I put off looking into this option because I was afraid I'd find nothing, but I got pretty excited because right away I saw a "new-with-tags" Men's medium Pendleton shirt that said it was "Brown/Tan Ombre." It was a Board shirt, not a Canyon shirt, but I went ahead and impulsively bid on it, thinking this could be it and that it was meant to be found by me that day. When it arrived in the mail, I nervously waited a bit to open the box, only to find a shirt of a much darker brown-tan ombre fabric. My heart squeezed with a flash of disappointment, and then I got mad at myself for making such a rash purchase and for thinking it would be so easy. I was ashamed to show Dustin, but when I eventually did he was sweet and said he could see how I thought it would be a match. I wasn't sure what to do with the shirt, which sat in the priority mail box under my desk for a few weeks as a reminder of my folly and my obsession.

It was still there when Frances came home from osu for summer break in June of 2024. She spied it and asked me what was in the box—she loves online shopping and has a keen eye for packages. I told her what I had done. We looked at the shirt together—it was in perfect condition—and I brought Owen's shirt down from his closet to show her how they really didn't match. We had a minute together remembering Owen and how dedicated he was to his favorite shirt. Then she quietly suggested maybe she could wear the new shirt when she has to go into the forest for field study days (she is studying forestry at Oregon State), that it might be just the right layer to help keep her warmer and drier than she had been on some days last term. I loved that idea and promised myself to be more careful before I bid on anything else!

I have stayed away from eBay since that snafu, but I've been lurking around the Pendleton Facebook groups. I haven't posted anything in there yet about my quest. I'm anxious about running out of options, so I've left this one still untouched. Does that make any sense? Maybe now that I have written all this about the search for his shirt's clone, posting something might come easier. For now, I will keep looking on eBay and at Goodwill (though not many Pendleton shirts make it to the racks of Goodwill as they are so highly prized by collectors!).

I am also thinking that maybe—just maybe—we could try wearing Owen's shirt a little. I don't want to wear it out or damage it, but it's a really good shirt and so very sad to see it hanging all wrinkly and empty. Owen might want us to wear it out into the world because he loved it so much. It might be just the right layer to keep me warmer and drier when we are out at Panther Creek, Owen's favorite place. Would it be sadder for my family to see someone else wearing the shirt? It's hard to imagine being sadder, as we have already cried so many tears over these years. Maybe I could wear it at the beach where I never see anyone, or throw it over my shoulders as I sit at Owen's laptop, typing my post for the Pendleton Owners Facebook group.

18 Birthdays

July 2024

This year we passed Owen's golden birthday. He would have turned 23 on July 23rd, and I know Owen would have loved that special numerical synchronicity. (I wonder why I didn't know about "golden birthdays" sooner. I would totally have loved turning four on the fourth of June, but maybe golden birthdays weren't a thing in the '70s.) Owen's special day in the middle of the summer was always packed with fun and treats. It was something we all looked forward to and excitedly planned for. When Gabe was six years old he said, "You know what my favorite part of summer is? Owen's birthday!"

It's very different now. We really don't celebrate it as a family anymore, though heavy thoughts of Owen start to accumulate on the horizon as the day approaches, building like the thunderclouds of a summer storm. I try to make sure this day holds at least a little sweetness for everyone in my family, and I always spend time remembering how much Owen loved his birthday.

Owen only had 18 birthdays. Owen *got to have* 18 birthdays.

He had 18 special home-baked cakes shaped like basketballs (two years in a row!), a soccer ball, campfire logs, an elephant, and a giraffe. Cakes decorated with Pokemon, pirate treasure, sparkler candles, lions, soccer players, rainbow jelly beans with marshmallow clouds. Towers of powdered donut holes and waffles with fresh-picked blueberries and birthday candles. Cakes that were chocolate, lemon, and vanilla. Cakes with layers of ice cream, and always lots of sweet frosting.

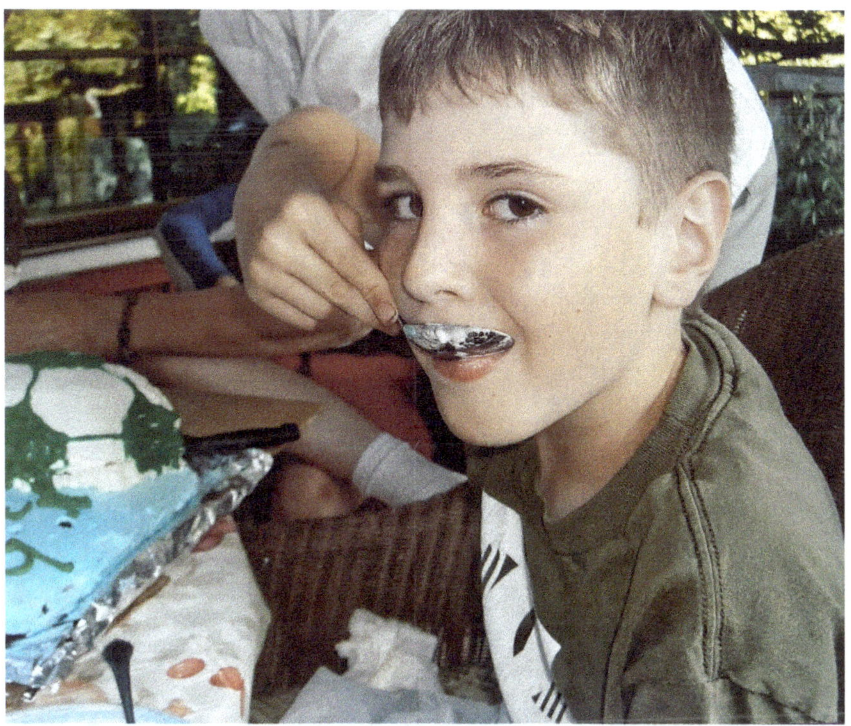

Owen had 18 birthday parties in the middle of summer. We always tried to make things fun regardless of the guest list. Some years, his friends couldn't be there because of their own summer plans. We invited Gabe's and Frances's friends to fill in the extra seats at the cake table, or we celebrated with just our family plus some grandparents. We played backyard ball games and ran front yard relay races. We threw water balloons at targets, blew the biggest bubbles, went on silly scavenger hunts, and broke open a piñata stuffed with Owen's favorite candies. We marked the occasion with sidewalk chalk and face paint.

Owen loved the year Granny B let him help drive a front-loader around on her rural property as her present to him. (It was a dream come true for a boy who loved trucks, trains, and big machines.) Splashing in sprinklers and backyard wading pools evolved into big-boy water play in ponds and creeks. A cornhole tournament with his high school friends at our cabin and daredevil cold water challenges in the icy waters of Panther Creek seemed like cool teen celebrations in high school, but looking back I imagine Owen and his friends were likely trying to make the parties even "cooler" by sneaking sips from cans of beers around the campfire after the adults went to sleep. I guess I couldn't expect the kids to want lemonade or sparkling water forever, though the year I served Mexican Cokes I felt like the best mom ever.

On Owen's fifteenth birthday, I had him all to myself. We had traveled to Central Oregon for a lacrosse tournament and stayed at a random hotel in the city of Redmond near the playing fields. I wanted to do something fun for him since he was away from his other friends and family, and on the road with his boring mom, so I took him out for a special steak dinner at Tumalo Feed Company Steakhouse. They offered buckets of onion rings, cheap root beer floats, good steaks, and an amazing cowboy cookie pie dessert that Owen devoured. (Oops, I forgot that in the photo you can see the extra spoon. I might have had one or two bites!)

This was the dessert my cooking group tried to replicate when our theme was Owen's favorite comfort foods. It was my favorite of Owen's birthdays because I didn't have to produce a feast for the neighborhood and goody bags for a gaggle of friends. It was just the two of us, lots of sunshine and exercise, some good steak and a sweet dessert at the end of the night.

Owen had 18 birthday wishes, made with sweet, long eyelashes closed against tanned cheeks. What did he wish for? More ice cream? More presents? More screen time? More brothers and sisters? Or fewer? Did any of his wishes come true? I wonder if he wished for a dog before we got Bella. What would he have wished for if he had been granted more years of birthday candles? What are we wasting *our* wishes on? They are precious, these birthday wishes, and I am suddenly thinking I should take them a little more seriously—especially since I am the mom of a boy who only got 18 wishes. I vow to be more thoughtful on my next birthday, dreaming big with my one wish since Owen can't wish anymore.

Owen was born on my dad's 60th birthday. I thought it was wonderful because I didn't have any other gift for my dad that year. I said, "Happy Birthday, Dad! Meet your grandson, Owen!" I could never recall how old my dad was before, but now I had an easier way to remember, with Owen's birthday resetting the count. Owen seemed to enjoy sharing his birthday, though there were some years my dad didn't celebrate with us, or we had a separate dinner with him because my mom's boyfriend (I'm not making this up!) was also born on July 23rd! Happy Birthday, Ron! Owen always shared his cake with good cheer—and he always had a big pile of presents, which made sharing the cake easier—but we never imagined as we sang "Happy Birthday, dear Owen" that he would be gone before the two older men we celebrated on that day. My mom and Ron are no longer a couple, so I don't really think about Ron's birthday anymore, but my dad's birthday is hard to celebrate now. Dustin and I try to plan something on a different day with him so we can be more present.

Owen's 18th birthday was just a month before he left for college, two and a half months before we lost him.

* * * *

Owen's 18th (and last) birthday 2019

It's hard to imagine what Owen would be like as a 23-year-old (25-year-old, 30-year-old, etc.). What would he be wishing for? A car? A better job? A romantic partnership? Would he still request a dinner of homemade Philly cheesesteaks? Would he want an ice cream cake? Maybe he wouldn't even be celebrating his birthday with us, though drinking beer at the cabin by the creek is a pretty sweet way to celebrate now that he would be over 21. Maybe he'd be living somewhere else, making birthday memories with new friends in a new city or blowing out candles on a cake by a different creek. I try to remember sometimes, that even if things go well, we won't always have our young people with us. Even if they don't tragically disappear from our lives when they are 18, they will most likely leave home and eventually build their own lives separate from their parents. We were going to be "losing" at least some of Owen as he grew up.

I want to believe that thinking this way will help lessen the pain of losing him, but—nope, I just did a quick check-in and it's still unbelievably heartrending and wrong that he's not here. However, I also have room in my heart to think that Owen *got* to have 18 birthdays and I *got* to be his mom and celebrate him through all of them. My wish is that one day his birthday will be our favorite part of summer again.

The Club No One Wants to Join: Mothers Who Have Lost a Child

FAQ Sheet for the Newly Bereaved Mom

August 2024

Welcome to the club. Membership has its privileges; the challenge is learning what they are.

I'm so very sorry you are here.

I know you have probably heard it so many times, "It's a club no one wants to join." But if you are here, there are a few things you need to know about our club...

Is it even a club? Wouldn't a club have dues?

OK we all paid the ultimate price* for this undesirable "membership" so we won't be collecting any further dues, unless you suffer collateral damage from this loss and also lose your partner, your marriage, or your job. Since our dues were paid in tears, we won't have much of a budget for splashy

---

*Disclaimer: Just because you already had your heart smashed into pieces once with the loss of a child, you are not safe from having this happen again. (If the loss that qualifies you for membership in this club was your only child, please see the attached application for sainthood. We are so very sorry for your loss.)

special events; perhaps we should plan some fundraising? Oh GOD, what if we have a car wash?! Can you imagine grieving moms standing at the edge of the parking lot in cutoff denim shorts waving signs and shouting for people to come and get their cars washed? Um, no. Maybe no fundraising, but even without much of a budget, we will persevere. Because that's what we do. Everyone is always telling us we are so strong, right?

What about club leadership?

1, 2, 3 ... not it. Oh, shoot, my reflexes were slowed by the bottle of wine I drank last night while scrolling through my son's saved Snapchat memories. I guess I will step in as acting president until we are able to get a little more organized and hold elections. You're welcome? Again, it's a role I never wanted to take on.

Are there even meetings? How do you set a date?

We haven't had a meeting yet, but we are working on the schedule. It's very complicated. I know this summer we've all been busy sitting inside in the dark while friends take vacations to Europe or wine country. Let's look ahead on the calendar. Hmmm. I can't meet on the 23rd of any month since July 23 was Owen's birthday. September 27 is the date I saw him last so I'm out for any 27th too. October 6 is when he went missing, but we didn't *know* he was missing until October 7 so I can't meet on the 6th or the 7th. His body was found on the 20th and his funeral was on the 30th so that's two more dates I can't make. Honestly, as soon as things start feeling a little like fall (pumpkin spice latte trigger, anyone?) I might have a harder time doing *anything*—after all, the body keeps the score, right? Fall is a season of trauma and tragedy for me. So maybe we should meet during another season. Winter? Um, that might also be hard with family gatherings feeling pretty empty for all of us with one less kid at the kids' table at Thanksgiving or one less stocking for Santa to fill on Christmas. And where I live, it gets dark so depressingly early. Maybe we should look at dates in the new year...

Are there attendance requirements for club meetings?

Assuming we were able to set a meeting date, I doubt other members would be interested in or capable of putting that date on their calendars in light of their own new sets of personal limitations. No one has to come to any meeting, ever. If we did have a date planned, we'd probably have to cancel at the last minute. Maybe some of the grieving moms would be stuck watching home videos in last week's sweats or digging around in the attic for that photo they thought was in an old album. Some might be kneeling by the empty crib in their baby's room, rocking a stuffed animal their child never got to play with. Others might be putting fresh flowers at their accident site vigil again. Those things are way more important than any meeting. Keep doing what you feel you can do. There will always be another meeting—that's *if* we can choose a date.

What about transportation?

Carpooling is encouraged!

Sorry! I forgot, some of you lost kids in car accidents and have some new reservations about getting in a car with someone else behind the wheel. Others probably don't want to share a car with anyone at all, since that's the place where you can safely scream and cry and let it all out. I totally get it—I'm glad my car has such darkly tinted windows! Never mind about carpooling. We can circle back to that. Or not.

What kind of refreshments are served at meetings?

Not sure about this one, we might have to make this potluck because hosting is so hard now. I used to host all kinds of PTA board meetings, dinners for my cooking group, and wine and dessert nights for my book clubs. I made a fancy dinner for Owen and his friends on their senior prom night when none of them had dates for the dance. I set the table with all my wedding china and crystal and the boys loved the Thai pork lettuce wraps I made. I know I'm preaching to the choir, but I will say it again: hosting is so hard now. I never know what I will feel I can offer energy-wise.

I guess if no one feels like eating* (it's too hard to swallow anything with the ever-present lump in my throat), we don't need much food. I used to always bake my famous chocolate chip cookies for board meetings, but now they bring up too many sad memories.

To drink, I'll make sure to have half a cup of cold coffee per person. I'll also bring opaque coffee cups so moms can put their whiskey or red wine in the mug without judgment. I was thinking I'd make sure there are a few bottles of wine...for me. What are you all going to bring for yourselves to drink?

Is there a dress code for meetings?

Our meetings are clothing optional. No! Not in that sketchy nude-beach way! I'm only saying clothes are optional because I know you might feel more like wrapping yourself in a blanket instead of actually getting dressed. Maybe I should have said, "Blankets are welcome." Also, it's a safe place for you to wear your son's lacrosse jacket—yes, the bright blue one with his name on the back. I would know.

What does a typical meeting look like?

Most of our time together will be filled with members sharing the stupidest things their friends and family or complete strangers have said or not said (with particular attention paid to stories of people unbelievably comparing loss of a pet to the loss of a child). We also cover milestones our children's friends have passed that our kids will never experience. If there is any time left, we try to rally and talk about hummingbirds, butterflies, and license plate signs. Show-and-tell of memorial tattoos and heart-shaped rocks optional.

---

*For members who have found that food helps numb the pain, I will bring a sheet cake from Costco and some forks. I will scare the people in the bakery by ordering black roses on the cake and asking them if they can fit all the names of our deceased children in pretty frosting script on the top. There will be a lot of frosting.

Does the club have a mission statement?

We haven't been able to agree on one that doesn't contain profanity, but here are a few unofficial mission statements we are playing around with (censored):

"Yes, we are strong, but we are ****ing terrified and live in fear that something horrible is going to happen to someone else we love at any moment and we won't be able to survive more loss."

"Grief is my superpower, b****! Don't mess with me!"

"Why isn't there a ****ing word for this in the English language?"

"This ****ing sucks!"

"**** this."

"****!"

Is there a club logo? Or theme song?

We have been taking votes on a logo, but it's been very difficult to come to a consensus. So far we have been able to agree on:

No rainbows

No hearts or broken hearts

No butterflies, hummingbirds, or dragonflies

No angel wings

No feathers

No praying hands

No straight line*

Regarding theme songs, I've been listening to my son's Spotify playlist of 23 different versions of Johnny Cash performing, "Ring of Fire." I might have to recuse myself from voting on a song for our club. "It's so complicated." Oh, sorry, no, that's not a song title. But maybe it should be. Does anyone want to write that for us?

---

*So many ideas have been vetoed I thought I had a secret winner with my simple straight line idea, but then a mom who saw her son's heart monitor stop when he passed away told me *that* was triggering, so I had to tell the graphic artist to stop working on that idea. Back to the drawing board…

Ways of Knowing: Spiritual Connections with Owen

August 2024

Owen and Gabe washing dishes at church

We used to be a family that was pretty involved with our church. Owen's "Where I'm From" poem had a neat way of describing how his religious life developed: "I am from Our Father, who art in heaven, most Sundays until I got busy with high school." Over the years at St. Philip Neri parish, our family volunteered in many different ways. Dustin served on the Finance Committee and as a lector at Mass. I helped as a Eucharistic minister, taught some Sunday school, counted and deposited money from the collection baskets, answered phones in the office, and sang in the church contemporary music group. All three of our kids washed dishes at parish spaghetti dinners and pancake breakfasts. Owen helped run sound for my music group, and Frances and Gabe were altar servers.

It was a rare Sunday that we were all sitting together in the pews, but one week I was glad I was next to seven-year-old Owen, who was doodling on the offertory envelopes when he fainted and hit his eyebrow hard on the heavy wooden pew. A doctor friend of ours was sitting a few rows away and rushed to help. Dustin and I took Owen to the local children's hospital emergency room, where he was thoroughly checked out and later released without any obvious or ominous explanation for what had happened. I thought maybe he hadn't eaten enough breakfast (sometimes it was a crazy scramble to get all five of us up and out the door in time to make it to church) and I fussed over him for a few days after the incident before our busy family life carried on.

On a warm summer morning at church a few years later, Gabe was standing next to the priest in front of the congregation, clad in an altar server's heavy white robe. During the Eucharistic prayer—a time I usually wouldn't be talking during Mass—I suddenly felt compelled to lean over to Owen and ask him, "Do you remember when you fainted in church?" Before he could answer, I heard a loud *ka-thunk* and looked up to see that Gabe had fainted, falling straight backwards on the elevated altar platform. Again, our doctor friend was there to assist, and luckily Gabe hadn't hit his head on anything hard like Owen did. We took him into a room behind the sanctuary, helped him out of his robe, and gave him a glass of cool water to drink. Thankfully, he was fine.

What I have always wondered is what moved me to be talking to Owen about his fainting incident right before Gabe had his? It wasn't as if I was thinking, "Gabe is going to faint," so I don't feel like I was having some kind of psychic prediction, but I must have been feeling *something*. I have thought a lot about this church fainting experience since we lost Owen, and since we lost our way at church.

As I explored earlier (and continue to be aware of), my lack of knowledge about Owen's life just before he went missing, and my family's life after, led me to wondering: how do we know if we know anything?

I never would have thought I would be someone exploring spiritual connection with loved ones who had passed away, but when Owen died I had so many questions. I needed to do everything I could to learn about what had happened to him; the physical answers we got from the police and the medical examiner weren't enough.

In one of my attic searches for more Owen, I found a paper I had written for a philosophy class at Notre Dame called "Ways of Knowing." My professor spoke English with a heavy Eastern European accent, and the assigned readings were academically dense. At the time I didn't really get what he was trying to help us understand (maybe because as a confident college student I thought I already knew it all!); I'm still not sure I get it now. I reread the twelve double-spaced pages of my paper titled, "Are Beliefs About Our Sensations Incorrigible?" hoping to be enlightened by my all-knowing nineteen-year-old self. Along with abundant (too many?) quotes from supporting texts, I discussed an example of someone believing he was having an itch sensation when he was really having a pain sensation, and therefore he could not trust his beliefs about his sensations. There is also a section about my brother and his friends telling me I was feeling a bowl of eyeballs in our dark basement-turned-haunted-house which was really a bowl of peeled grapes. Somehow, I received an A- on that paper and did well in the class, but I still had a lot to learn about the way we know things.

When Owen went missing, we simply did not know what had happened to him. Well-meaning people asked me if I could *feel* that he was gone, or if I could sense that something had happened to him. I could not. All I could feel was terror, fear, and pain (*not* the itchy kind). And then I also felt bad that I didn't have any feeling about what had happened. What kind of a mom was I if I didn't have those extrasensory connections and feelings about my son? There are many stories about people sensing something happening to a loved one, even waking up in the middle of the night with a sudden intuitive feeling, but this is not what happened to us. We did not know what happened to Owen, and we didn't have any intuitive feelings guiding us. We needed all the help we were being offered—and more—to find him and we *still* need help to figure out how and why he died. Because we still want to know.

We trusted police and campus security to help us find Owen and discover factual evidence about what had happened to him. They didn't do much, or couldn't do much. Owen was 18—an adult!—and appeared to have left campus on his own. Along with thousands of friends and concerned citizens of Portland, Dustin physically searched for him in areas near campus and well beyond. We posted flyers with his photo all around the city, eventually even on digital billboards throughout the region. We talked to his new friends on campus and his old friends from high school to learn what Owen had been talking about and doing in the weeks and months before his disappearance. We scrutinized his internet search history to see what he had been looking into on his laptop. As I've mentioned, we never found his phone, but we researched the numbers he had been texting or calling that showed up on our cell phone statement.

Dustin and I were desperate for help. The police found a video taken from a TriMet bus that showed Owen walking at the edge of campus. This seemed like a promising clue, but their misinterpretation of the direction Owen was walking led search efforts in the wrong direction for 12 days. (When they finally showed me and Dustin the video, we were able to *immediately* tell which street Owen had been crossing and which way he was really heading.) It was so frustrating and we were so desperate, we consulted some more unconventional sources for help.

At my urging, Dustin met with a man who had search dogs of dubious ability. Heading down the street that Owen didn't walk on (the street the police incorrectly identified from the bus video), the man believed his dogs had led Dustin to a house where something bad might have happened. Owen wasn't there, but there was a group of sketchy young people in that house who were eventually arrested for their connection to some other violent crimes in the neighborhood. We still didn't know anything about Owen, we were out $600, and I felt pretty foolish. I still have the blue sock we let the dogs sniff to catch Owen's scent sealed in a Ziploc bag. It doesn't really smell like Owen anymore, and since those dogs weren't even really following Owen's path, maybe it never did. Who knows?

Someone named Marcus (was that even his name?) reached out to us and said they could sense where Owen was if we could give them something of Owen's, so Dustin coordinated the handover of another sock (oddly not the mate to the one we used with the dogs) and now *that* sock is somewhere with Marcus, who never came back with a lead for us. That was two strikes for these alternative ways of knowing, but I couldn't give up. We needed to find Owen.

A neighbor, an intelligent woman working in public relations for Intel, offered to contact her personal psychic to help us find Owen. Dustin and I were skeptical, but growing more despondent every day that Owen was gone, so we said yes. I remember talking to her on the phone up in my bedroom while the buzzing activity of our friends planning searches and brainstorming ideas carried on downstairs. The psychic believed that Owen was being held against his will at a motel somewhere close to the city. The psychic glimpsed highway signs and thought the motel was near an open grassy field. I felt my hopes rise and wanted so badly to believe that this was true. Friends (who are also Frances's godparents) went on this wild goose chase for us to try to find the motel or the field, but they didn't find Owen. My hopes were dashed again, and since this had been my first time talking with someone who claimed to have the ability to see beyond the physical realm, I was quickly losing faith that this "woo-woo" way of knowing would be our path to finding Owen.

One of Dustin's best friends from childhood is a Catholic priest in a neighboring city. About a week into our search for Owen, Father Tom wrote to us to say he had reached out to someone at his church known for having prophetic visions. Coincidentally (or not!) she had actually dreamed about Owen the night before, but she didn't have the context to understand the vision until she heard from Tom.

She told Tom about her dream and he emailed us the following:

In her dream, there is a person in a river and people see him. There is a crowd of people that are worried about him. The person in the river is not alone and there is a sense of being chased. The person is trying to reach the other side, but the current is too strong. The person in the river is about to hit rocks and reaches out his hand in a very visible way.

There was also a priest in the dream, maybe Father Tom, who was able to interpret this "prophecy."

Years later, I still feel chills reading this exchange. Tom urged us to search the river in a boat, maybe even one equipped with underwater lights or people who could search underwater. It was not what we wanted to hear, but when Owen's body was recovered from the river a week later, I remembered this vision and thought there might be something to this different way of knowing.

Once Owen's body was found, my focus shifted to wanting to know how he had died. How did he get in the river? Was anyone with him? Was it an accident? Did someone harm him? Was he experimenting with heavy drugs? Did he mean to end his life that night? The medical examiner's report took several months to be completed, and I had high hopes that it would answer at least some of my questions.

No broken bones were noted, and the medical examiner found only a trace of cannabis in Owen's system, not any scary drugs. Sadly, the report only seemed to raise more questions for us: was Owen conscious or un-conscious when his body entered the water? How long was his body in the water? Was the damage to his chest and lungs caused by falling from the bridge or from the accumulation of fluids as his body began decomposing in the river? We asked a few medical experts to review the autopsy results without learning anything more. There were no obvious or immediate revelations that led detectives to quickly solve the case, as you see on TV; no detectives were working on Owen's case anyway.

We hired a private investigator, and I kept my heart open to any way we could learn more about what happened. She interviewed more people than the police did and her report confirmed that along with wide acclaim for Owen's thoughtfulness, his humility, and his kindness, there was also much distrust for one of Owen's roommates. Unfortunately, her probe didn't reveal what had actually happened.

Just a few weeks after Owen's body was found, my friend Michelle connected me to a medium named Jessica in California. I don't remem-ber making the phone call, but I made a recording of the session and remember Michelle coming over to listen to it with me. We sat on the couch in my living room, where Dustin and I had recently been holding press conferences about the search for Owen, and balanced coffee cups on our laps as we leaned close to the phone to hear what the medium said.

Jessica came up with some surprisingly accurate things to say about Dustin's dad, (who had passed away in 2007) and their relationship, but she didn't come through with much about Owen. She said it might be too soon. Dustin was very skeptical and thought it sounded like a waste of money, but I knew that the details about Dustin's dad weren't things we had ever shared online.

This meeting gave me hope that there was still more Owen out there somewhere that I could connect to, but I didn't want my exploration of spiritual connections with Owen to make Dustin uncomfortable. I kept some of the other meetings I had with psychic mediums to myself until they were too juicy not to share.

Moms from my old neighborhood playgroup made an appointment for me to meet with Renee Terrill, a Portland psychic with a business called "Ask Renee." I met her over Zoom and was blown away by the way she sensed Owen's energy, his sweetness, his quirkiness, and his humility without me having to say a word. She seemed to see very quickly that Owen had gone missing and that his loss was sudden and unexpected. The evidence she came up with made me believe she was really connecting with Owen's spirit.

During my sessions with Renee, I didn't receive many definite answers for my questions about what happened to Owen when he left campus, but when I asked the big one, did Owen jump to his death on purpose from the St. Johns Bridge?, she said she is "a million percent sure it wasn't suicide." In her practice, she has read for many other families who lost loved ones to suicide, and she said Owen did not come across to her as having ended his life purposefully.

She said he seemed to be feeling confused by bad effects from self-medicating efforts that had gone sideways. She said it feels like he just fell and didn't know what was going on. "He felt nothing. He blacked out." Even though I didn't understand how it could be possible that she was sensing and feeling Owen, I wanted to believe her, as the things she was saying lined up with my own thoughts about what might have happened. However, it was still difficult for me to trust this very new way of "knowing."

In the spring of 2020, I started listening to a podcast called *Moving Beyond* with Medium Fleur. The show features a world-renowned psychic medium doing blind readings with people experiencing all kinds of losses, followed by a discussion between the medium and the guest about whether the reading had been accurate and helpful. The departed loved ones in each episode came through as unique individuals; it wasn't generic "you have a grandmother who has passed" kind of stuff. People were obviously helped by the messages Fleur was able to deliver from their loved ones in spirit, and as I listened from my own dark and lonely cave of early grief, my heart was lifted, too. When the producer announced they were looking for more stories to be featured on the podcast, I wrote to them about Owen, and about a year later I was selected to have a free reading with Fleur.

Over Zoom from Portugal, Fleur quickly recognized me as a mom with a son in spirit who felt like a young adult. She said he had really nice long hair, a gentle heart, and real compassion for other people. He came across as quite social with "a million friends" and a strong connection to his family. She clued in right away about Frances and Gabe, being his younger and older siblings, saying Owen watches over both as their guardian angel. Owen was now getting to know a grandfather in spirit that he didn't really know well in the physical world. I thought this referred to Grampy Bruce, Dustin's dad, who passed away when Owen was only four years old. So many details about Owen and our family were 100 percent correct. I had goosebumps the entire time.

When details about Owen's passing were coming through, she also said that it didn't feel like intentional suicide. She knew he had been walking around outside by himself at night. She said he was intoxicated and confused. He was possibly hallucinating and not acting logically. He passed suddenly but wasn't found for quite a while. She said there was a sense of naivete in his experimenting with intoxicants. I asked her if there was anything about Owen's life that he wished we knew, and she said it was really quite the opposite: "There's a sense of him wanting you to know how much you really did know him. You do know him."

This session was recorded in the summer of 2021 but wasn't released as a podcast until January of 2023. Every time I listen to it, I am struck anew by how quickly and confidently she seemed to be connecting with Owen. I like thinking about how Owen's journey continues, but it's just not in the physical world with us. She made some suggestions on how I can strengthen my spiritual link with Owen that aren't mind-bending but seem doable—a lot like stuff I used to do at church.

Some people have scoffed at connecting with the dead as sacrilegious or somehow the devil's work, but it seems to me that it is very much in the same realm as believing in and praying to "all the angels and saints," which I've done for years at the Catholic church. I might as well use that faith in the world beyond my physical ways of knowing to believe that Owen's spirit is still journeying and connecting with us. It feels better to believe he's not just all gone.

The medium I've connected with most recently is Maureen Hancock from Boston. A friend had suggested her podcast to me, and the day I finally tuned in to listen, it was the second anniversary of Owen's disappearance. The episode was about what to do when a child goes missing. I had chills!

I listened as I walked down familiar neighborhood streets with my dog on an eerily foggy fall morning. Maureen explained, in her heavy Boston accent, all of the things our friends had helped us do when Owen was lost: set up a command center, have someone take charge of volunteers, use social media to spread the word. In that episode she also spoke about how she works with police, FBI, and parents to help discover a child's body and explain what had happened. It might be hard to believe that I can listen to stuff like this because the content is so triggering, but somehow facing the biggest monsters sometimes gives me strength to carry on.

When I got home from that walk, I wrote an email to Maureen, asking if she could help me and Dustin learn more about what specifically happened to Owen on the night he went missing. Shockingly, she contacted me that same day and scheduled a free Zoom session with us for the following week. Dustin was very skeptical but agreed to sit next to me and listen. When we got on the call with her, she seemed so down to earth, corralling her dogs and moving around her home to a spot with better Wi-Fi. (Mediums! They're just like us!) In her introduction she said, "I try to take something that's so 'ooga booga' and help you know that we all have abilities. It's like you are creating a non-physical relationship with them." Explained so succinctly, it sounds simple and easy, but I knew Dustin would not be easily swayed. I was also struggling with feelings of doubt, wondering when enough would be enough for me.

Maureen immediately seemed to be accurately describing Owen, laughing about his personality and our family dynamics. She saw how he had gone out walking that night for a long time. She saw that he did not mean to end his life, that he was just out trying to clear his head and get away from "the pressure." She said he slipped and fell into the river in the dark and he was confused. She said he had plans for his future, not plans to end his life. She thought he was feeling pressure at school, not that he wasn't a good student, but that he was maybe in a fight with someone.

At this point in the Zoom, she abruptly asked, "Do you have his hair?" Dustin and I quizzically looked at each other with this abrupt change of topic and tried to think, finally remembering that we actually do have a lock of his hair in a crystal Christmas ornament. I also realized that I had just been looking at my own image on the screen (it's so hard not to do that when you are on a Zoom, right?) and I had been THINKING "I have Owen's hair!" She said "Oh, yeah. Owen heard what you were thinking and he told me."

I know this seems really out there and hard to believe, but she hadn't seen any photos of Owen and didn't know anything about his story until we met online that day. Some of the specific things she brought up to us are sensitive topics we haven't widely discussed. She described one of Owen's new connections at college as a "party boy" and how Owen didn't like injustices, but he was being pressured to support this person in a lie. She said Owen is very truthful by nature and really couldn't be a witness to something involving this person because he didn't see anything.

She used more colorful language and said the word "pressure" seven or eight times in relation to this situation, and it clicked big time for me: the sexual assault accusations one of Owen's roommates was facing. (Yes, that untrustworthy one from the PI report! He actually asked Dustin to be his lawyer, but we, uh, were a little busy looking for our son!) This "party boy" had pressured Owen's other roommate, Justin, to support him during the investigation, and we made the leap that it was quite likely Owen was also being pressured to be a witness for him in the administrative proceedings.

Maureen's feeling was that Owen left campus to walk around that night and get away from this pressure, to clear his head, and have some space from a "hot-tempered person." This was very sad and frustrating to hear about. Owen really had a big heart and trusted others easily. We also had trusted this roommate early on in our search for Owen, as he was the source for many "details" of Owen's departure from their room on the night he left. This person changed their story with us a few times, however, which made it difficult for us to continue to trust him. I told Maureen we were no longer in contact with him, and she laughed as she barked back Owen's reply, "Don't be!" Oh, how I wish Owen would have just come home that night to talk to us about what was going on. Actually talking to Owen is the only way we could ever know exactly what happened that night, and hearing from Owen through Maureen that day felt as close to that as I've experienced. Dustin still isn't persuaded and simply said, "It's interesting how she came up with that information." (You can't see me, but I am rolling my eyes!)

Thinking about these mediumship experiences and looking back to my philosophy class about the ways of knowing, I know I cannot persuade Dustin or anyone else to have the same belief in these connections as I do. Your own system of beliefs might not allow for even a hint of any connection with the spirit world. The intuitive moment I had before Gabe fainted in church added to the faith I have long held in a spirit or energy greater than all of us (God!?) and primed me to be open to these experiences. I view the changing waves of light I have seen when I am meditating and thinking of Owen as evidence that Owen's spirit is here, somehow, still journeying with me.

Even as I proclaim my belief in his spiritual continuation, it's also still so hard to accept this "ooga booga" way of seeing Owen as all we have with him. The longing I have for a physical hug or the sound of his laugh brings tears to my eyes at unexpected moments each day, no matter how many heart-shaped rocks I find. I don't want to become dependent on mediums to continue my conversations with Owen. I want to feel him and hear from him by myself. I will continue to look for him in the "flow of life" like Fleur suggested, keeping my heart open as I spend time outside in nature. I will listen for him in songs on the radio, pick up every heart rock I see, and hug him whenever I can in my dreams. I want to embrace my opportunity to enjoy human experiences, *and* I will continue seeking more Owen wherever I can find him. And when I do get to see him again, you can bet I will ask him, "What happened to you that night!?"

Psychedelic Healing

September 2024

Everything is blurry without my contact lenses. I can't see anything clearly unless it's just a few inches away. I'm super nearsighted, and taking my lenses out (or removing my glasses) signals my body that I am off duty. I feel more vulnerable this way, but I also like how the softening of my surroundings enhances the mystery of the journey I am beginning.

I feel safe and held by the chair I recline in, and I'm comfortably covered with a soft fleece blanket of just the right weight. The delicate colored lights on the ceiling twinkle and wink at me like warm lights on a Christmas tree. There's a quiet glow in the room, like the embers of a campfire burning low, late into the night. I do not feel alone. I am not alone. Calming wisps of aromatic smoke from burning palo santo wood infuse the air with a holy reverence like I'm at church (in a good way). And there *is* a reverence: a sacredness and honoring of my courage to explore a new level of consciousness in my sessions at Cascade Psychedelic Medicine.

Before my IV ketamine infusion begins, I talk with the doctor about my intentions for the session. He knows about Owen's death and the anxiety I carry parenting my two other children. I hope to surrender some of my sadness and relax (or shatter!) the lens of judgment I often look through. I want to open my heart and mind to deeper spiritual connections with Owen and my surroundings. I'm nervous, but the doctor leads me in meditative breathing and I feel my nerves settle. The medicine begins to flow in through my IV, and I surrender. My mindful inhales and exhales evoke the rhythm of the ocean at the beach. I know I'm not at the beach, yet I feel the energy and movement of water. I feel the certainty of its continuance—it feels like something I can trust. Somehow I *am* the water. I'm floating, yet I feel more grounded than I have in a long time.

There is music all around me. Within me. It somehow holds me up, keeps me centered, and beckons me to follow it to somewhere beyond, somewhere deeper. It's evocative music like I've never heard before, played on instruments I can't name—appropriate since there is no name for a mother who has lost her son. When the music changes, gradually melting into a different sound, I find myself wanting more of what I was just hearing. Soon enough the new instruments carry me somewhere fresh, and I become a part of a different scene. There is a feeling of love all around me. My hands feel strong like I could hold anything, like I am holding everything. At the same time I sense that I am being held by the earth, supported in a perfectly balanced way. I don't have to do anything but love and be loved.

I know Owen is with me.
Owen is *with* me.
Owen is with *me*.

I see the waves of light and warmth I associate with his spiritual presence. It's not exactly like I *see* him, but I feel like I am *with* him in the last moments I spent with him behind his dorm. I'm there even as somehow I'm also above the scene *and* looking back on the moment. I feel myself hugging him goodbye, letting the question "Did we hug that day?" float away. The answer doesn't matter. We are hugging now. We are always hugging. There is no guitar in the music being played in my session, yet I hear songs Owen and I could have written and played on guitar together. It is the most beautiful music.

Tears run down my face, but they feel good, not sad. The sensation of gently moving in and out like the ocean morphs into flowing like a river. I'm continuously flowing with the current—I am the current—slowly circling at times and then rushing down a small rapid. I hover in midair alone as my rivulet launches itself over a rock in the stream, but then

I'm seamlessly combining with the body of water again. The river keeps moving forward: always renewing itself, accepting change, and carrying on. The river absorbs my tears. I think about Owen in the river. Owen's body being found in the river, being found in a river of my tears. I imagine I am the one finding Owen in the river. I picture Mary taking down the body of her son Jesus from the cross. I never had that moment with Owen's body. I wonder what that would be like, but I somehow feel it's OK that I didn't see his lifeless body. It's not how I would want to remember him. The river keeps flowing, and I flow on. I am with Owen. I am OK.

I am pulsing with life, pulsing with love, pulsing with passion and purpose. Ideas bubble up about art and writing, supporting Frances and Gabe, sharing all of this life and love with Dustin. I see an illuminated heart with glowing electric lights shining in the darkness. I feel warmth and love radiating out in all directions from me, from this heart. There is love all around me, and I am so grateful I have found it again.

* * * *

I was very nervous to try treatments with psychedelic medicine. I never experimented with drugs or was even particularly curious about any mind-altering substances while growing up (remember, I was trying to be perfect). Even if I had been susceptible to age-appropriate peer pressure, no one ever offered me weed—or anything stronger—in high school or college.

I was worried I would become instantly addicted to drugs after one puff of a joint or one pill. The "this is your brain on drugs" ad campaign with the poster of eggs frying in a pan during my adolescence got to me: I did *not* want to fry my brain like eggs. I liked my brain. It got me noticed in a good way. I was a smart student and enjoyed having that reputation in my family and among my classmates. I didn't want to mess that up or risk my future in any way.

So how did I end up under a blanket in this beautiful "hippie spa" crying tears of joy about all the love? My dad was a pathologist and my mom was a nurse in surgical recovery; I grew up believing that drugs and medications were serious tools for healing, not for recreational fun. I hope that by sharing my experiences, others might be encouraged to open themselves up to this type of life-changing therapy.

When we lost Owen, I wept openly for months and months wherever I went. I remember crying at the dentist's office during painless x-rays of my teeth and in the waiting room at the eye doctor where I sat with my older son, Gabe, who, even though we had recently lost his brother, needed an eye exam to renew his prescription for contact lenses and we couldn't reschedule. (IYKYK)

I found a gifted and compassionate grief therapist who probably spent a good chunk of my hourly fees on restocking the fancy herbal tea I drank to keep up my hydration while I cried an ocean of tears into box after box of her soft, expensive Kleenex. I wasn't eating. I wasn't sleeping. And it went on like this for a long time. "It feels right to feel wrecked," was my mantra. As much as anything felt "right" during that time, the confusion, numbness, anger, desperation, and sadness that took turns swamping my drowning heart felt deserved. These were appropriately debilitating emotions, my body's innate response to the inconceivable loss of my beautiful 18-year-old son, and I didn't want to feel anything different.

I did not want to take medication to help me sleep. I did not want to take medication to mute my pain. Every tear felt precious and necessary. My mom said Owen was worth every tear. I kept going like this for a long time, lying on the floor of my family room when I was home alone or crying in my car while driving down all the streets of our city where Owen used to drive.

Ever so slowly, things started to shift for me. Going to tennis, where I could set my grief aside on the bench for an hour or two of focused competition, helped. Joining an online grief writing group in 2022 helped me craft a container for some of my pain. And I found ways to lovingly remember Owen and mourn his loss while still supporting and celebrating Gabe and Frances. We adopted a puppy. It was better, but still not ideal by any means.

Meanwhile, my friend Michelle's husband, a former emergency room physician, opened a clinic in our neighborhood treating people with depression, anxiety, and PTSD. Following an evidence-based protocol, he uses IV ketamine in a supervised and controlled setting to help improve his clients' symptoms. (Ketamine, an FDA-approved anesthetic, can cause problems if abused and was linked to actor Matthew Perry's death, but this clinic was moving slowly and carefully to ensure client safety.) My friend and her husband wanted to help me—and they even offered me a job at the clinic supporting other anxious and grieving clients—so I said yes when they suggested psychedelic medicine might help me.

The feelings and sensations I described above are only some of what I experienced. I went through a series of six sessions and then in the days, weeks, and months after the series ended, I worked with my grief counselor and an integration specialist, a therapist with special training in working with the psychedelic experience as a valid and useful modality that can help a person grow, process, and heal. I still reread my journal entries and listen to some of the music from my sessions to rekindle the positive vibes and ponder some of the gleanings.

Recurring themes of connecting with Owen's spirit, surrendering control, and basically moving with the flow of life unite my experiences, yet they were all unique and different. I felt an incredible sense of oneness with nature: water, sky, mountains, sun, ocean. I witnessed shifting colors and patterns resembling watercolors of topographical maps; I saw jigsaw puzzles missing a piece until I became the missing piece and completed the picture, dissolving into the scene. Fragments of other music somehow slipped into my mind over the live chanting and drumming, and I found myself thinking of "The Hebrides Overture" by Felix Mendelssohn, a favorite classical piece of mine. Being reminded of it in these sessions was a surprise, and yet it seemed like an important signal that even as I am significantly changed by this loss of Owen, I am still the person who loves this music. I'm still here AND I'm changing. I don't have to do everything perfectly. There is so much love and beauty all around us if we can find a way to be present and surrender ourselves to that love.

A big takeaway for me is increasing my acceptance and openness for simultaneously experiencing grief and joy. AND. It's human to feel both *and* we need both. I am still the mom of Owen *and* he is gone. I feel like I am carrying him with me *and* it feels like he is carrying me. I can miss Owen *and* love the life I have now.

Now I work part-time at the clinic, communicating with potential clients to answer their questions and help them navigate the intake process. I welcome clients to our cozy, inviting space and sit with them after their sessions if they want to talk or make them comfortable with a snack and a cup of tea while they write in a journal or create art. (There's even a bowl of Owen's heart-shaped rocks clients can draw on and take home.) I know that psychedelic medicine is still edgy and a little "out there," but I am hopeful that if this experience was so positive for me it can definitely help others. Wouldn't everyone feel better with a little more love and acceptance? A little More Owen?

Postscript

The wound is the place where the Light enters you.
—RUMI

When Owen died in 2019, I wasn't ready for anyone else's interpretation of what I might experience. I needed to live through every painful minute of every unbearably sad day, honor every tear, and rejoice with every sweet discovery of more about Owen (of More Owen). Looking back now, I realize that losing my son in the traumatic way we did, without knowing what really happened and without understanding who or what was to blame, narrowed my focus and left me unable to engage in bigger national and international news issues. His loss eclipsed much of the world outside our family for many months, leaving us shivering on our own in a cold, dark twilight of grief, yearning to see the sun. Slowly, through living, writing about, and sharing my ordeals, I have been able to open myself up to the experiences others have had with grief. My curiosity about people is reemerging. I can see and feel the light beginning to enter me.

Losing Owen completely reset my perspective on what truly is a problem in life, and for me it's this: there's child loss, and then there's everything else. Do you know the adage, "Don't sweat the small stuff"? In some ways I *can't* sweat the small stuff anymore because I know how bad the big stuff can be. I don't have any energy to spare for trifling problems. I'm calmer at airports, I'm more patient in traffic, and I think I handle formerly ego-bruising miscommunications between friends with more grace. I'm letting go of my perfectionistic tendencies and allowing drifts of dog fur and dust to accumulate in the corners of my home. Even after this terrible, horrible, unimaginable thing happened to our family, I'm beginning to feel lighter.

At the same time, surviving the death of my beloved son—the experience that is my biggest and most enduring problem—has united me with all the pain and sorrow in the world, even if it's pain that may seem small. Discovering a connection to all human suffering seems an unlikely path towards healing or letting the light in, but that's what it feels like. I have more compassion for everyone who is struggling, even if it's chump change compared to child loss. I wish they weren't hurting (and I am glad they don't know how much worse their pain could be), but I know these experiences of loss and anguish are an important part of each of our soul's journeys here on earth.

This is the end of my book, but it is not the end of my story—nor of Owen's story. I know there are things I haven't been completely able to delve into here. I'm aware I might never be able to find many of the answers I'm searching for. I'm attempting to be OK with not knowing exactly what happened to Owen. I'm striving to be open to the new way my relationship with him continues, even without his physical presence. When I close my eyes, I imagine him smiling and giving me two thumbs-up on whatever I'm doing or feeling, even if I'm not feeling very thumbs-up about it. I know he will always be with me, that there will always be an outlet for me to share my love for him.

The most painful thing for me to think and write about remains the question of suicide: Did Owen choose to end his life when he left campus that October night in 2019, after buying some snacks for midterm week and taking money out of the ATM? I still don't believe so, but I know that many others did, and do. The possibility that this was suicide still haunts me, but I am trying to let it go. I hate thinking I might have missed something Owen was struggling with, that there was something so terrible or terrifying about his life that he felt like he couldn't share with me.

I tell myself that it doesn't matter how he died, that the important part is that he is no longer physically here, but not knowing still torments me. As I touched on a bit earlier, visits with mediums have shifted me more toward understanding Owen's death as an accident and have kept me (most days!) from fruitlessly searching for a murderer. Integrating lessons learned in my psychedelic healing sessions continues to help me simply keep living every day, missing Owen AND finding glimmers of joy. It's grueling, AND I am going to survive.

My belief that I'll be OK is tenuous, because off and on throughout this grief journey I have believed it was correct for me to be shattered by Owen's death. At times I wanted to wallow in my pain because it proved how special Owen was, how much I loved him, and how much I was missing him. Feeling "better" felt like I was diminishing the importance of Owen's existence and erasing the impact of his loss. Those feelings still well up from time to time. If one were to chart a graph of my healing journey, it wouldn't be a straight and steady line climbing up from darkness into sunny days and smooth sailing. I continue to endure volatile ups and downs that have me dancing goofily around while playing pickleball one hour, then weeping in a friend's kitchen as we reminisce about the disappointing police report from Owen's case the next. Sometimes the pain ambushes me out of nowhere, and other times I stare it down intentionally, like watching a movie about a child who goes missing, to see how much it hurts, how much I can take, how strong I am now—or maybe just so I can release some more tears.

While writing this epilogue, for example, I Googled Owen's troubled roommate—the one who was under investigation for sexual assault—to see if there was anything new on that front. The search led me down a rabbit hole into an "unresolved mystery" forum on Reddit* and pages and pages of theories and opinions about Owen's disappearance on Websleuths. com. I sat at my computer reading close to a hundred comments written by strangers about Owen's death and what they thought might have happened: how things in his case didn't make sense, how sketchy the details around this roommate look when scrutinized, how Dustin and I were indulgent (and oblivious) parents, how this was obviously suicide...a drug deal gone bad...an accident...a homicide.

I wept again rewatching recordings of someone who looks and sounds like me speaking to the media about Owen in press conferences and local news shows. I am not that person anymore. That Mary is gone, and yet I am still here. It doesn't take much picking to break the scab open again and bleed profusely from this wound caused by the loss of my son, the loss of how our family was when he was here, the loss of who he might have become in the future. I don't want to hide my tears or my bleeding heart, but maybe I need a box of cute bandages so the blood won't get all over everything else in my life. (Oh, and I'm still going to get that tattoo! Maybe that can help seal the scar a bit...)

---

*An unknown author posted this comment about Owen on Reddit 3/18/2025: "He was a really good guy. He was kind and funny, and he died too young. Maybe I'm just posting this because death does weird things and I was reminded about him today, but I never expected him to die like this. No one who knew him did. I still remember finding out because my friend sent me the article saying 'it's Owen from biology'. But I knew him for longer than that.

I use[d] to really like reading about true crime, and then this happened. And now it just feels incredibly strange.

To anyone who finds this Owen lit up every room he walked into. He went out of his way to make space for people around him. I'm not saying he was a saint or perfect because no one is, but a lot of people cared about him and still miss him. Just remember that before theorizing about what happened."

Owen is gone and I am still here. I am grateful to still be married to Dustin. (Until I accidentally pull the on/off cord out of the light in our basement's furnace room again. I've done this a few times lately, and it really annoys him! He might want to get a new wife!) I cry every time we make love, but I'm grateful we can still connect in this way that is essential and nourishing for our relationship. I know that many couples do not survive the loss of a child. I know that Dustin wanted more than anything to find Owen for me and bring him safely back to my arms.

Together, we still worry about Gabe and Frances more than they are comfortable with. I hope they understand why. I want them to know they are as precious to us as Owen was (as Owen is!) and that they don't need to shield us from any of their worries or problems. It's not fair that they have to continue growing up without Owen. Your siblings are supposed to be with you through your entire life, forever teasing you about your ugly duckling stages, teaching you how to share and compromise, and helping you deal with your annoying and embarrassing parents. They are not supposed to disappear (and take the best parts of your parents with them) when you are still coming of age yourself. I hope that Frances and Gabe can continue to have a relationship with Owen's memory and his spirit, finding more Owen in each other and the people they surround themselves with.

Frances was recently home from college for a few days of spring break, and we used Owen's record player to play some of our old favorite (The Beach Boys) and newly acquired (Paul Simon) LPs while she and I worked on making some crafts with a few heart-shaped rocks. My heart fluttered with hope when she wanted to take the mobile she made back to the off-campus rental house she's sharing with three friends this year. We were lucky to see her at all over break, as (like many her age) she likes to spend most of her free time with her boyfriend. He's studying culinary arts and earned our admiration when he stayed up late with Frances last fall making delicious gourmet sandwiches (on bread rolls he baked from scratch!) for all the guys playing in our Thanksgiving weekend Owen Klinger Memorial lacrosse Game. We are grateful that she can have some age-appropriate and "normal" experiences at college after the trauma and struggles of the past few years.

Gabe is working full time at Oregon State University, living with his girlfriend, playing computer games, planning fun outings, taking classes, and playing sousaphone in the alumni band at occasional OSU sporting events. (Most recently, he played in the pep band at a gymnastics meet!) He doesn't share many thoughts about Owen—and declined my offer to let him read these writings with a quiet, "I'm good"—but last Christmas he gifted me with a special adapter to connect our old video camera to the computer so I could watch and digitally record all of our old home movies. There were hours of boring baby stuff, but Gabe tuned in with me to watch some pretty chaotic scenes of Owen and Frances foiling his attempts to seriously practice songs for first grade Japanese class. I was very touched by his thoughtfulness and grateful for his tech-savvy mind. Gabe's girlfriend says Owen's La-Z-Boy is the most comfortable chair in their apartment, the one she always looks forward to sitting in when she comes home from her job as an elementary school educational assistant. (And she needs a soft place to rest: a kindergartner recently punched her in the stomach and bit her!) Even though I was hoping Owen's chair would move with Gabe, I was worried it would be unbearable to see it go. Instead, I am just so happy that this faux suede chair Owen was so proud to purchase for himself is bringing comfort and joy, not sadness, to Gabe and his girlfriend. I'm hopeful there might be hidden joy in some of Owen's other possessions I have been clinging to.

This brings me to my guitar, which became Owen's guitar and is now my guitar again. I haven't made much music since we lost Owen. I'm not the same musician I was; familiar songs don't sound the same and are uncomfortable for me to play. However, I know there is medicine in music, and I am beginning to find that it can be a pathway to joy and a way of discovering more Owen.

For Christmas in 2020 (that year we spent so much time at home due to Covid), I picked up the guitar we had shared and taught myself to play "California Stars," a folk song originally written by Woody Guthrie and recorded by Billy Bragg and Wilco. In the weeks before we lost him, Owen had Googled how to play this song. I don't know if he learned it or played it for anyone, but I thought it would be a good distraction in those emotionally fraught pre-holiday days and something I could surprise Dustin with at Christmas. It was not easy, and I cried many times by myself while I practiced. I also cried when I finally played it for Dustin and my family, choking out some of the words as I sang through extra verses I made up about "Owen's Heart-shaped Rocks" (too cheesy to write down here for you), but I made it through the song. I didn't realize it at the time, but the instrument that Owen had most recently played added something special to my performance. There were scratches on the back of my guitar from where Owen had held it close to his heart and the pearl-covered snaps on his Pendleton shirt scuffed the shiny surface. When I saw these marks, I felt Owen was with me in the music, that these scratches in the lacquer were proof Owen was here enriching our lives in every day and in every song. I know Owen cradled this guitar as he sang lyrics he wrote about his favorite place on earth. No one sees those scratches when I play, but I know they are there, and they make my music richer, sadder, and more meaningful. A little more light sneaks into my life and music through these scratches.

My heart, shattered by the loss of Owen and then stretched to somehow hold more love for him and more love for Gabe and Frances and Dustin, is all scratched up like the back of my guitar. People I meet now might not know of the damage hidden there, but this experience of loving and losing Owen, right when he was about to take off to his Great Big Unknown Future, colors every interaction I have with other humans.

So, no, the story isn't over and the jury is still out on how my little tribe and I will be able to carry this grief moving forward. Mentioning the jury, though, reminds me of something, reader! I didn't tell you about my jury duty experience when I was seated as the #1 juror in the box before *voir dire* for a trial in which Portland Police officers would be giving testimony in April of 2023. I was excused after the defense attorney asked if anyone would have difficulties believing a police officer and I had to answer yes. So in addition to opening my heart in ways I never thought were possible, losing Owen also got me out of jury duty.

The hole left by Owen's death is where the light gets in. I hope I can continue to shine like Owen did. I want to share the music from my scratched-up guitar, to share the love from my lacerated heart. I want to share More Owen with you and everyone.

In Owen's dorm room with the afghan I made for him in UP's school colors

Acknowledgements

As a lifelong striving perfectionist, I once was a dedicated writer of thank-you notes, but in the aftermath of Owen's death I found myself owing such a deep debt of gratitude to an overwhelming abundance of people I had no idea where to begin.

This book is essentially my thank-you note to Owen. I know he isn't physically here to read it, but his love, energy, and special zest for life inspired every word. It was an honor and a delight to be his mom and to see his face light up whenever I cooked bacon. I am eternally grateful for the ways he brought more of everything to my life and for the ways his death is opening me up to new ways of living and connecting. Thank you, Owen, with all my heart.

I will take this opportunity to say thank you to *everyone* who helped search in big and small ways for Owen, the people who supported our family for many months after Owen's body was found, and the community of #moreowen followers who continue to reach out to me online with kind messages. You have all helped me and my family more than you could ever know.

There are many, many people I would like to thank more specifically. My fear of leaving anyone out or making this list way too long is almost paralyzing, but I must try. If you don't see your name here, believe me that you are not forgotten in my heart.

I want to extend special thanks to the core members of our "Find Owen" team for harnessing your brain power and skills to coordinate and execute the search to bring Owen home. Shout outs to Bill for wrangling countless volunteers and to Susan and Kevin for guiding media relations. Anthony Kautz, I will be forever grateful that you were on the river that morning. Finding Owen and then finding More Owen would not have been possible without all of you.

Thank you Joanne Radmillovich Kollman and Micah Kassell, for capturing such different aspects of Owen's likeness and life in your paintings. Thank you, Justin Tong, for sharing your digital portraits of Owen and stories of your brief time with him at UP. (I think Owen would be delighted that he inspired all these creations!)

I'm grateful to the photographers, especially Ron Cooper and John Davenport, for generously documenting and sharing precious moments of Owen's life. Thank you also to Beth Nakamura who so reverently photographed Owen's baby blanket for *The Oregonian* and who cut through frustrating red-tape so I could include that photo in this book.

Thank you, Melinda Laus and the Nature of Grief group, for giving me new ways to explore my grief and for letting me witness your own beautiful sadness (and for seeing mine).

I say thank you from the bottom of my broken heart to Mila Liessler for permission to share her daughter Natalie's story and send a big, healing hug to her and all the grieving parents I have met since losing Owen. I'm so sorry that you know the pain of child loss too.

I raise my coffee cup in a toast of thanks to Anne Gudger and Maria Gibson for their grief writing workshop "Write Your Grief Out." Writing with this group in 2022 created the acorn from which this book grew. Reading pieces of my writing during their online zoom groups and speaking on their podcast, "Coffee, Grief, and Gratitude," gave me a tantalizing taste for the microphone and bolstered my confidence to continue sharing my writing.

Thank you to Nancy Jean Burns (www.lilmcgil.com) for something I didn't know I needed: creative guidance that helped me see myself as a Writer, an Author.

Through linked comments on my manuscript, in emails, and over the phone, my Seattle-based editor, Karalynn Ott, offered tender and tough suggestions that helped me winnow and weave these bits of More Owen together. Thank you, Karalynn, for loving Owen though you never met him, and for improving every page of this very personal project with your impressively professional skills.

Thank you to Valerie Blanton for saying yes to the inopportune opportunity to be my proofreader. Your sharp eyes caught some big mistakes (things you can't unsee, sorry!) and gave me much needed peace of mind that the commas were in the right places. Any remaining errors of fact or punctuation are my fault for sure.

Thank you to Kimberly Parks for design work that gives me chills. Along with this stunning book cover, she developed the search posters for Owen and several #moreowen stickers I've shared with friends and supporters. Thank you, Kimberly, for being in this with my family from the first day Owen was missing, for listening with your heart, and creating these stunning graphics so we can all have a little More Owen.

I'm appreciative of the generous guidance and support I received from Portland-area writers, including Amy Baskin and Laura Stanfill. I was clueless about the path to publishing before reading Laura's book *Imagine a Door*. Thank you, Laura, for this entertaining and thorough tutorial and Amy, for introducing me to Laura and to Ali Shaw at Indigo.

To my team at Indigo: Editing Design and More—Olivia Hammerman, Jenny Kimura, Deborah Jayne, and Ali—your direction and knowledge came at a perfect time to help me and Owen cross the finish line.

Thank you to my mom and my dad for raising me in a house full of books and letting me study English at Notre Dame. These foundations in reading and writing helped me work through my new reality and, of course, tell Owen's story. I'm also forever grateful for the special family memories we made at the apartment in New York (Dad) and at the beach house (Mom).

I want to express my gratitude to the journalists who took Owen's disappearance as seriously as I did and who treated my family with kindness and compassion.

Thank you to students and staff at the University of Portland who searched for Owen and mourned his death with us. Thank you for including Owen in your prayers and your memories of your time on the bluff. I'm also grateful to UP for planting a beautiful tree for Owen and for hosting our annual Owen Klinger Memorial Lacrosse Game on campus.

I've enjoyed learning more about Owen through his Japanese Magnet Program friends and sports teammates. I know no one knows what to say to the dead boy's parents but thank you for reaching out to me with your stories and photos. I'm always here for More Owen and updates about your own lives.

Tennis is life-saving therapy for me as I navigate a new path forward after Owen's death and I am grateful I get to play this addictive game with so many quality humans. Thank you to all who captain the tennis teams I play on and those who invite me to drills and practices. Sorry to anyone who must play against me now, I have some secret weapons: Owen's grit and determination. "C'mon!"

Thank you, Michelle and Seth Mehr, for transformative sessions (and now part-time employment) at Cascade Psychedelic Medicine. It's a privilege to support the healing work you do.

I'm incredibly fortunate to have an abundance of supportive female friends in my life; thank you for letting me cry tears of joy, sadness, and laughter with all of you over the years. Wendy and Heather, dear friends from my youth, you keep me in touch with my younger self and accountable to her passions. To Michelle K., thank you for frequent dinner invitations and for never shying away from talking about Owen, Gabe, and Frances, even when there are no words. My Farley Hall roommates from Notre Dame generously share their hearts and love from across the country; I hope we can keep getting together. Thank you to the women in my cooking group who have supported me in countless ways over the last 25 years. It's my turn to give back after I received so much help from you! To the women in my book clubs (yes, I'm in more than one!), thank you for appreciating (and adding to!) my heart-shaped rock collection and for offering me endless Kleenex and refills of wine. Thank you for grace and understanding during the time when Owen's death robbed me of my ability to read.

To Dustin, Gabe, and Frances, thank you for giving me space and time to grieve and to write about Owen. It's been a lot (all?) about him since he died, but I want you to know you are each just as precious to me. I know I am not the same wife and mom you knew before, but hopefully I can be even better with More Owen.

Photograph Credits

Most of the photos in the book come from the Klinger-Pozar family archives except for the following images friends and photographers generously granted permission for me to share:

Introduction: Owen bodysurfing in Hawaii—Ron Cooper

Skydogs and Panther Creek: Owen with his ukulele at Panther Creek—
Ron Cooper, Owen sharpening sticks with Gabe—Ron Cooper

Missing Kids and a Box of Crackers: More Owen—Justin Tong

Do Not Work as a Referee: Owen's tree at UP—Father John Donato

Owen's Camera: Photos by Owen Klinger except for Owen behind
the camera in Hawaii—Ron Cooper and Owen photographing
the sunset—Ron Cooper

List of Fun: Owen flying at the swimming pool—Ron Cooper,
Baseball catch—Ron Cooper, Snow fort—Ron Cooper, $100—
Ron Cooper, Owen bodysurfing in Mexico—Ron Cooper, and
Owen smiling at Baseball—Ron Cooper

Owen's Baby Blanket: Owen's blanket ("Fuzzy")—Beth Nakamura
for *The Oregonian*

Letters of Thanks: Columbia River at dawn—Anthony Kautz, Owen
kanji—Kimberly Parks

The Last Lacrosse Game: Owen with the ball—John Davenport, For
Eyes Photography

The Oil Portrait: Owen's senior water polo portrait—John
Davenport, For Eyes Photography

My Pink Shawl and the Emotional X-Ray Machine: Me in my pink
shawl—Kimberly Parks

Tennis as a Grief Sport: Marco Pineda on court with me—Ann Skoog

Flow: Owen's flow—Sylvia Jiminez

The Photographers: all photos by John Davenport, For Eyes
 Photography
A Season of Water Polo: Owen with the ball—John Davenport, For
 Eyes Photography, Owen as the goalie—John Davenport, For
 Eyes Photography
Things Seen on a Jumbotron: Owen's yellow swimsuit—Ron Cooper
His Favorite Pendleton Shirt: Klinger kids walking on campus at
 Oregon State University—Johan Reinalda